Interaction rhythms

DISCARDED

INTERACTION RHYTHMS
Periodicity in
Communicative Behavior

Edited by
Martha Davis, Ph.D

The Institute for Nonverbal
Communication Research Inc.

HUMAN SCIENCES PRESS, INC.
72 FIFTH AVENUE
NEW YORK, N.Y. 10011

CONTENTS

7

ACKNOWLEDGMENTS

First, I would like to thank those who supported the development of the Institute for Nonverbal Communication Research which sponsored the conference on *Interaction Rhythms*. The speakers at the conference put in tremendous efforts, both on their presentations and in later rewriting for this book, and I thank them especially. I am grateful to those who helped prepare the manuscript, Susan Morance and Nora Owens. I particularly wish to thank Norma Fox, editor-in-chief of Human Sciences Press, for her support.

Finally, words fail to capture how thankful I am for the gracious dispositions of Sergio and Elizabeth Rothstein.

Martha Davis
Editor

COMMENTS ON THE SIGNIFICANCE OF INTERACTION RHYTHMS

Albert E. Scheflen

I first consciously observed an instance of interactional synchrony over a generation ago when Ray Birdwhistell pointed it out to me. About that time Arensberg and Chapple were studying interactional tempos. Then pioneers such as Byers, Condon, Lomax, and Kendon described interactional rhythms. In those days few people were interested in these phenomena, and even fewer grasped their significance. So I was pleasantly surprised when Dr. Davis told me we would have a conference on the subject. I was even more pleased when so many of the pioneers prepared papers along with the relative newcomers.

With this volume I guess we can say that our small science has come of age. But now that we are on the map, we have some rather serious responsibilities. We have a lot more research to do, and we must define what interactional synchrony is more clearly. But I think we also have to realize the significance of what we have discovered, for it forces us to a new methodological, personal, and theoretical perspective. This is what I will write about in this preface. I want to address the perspective or context of these fascinating papers rather than review each separately.

First, the discovery of interactional rhythms has implications for our personal views of shared human experience and our
own participation in human affairs. We can begin to discuss this
aspect by looking backward to the history of our modes of
Western thought.

It is striking how belatedly we have discovered the obvious.
Any dancer or musician could have told us that we must share a
common rhythm to sing or play or dance together. So could any
athlete who plays on a team. And privately we have always
known that a common rhythmicity is essential to consummate
sexual union. But why didn't we realize earlier that interaction
rhythms were essential in every human interaction? Are scientists
always the last to know what artists and others have known all
along? There seems to be but one feasible explanation for our
blindness. Academics have been caught in a mode of observation and conception that was too narrow for a vision of co-
action.

Julian Jaynes (1978) argues that Western peoples did not
develop a sense of self-awareness or personal differentiation
until maybe 3,000 years ago. A few centuries later Plato argued
for the primacy of the human idea, and Aristotle suggested that
we explain our experience by finding the main and causative
agent. After the inundation of the Athenian state, a series of
religions claimed that God originated ideas, and the main and
causative thing was divine. For almost 2,000 years, then, the
focus of philosophical attention was upon the relationships of
person and God, not on person and person. Then in the Renaissance we Westerners developed a cult of individualism befitting
an age of conquest and colonization in which people were
needed to sail off to distant lands. But this focus on "the
individual" has not abated since the Renaissance. In fact, it has
culminated in modern times with two prestigious paradigms that
have dominated our explanatory systems—the paradigms of
organismic biology and of individual psychology.

In such a tradition it was inevitable that we watched one
human subject at a time and conceived of individual actions in

isolation. Even in the 1950s when we did begin to conceive of communication and better appreciated that more than one person was present, we were still stuck with the habit of focusing on one person. So we watched one person *and then the next one*, as if we were watching a tennis match. At this point we began to conceive of communication as an interaction, as an action and reaction sequence between two "individuals" who took turns.

If we observe only one person or one person at a time, there is no way we will observe synchrony or co-action or interactional rhythm. It is interesting to note that even today we title the phenomenon of shared rhythmicity "interaction rhythms" instead of "co-action" rhythms, thereby hanging onto the notion of alternative actions in sequence. We could, of course, conceive of interactions as simultaneous as well as sequential, but few communication theorists do so.

So much for the history of narrow observational foci. The fact is that we now notice that people move in shared rhythms, and we can no longer go back and act as if we did not know this. On this account we can never be quite the same even at the simple level of the mechanics of watching a human event. We can no longer point our foveal vision at one participant *and then* at a next one. *We must learn, consciously and purposively, to look at more than one person at the same time.*

Some of us have already learned to watch film or video this way, and that is the mechanistic reason we can write research papers on interaction rhythms. I am suggesting more than this. I am suggesting that once we know about co-action, we are enjoined to watch multiple people at the same time in everyday life. And I am also suggesting that we learn to watch (and listen to) all of the participants in a small grouping *including ourselves*. We must learn to watch our own bodies in relation to the bodies of the others, instead of looking (consciously) from the face of one speaker to the face of a next one as we have done in the past.

If we can learn to do this, we can more readily employ a co-actional and social level of explanation. When things go wrong, we can ask what is wrong between us instead of what is wrong with me or with that other person. And we can consciously observe the bases of our interpretations. We can learn, for instance, to examine dyssynchronies, and we can think about how to correct them on purpose. We might even want to learn how to be dyssynchronous on purpose in order to break up an unwanted degree of involvement.

When we have learned better to do this, we can teach it. We can help people who participate inadequately without having to rely solely on personal self-examination. And I think we will be able to help a group of people we now call schizophrenic in a much more purposive way. At present we give these people insight therapy or drugs with doubtful results, or we do try to engage them in shared activity, such as dance therapy, hoping that they will somehow achieve an ability for co-action in some automatic way. I am suggesting that we can and should learn to recognize, demonstrate, and correct the severe dyssynchronies of autism and schizophrenia in a more purposive and comprehensive way. I am suggesting that we help patients and clients with dyssynchronies in all forms of social participation, from greetings to sexual consummation.

In short, I am saying that, now that we have realized the importance of interactional rhythms in *any* shared activity, we should extend our awareness and use it to enrich our social participation in everyday life. And we should use this insight to help other people enrich theirs.

I think there is a second use for our discovery. If we can learn to watch the movements of several people simultaneously, we can further extend our observational focus to gain a more and more comprehensive view of communicational activity in general. For example, we can learn to watch *and* listen and lay to rest the useless dichotomy between ''verbal'' and ''nonverbal'' communication. We can learn to study the simultaneous relationship of all modalities of the communication code. And, when we have achieved a more holistic and less reductionistic ability to observe, *we must turn this ability to the study of interactional rhythms themselves*. Then we can realize that we are studying a complex, multifaceted, and often changing phenomenon which is not to be comprehended by old-fashioned atomistic approaches. We will not again argue that there is a single human interactional rhythm or even a single one for a given culture. And we will no longer get into arguments about whether interactional rhythms are genetic *or* psychological *or* cultural. We will no longer be able to say they are in voice *or* in movement. These phenomena are of a systems nature. They are all of these and more.

More specifically, I think that these papers and our general experience demonstrates that at least the following levels of complexity are minimal for the understanding of interactional rhythms. First the participants in any interaction show a rhythmicity, and these participants can change tempo according to a variety of contexts. There is not, therefore, *a* rhythm. Each of us has a *repertoire* of them—a repertoire that is contingent upon ethnicity, region, class, and probably occupation. Second, a group of people can automatically share a rhythmicity according to a context, and they can change it together in accordance to changes in situation or context. And, third, people can in some measure alter each other's tempos and rhythms, and in some degree they can do so consciously. People can sound or tap a beat and thus manipulate the rhythmicity of the occasion.

We should not make the matter simpler than this to fit our favorite research methodology or our favorite paradigm of human explanation. We may work on a single facet of the subject, but we cannot on this account act as if we have said what interactional rhythms *are*.

Discoveries of interaction rhythms lead us to another sort of sophistication. It is no coincidence that we discovered interactional synchrony and shared rhythms at this particular time in the history of the human sciences. It is no coincidence that we discovered them at a time when we are moving away from an individual-centered epistemology to an epistemology of fields and then of systems and cybernetic relations. We discovered them in an era when we began to study relationships—an era of social psychology, behavioral sociology, ethology, and social biology. And we discovered them at a time when we moved from linear cause models to conceptions of simultaneity, feedback, and feed forward.

There is a system relationship between the change in our epistemology and the discovering of interactional rhythms. As we looked at relationships among participants and at fields of simultaneous occurrence, we were able to see interactional rhythms. And, when we saw such rhythms, we were further forced to an epistemology of relations and co-occurring changes.

On these accounts we can no longer ride on a kiddie-car model of human communication. In the 1950s we used terms such as "I communicate" or "He does not communicate," as if communication could be the action of a single person. And without blushing we could use a word like message to describe all of the complexity of a multimodal media. Then in the mid-1950s we were taken with information theory and said that communication was a process in which a sender transmitted a message to a receiver who decoded it and so on. We spoke of ourselves as if we were telegraphs, but at least we achieved the recognition that communication was a transitive occurrence. Then we took another little step toward complexity. We said that communication involved a sequential action and reaction between senders and receivers.

In formal terms each of these simple models consists of various modifications of the Aristotelianisms which have dominated formal academic thinking since the Middle Ages. In this world view it is assumed that (1) any phenomenon is the action of *a* central and causative entity or agent (a gene, a star, a person); (2) the action is an emission or expression from within the subject; and (3) that this action represents an unseen force that resides within the subject until it is expressed or emitted (for instance, phologiston, gravity, instinct, will, or motive).

Centuries ago the failure of a simple Aristotelianism to explain all phenomena was recognized, and various elaborations were introduced. For example, subjects were sometimes seen as acting upon an object. Or sometimes one focused upon an object and took the view that objects received an action, such as a stimulus. Eventually stimulus and response models evolved. And about 1950 we adopted a quasi-Newtonian model in which two or more bodies are seen to react *to each other*.

Biology, psychology, and sociology adopted and held on to various versions of Aristotelianism, and in the main, they still do. That is why expression and interaction theories of communication are still popular in both academic and clinical circles. *But no matter how much you elaborate on a thing-action model, it is still subject-centered, and it still depends upon the postulation of heuristic forces.* It still depicts the world as boxes representing things or people and lines that depict abstracted actions. An Aristotelian epistemology still ignores the observables, that is, *the patterns of action and change*, and keeps us in a conceptual universe of imaginary forces.

This recognition brought Maxwell, then Einstein, and then others to a field theory or an epistemology of pattern. The focus was first changed to the form or structure of the field of actions and changes and then one moved back to a view of how the physical bodies evolved, took part, and shared the field. But back at the ranch, we human scientists were still relying upon Aristotelianisms — as late as the 1950s. In fact, to be sarcastic about the matter, we had not yet achieved a Newtonian version by the late 1950s when we postulated interaction as taking turns. Even Newton recognized that interaction was a mutual and simultaneous relation. We did not get that far until the 1960s.

This, of course, is where the discovery of interactional rhythms and synchrony plays a critical epistemological role. *Once we recognized that participants regularly, continually and generally act in synchrony, we could no longer entertain an action-reaction mode or any simpler Aristotelianism as a basis for our theory.* We were forced to adopt an alternate epistemology. We were forced, as were Einstein and Weiner and others three generations earlier, to adopt a field epistemology.

The point can be put in less fancy language. There are occasions when all participants in a scene turn at the same moment to countenance an interruption or a noisy stimulus. In such cases we can say that they co-act in a common response. But in most kinds of interactional synchrony discussed in this volume there are no perceivable, external cues. One explanation of this is obvious and unavoidable. *The participants have in common adopted the same tempo, and they are following in common an agenda, a script, a program, or a scenario that each has already internalized.* Participants are not merely reacting *to each other.* They are not merely identifying or copying *each other.* They are co-acting in a common, prewritten, or culturally traditional drama.

There is now no turning back. Some traditional scenarios do feature self-expression. The scripts of the psychotherapy session are an example. And some feature turn-taking. Ping-pong, bridge playing, and formal British debates are an example. And some people do violate traditional scenarios by expressing themselves when it is gauche to do so. And some react, not to the expectancies of the context, but to what they had for breakfast. But whatever the contingencies, we now realize that people follow internalized scripts and tempos when they come together. Otherwise they do not ''get it together.''

That is what has belatedly happened to our conception of human communication since the 1950s. We have come into the postEinsteinian world. Like Einstein we did not single out the main body in a system of events. Instead we saw bodies as being born, becoming red giants, and dying into black holes in a structured order that preceded the emergence of any given substance (as Aristotle would have said). In the field of communication we did not any longer see the processes as the actions of a Mary or a John. We observed Mary and John moving and acting in a system of ongoing events. The model of the opera or the theater or of the orchestra became more adequate than the model of things emitting forces.

I do not want to be systematically misunderstood on this point so that what I say might be lightly dismissed. I am not saying that the study of individuals or participants is not relevant to the study of communication. Nor am I saying that people move passively in communication fields like planets do in their orbits. I am saying instead that the study of individuals is a legitimate and important activity, if we want to learn about individuals. And I am saying that the study of how people participate in communication events is critical to understanding participation, but communication is more than participation.

Certainly participants do not ordinarily enact traditional scenarios in a passive or ritualistic way. On the contrary, participants make faces about what is going on, and they make comments too. And these reactions are also cues that can change the ways of participation. People express themselves in other ways, too. In fact, they change and modify and rewrite the scenarios of communication.

It was this recognition that has allowed us to move on in the 1970s beyond a concept of fields. Cybernetics and systems approaches allowed us to put the mechanisms of participation back into our view of the structure of events. Bateson's concept of metacommunication allowed us to envision how participants both enacted their parts in an event and how they simultaneously acted and reacted to the events. And then the new neuropsychology began to have an impact. Abstractions about cognition or ego were gradually replaced by constructs about information processing and then by constructs about images and plans. Pribram has offered us such integrative views of neural function. Now they are beginning to pay off with views of cerebral-corebrain relations and of left and right brain integration.

We must still do a lot more work to put all of these aspects together into a highly comprehensive view of human communication. We have yet to see clearly that anything people do together, whether to converse or to dance, is communication. But we did turn the corner. We attained a roomier epistemology. The discovery of interactional synchrony and rhythmicity played an important role in that development.

One valuable thing about a theoretical house of many mansions is the existence of room for residents of all persuasions. On this account, the question we must ask about each of the chapters in this volume is not whether they are true or not. The question is: Where does each fit into a larger view of human communication and human sharing?

REFERENCES

Jaynes, J. *The origin of consciousness in the breakdown of the bicameral mind.* New York: Houghton-Mifflin, 1977.

Pribram, K. *Languages of the brain.* Belmont, California: Brooks-Cole, 1979.

Scheflen, A. E. with Scheflen, A. *Body language and the social order.* Englewood Cliffs, New Jersey: Prentice-Hall, 1972. (Previously published as *Stream and structural communicational behavior*, 1965.)

Scheflen, A. E. *Communicational structure: Analysis of psychotherapy transactions.* Bloomington, Indiana: Indiana University Press, 1973.

Scheflen, A. E. *How behavior means.* New York: Doubleday, 1974.

Scheflen, A. E. & Ashcraft, N. *Human territory: how we behave in space time.* Englewood Cliffs, New Jersey: Prentice-Hall, 1976.

INTRODUCTION

Martha Davis

The *Conference on Interaction Rhythms*[1] brought together social scientists interested in recurring patterns of face-to-face interaction, particularly the paralinguistic and kinesic dimensions of communication. Whereas the participants shared an enthusiasm for understanding the intricacies and regularities of interaction, they were very different in their approaches to interaction research. This was an interdisciplinary conference. Anthropology, ethology, linguistics, dance ethnology, psychology, speech pathology, psychiatry, sociology, and ethnomusicology were represented. Understandably the terminology and methods of the researchers varied. It was a credit to the

[1] The *Conference on Interaction Rhythms* was sponsored by the Institute for Nonverbal Communication Research. Chaired by Conrad M. Arensberg and Martha Davis, it was held March 23 and 24, 1980, at Teachers College, Columbia University, New York City. The Institute is a nonprofit educational organization for those interested in nonverbal communication research and its applications. It currently sponsors several publications including *Kinesis; News and Views of Nonverbal Communication*, published six times a year by Trinity University. The Institute is located at 25 West 86 Street, New York, New York 10024.

conference participants that traditional academic factions did not develop and discussion was not reduced, as it well might have been, to a debate between experimental research methods and ethological or systems approaches.

Structural linguistics, systems theory, biorhythms research, and the rediscovery of the importance of the body in communication form the background for the research presented in this volume. And Eliot Chapple, Ray Birdwhistell, and Albert Scheflen are its pioneers. But, as Scheflen reminds us in the Preface, dance and music are the ancient and ever-present sources of insight into these present attempts to understand the role of rhythm and temporal regularity in social behavior. It is not a coincidence that the language of music or the movement analysis system of choreographer Rudolf Laban inform the work of some of these researchers. As the chapters by Lomax, Chapple, and Mathiot and Carlock indicate, music and dance rhythms are more than analogies for rhythms in social behavior.

At first glance the subjects of these chapters seem so diverse that they belong in different books. Yet they each deal with how people "get it together." There is a common concern with the regularities of interaction that serves social organization and helps people to sustain and negotiate myriad face-to-face encounters. There is a common interest in the behavioral manifestations of rapport and social bonding.

In a more technical vein, there are relationships between the studies in terms of the length of behaviors delineated. Each study cuts time in a particular way—from the "microbits" of motion visible in slow motion film as analyzed by Condon to the 90- and 180-minute cycles of conversation described by Hayes and Cobb. Condon reports patterns occurring in milliseconds. Beebe describes 1/4- and 2/3-second rhythms. Mathiot, Stern, and Duchan focus on sequences lasting from approximately 1/2 to 2 seconds before they are repeated. The behavioral segments described to Lomax appear to vary in length from a few seconds of dance movements which then repeat to several minutes of a complex song. The store transactions studied by Jones and von Raffler-Engel occur from about 15 to 75 seconds. The interaction sequences illustrated by Daubenmire and Searles last several minutes. LaFrance, like Crown and Siegman, sums her observations for statistical assessment irrespective of length and place in the sequence. But the positions she records appear to last several minutes. Finally, in a big leap up the time scale, Hayes and Cobb examine 90- and 180-minute cycles recurring through days and weeks.

One of the main debates at the conference involved this hierarchy from smaller to larger behavior units. Namely, how do the different levels of behavior interrelate, and are Condon's microbits of interactional synchrony the "atomic" unit on which other interaction rhythms of increasing length are built? Considering the hierarchy of levels of interaction in terms of the size or length of the behavior bit is obviously useful as a start, and there are suggestions here that we may be discovering the "natural" rhythms and cycles important to specific levels and contexts. But, as we move up the scale from micro to macro behavioral units, the types of behavior attended to change from tiny alterations in direction of body parts (e. g., Condon) or gradations of change of facial expression (e. g., Beebe et al.) to aspects of posture and orientation (e. g., LaFrance; Jones and von Raffler-Engel) to analyses of clusters of conversation over days (Hayes and Cobb). Future attempts to interrelate interaction levels will obviously have to consider many more aspects of speech and motion: more complex aspects of spatial patterning, group formation, posture intonation, movement intensity, touch, and so on.

Despite tangible relationships between the studies, the question persists as to why such diverse researchers, traditionally entitled to create a scientific tower of Babel for two days, were able to address this theme so coherently. And why does one find anthropologists underlining the biological basis of the interaction patterns described? Of course, they did not simply vote for nature in a nature-nurture debate. It would be more accurate to say several researchers, most of them anthropologists, articulated the position that there is cultural shaping of the interaction rhythms which themselves have a biological basis.

Perhaps one of the reasons people from such diverse disciplines could confer on this theme and display some accord as to the origins and functions of the interaction rhythms lies in the nature of the kinesic and paralinguistic phenomena they are investigating. No one here focuses on "content": what people do or say, the lexical meaning of their utterances, or the symbolic and instrumental character of specific actions. In different ways they all attend to the forms of interaction, patterns of coordination, tempo, alternation, and duration in behavior. Unlike speech content with arbitrary forms (i. e., there is no iconic or intrinsic relation between the sound or "look" of the word and what it means, onomatapoetic words being rather rare exceptions), the patterns described in this volume suggest their significance. They have what psychologists call face validity. There are recognizable or intrinsic relationships between the patterns observed and their presumed or discovered significance[2] (Davis, 1975).

Thus, it is not a coincidence that mothers use a repeated rising pattern of inflection to get attention (see Chap. 6). Or that individuals signal inattention by lowering head and gaze (see Chap. 7). Or that the members of cultures with permissive childrearing practices take long, "indulgent" speaking turns (see Chap. 9).

Theories of learning by association or conditioning have a disconcerting way of implying that the patterns learned and so transmitted can be arbitrary in form. In that framework it presents no problem if the greeting of one culture is a slap; the greeting of another a kiss. But the patterns described in this volume are not arbitrary. As Chapple, Stern, and Lomax each suggests, the forms of these interaction rhythms have obvious adaptive functions and biological substrates, although they vary greatly by culture and context and are profoundly sensitive to changes in the environment. Moreover, whereas the rhythms may be learned as Condon suggests, the fetus is absorbing the rhythms of speech and motion of his or her culture in utero; the

[2]Davis, M. *Towards understanding the intrinsic in body movement.* New York: Arno Press, 1975.

patterns themselves may be recognizable to at least a degree across cultures. That primary modes of organizing and regulating social interactions are rooted in adaptive actions is of course more parsimonious and logical than that the patterns are arbitrary in form.

The intrinsic nature of the movement and paralinguistic patterns described in these chapters may account for the sense that we can readily identify with them intuitively, visually, and musically, even though we are continually surprised at the intricacy and richness the forms take and respect the great range of cultural variation. When Hayes and Cobb offer evidence that couples talk in regular intervals of the diurnal cycle; when LaFrance reports that mirrored, but not identical positions, correlate with rapport; when Condon describes the "CVC" pattern in which consonant-vowel-consonant stress synchronizes with accelerations and decelerations of movement; there is a sense of "how extraordinary" mingled at once with "of course it could be that way."

If this book is a fair reflection of the state of the art of interaction rhythms research, one can see it is a subject on the threshold of becoming a topic of broad interest and investigation. It has moved beyond studies of a few contexts such as psychotherapy, and beyond the individual efforts of a pioneering few, to the active interest of those in many professions. There is a great deal of interdisciplinary communication and with it cross-fertilization of methods and observations. The speakers at this conference are really part of an informal "network." Kendon, Condon, Byers, and Lomax worked or consulted extensively with Scheflen and Birdwhistell. Stern and LaFrance have collaborated with Condon. The work of Feldstein, Siegman, Hayes, and Cobb is very directly related to Chapple's. Mathiot, Oliva, and Lomax each acknowledge an intellectual kinship with linguists Trager and Smith. At different times two or three of the researchers have worked for several years together in research teams. One sensed at the conference a respect for the arduousness of the research described by those who knew first hand what each had to do to produce these summaries of hours of film, video, or sound tape analyses.

But as the subject gains in broader interest and effort, there is a danger that researchers may become embedded in the details of their individual studies and the demands of their particular focus, losing sight of important questions raised by the work. It is easy to imagine myriad ways this research applies to our lives, but the step from pure research to valuable practice is one few are attempting as yet. Nevertheless, there are references to practical applications through the book, particularly in the discussions following certain chapters.

And the discussions of Scheflen, Arensberg, and Byers are broad sweeps that consider the philosophical and theoretical implications of this research. As they indicate, investigating interaction rhythms can transform our ways of knowing and our perceptions of human nature. Illuminated by such study, the ordinary bits of film such as were shown at the conference—a mother and infant at play, two men talking, a group dancing— can be startling. They can stir us to reconsider our most ordinary and fundamental assumptions about living systems.

The chapters by Conrad Arensberg, Paul Byers, William Condon, and Daniel Stern are based on transcripts of extemporaneous presentations, and although edited for clarity, the informal tone of each has been preserved. The other authors have contributed formal papers written for the conference or afterward, based on their talks. Two papers, not presented at the conference, have been included as invaluable contributions to this volume. They are the preface by Albert Scheflen and the chapter on nurse-patient interaction by M. Jean Daubenmire and Sharon Searles.

There were discussion periods after each presentation, and some of these are included. Comments of discussions not reproduced at the end of the chapters have been incorporated into the papers. At the end of the conference the presenters formed a panel for a final discussion. Given its brevity, it has not been presented here as a separate chapter. The principal sections of this panel discussion can be found in the discussions following Paul Byers' and William Condon's presentations.

Part I

Film greatly slowed down illuminates details of interaction largely out of our awareness. With slow motion film William Condon can demonstrate the exquisite synchrony of movements between people in conversation, and Beatrice Beebe and her colleagues can illustrate the subtle coordination of facial expressions and movements toward and away as infant and mother play a hand game. In these chapters the focus is primarily on "micro" interaction patterns occurring in fractions of a second. The section begins and ends with major theoretical discussions of the significance of interaction rhythms by Eliot D. Chapple and Paul Byers and is replete throughout with examples of the function of these rhythms in social bonding. With its stress on mother-infant interactions and the microrhythms of rapport and synchrony, it has a most extensive discussion of the biological bases of these interaction patterns. Another theme emerging in the chapters by Beatrice Beebe et al., Daniel Stern, and Judith Duchan involves the role of repetitive movements and intonation patterns in establishing and maintaining attention and cognitive expectancies. Disturbances in interaction rhythms and their relationship to psychopathology and disorders of communication is also a prominent theme here, particularly in the chapters by William Condon and Judith Duchan.

Chapter 1

MOVEMENT AND SOUND:
The Musical Language of Body Rhythms in Interaction

Eliot D. Chapple

I should say first, by way of preface, that I am unhappy with the term, "communication." Not merely is it a buzz word, but its primary denotation reminds us of that mandatory merchandising process by which every aspiring manager or public persuader is supposed to acquire the techniques of symbolic manipulation (and body movements), for a price. As we well know, there are hordes of experts anxious to sell their wares. Many years ago, when the sanctity of communication was first becoming fashionable, I wrote a short piece, " 'Understanding' Is Not Enough" (Chapple, 1949); *nor is it*, in therapy, in industrial relations, in managerial effectiveness or in national or international affairs. To understand in no sense guarantees that you have or will change how you act. It merely provides great opportunities for self-justification.

There are other usages (and meanings), however worthy and interesting to pursue, which distract our attention from the investigation of the interaction rhythms themselves. Great effort has been expended in trying to produce a vocabulary of body movement patterns in their space-time contexts. Whether or not these are to be considered paralinguistic, thus in some degree different from the analysis of language as we know it, they still reduce the patterning of movement and sound to lexicological stereotypes. Beyond that, as an expansion of linguistics, they focus our attention on the cognitive and denotive use of symbols and their logics. In so doing, they minimize the significance of movements and sounds as *direct* effectors of change in central nervous system states.

Interaction rhythms are the resultants of the interplay of the somatic, autonomic, and endocrine subsystems of the central nervous system (CNS), as we now understand it (Pearse, 1968; Pearse and Takor, 1976; Guillemin, 1978). They are primarily identified by observation of somatic (and particularly skeletal) muscle movements. They constitute the neurobiological configurations of the individual through which the learned cultural patternings of the interaction rhythms are expressed (Chapple, 1979). It should not be thought that since these neurobiological components are derived from the genotype, they are not modified experientially, from the moment of birth, and even before. "Learning," as a term, is perhaps liable to be taken in too restricted a sense, by psychologists at least, which is why those of us who have been concerned with biochemical and physiological genetics prefer to use the term, "experiential," to include all the interactions and environmental adaptations influencing the system.

Moreover, even today, there is a tendency to think of genetics as dealing only with structural genes, forgetting that it is the regulatory genes which control the rates at which neurobiological changes take place and through which environmental modification of patterns of behavior occur. At the same time, we must also realize that although experiential influence can potentiate, modify, or suppress genetic expression, the genotype also sets boundaries beyond which changes will not appear. This is why interaction rhythms are species-specific, and thus a universal property of humans, yet also capable of absorbing and elaborating on the cultural differentiations which experiential influences cumulatively provide.

In what follows, therefore, you must understand that, for me at least, interaction is not equivalent to communication. On the contrary, as I shall point out, interaction is the primary language affecting human beings. It has these properties because changes in its rhythms consequent on variations in its patterns of synchrony and asynchrony are mediated through the CNS even though they are evidenced directly for us largely by its somatic subsystem. Secondarily, and only at times, our verbal and non-verbal cultural vocabularies gain or lose their "communicative" impact to the degree their symbolic representations approach (refer to) these interaction rhythmic patterns.

Put another way, the language of the CNS (the brain) differs very considerably from mathematics as it presently exists, its logics and the logical structures of the language we use. This point was made very clearly by the mathematician, John von Neumann in the unfinished Silliman lectures he was writing before his death, published posthumously as *The Computer and the Brain* (von Neumann, 1958). One of the founders of computer technology, he put himself to learn as much as he could about the functioning of the nervous system since he, and many others, were struck by the apparent similarities between the two, each activated through electrical circuitry and digital switching. (As he discovered, this oversimplifies what goes on at the neuron level.) It became increasingly obvious to him that, though you could call the brain a computer if you wanted to, its properties are completely unlike those of any computer our science and technology can contemplate building. Consider a few of these differences and their implications which I shall summarize.

(1) Even when von Neumann wrote, and transistor technology had appeared, the reaction time was between 10^{-6} and 10^{-7} seconds. Since then, with bubble "memories" or silicon chips, the speed has markedly increased. By contrast, the transmission of pulses across the synapse of a neuron to its axon, and so along the neural chain, is about 10^{-4} seconds. But this is by no

means the whole story since once it acts, the neuron is fatigued and requires time to elapse before it can respond to another pulse. Von Neumann estimated this latent period as about 1.5×10^{-2} seconds. He thus concluded that transmission time itself only required 1 to 2 percent of the total time available, and that the balance was needed to enable it to return to its original, nonstimulated state.

(2) Computers, as we all know, are essentially serial in organization, that is, each step programmed has to be completed before the next can start. It is true that modern computer design can incorporate some parallel processing. By contrast, the nervous system can process an enormous number of items simultaneously, but at a much slower rate. It can, of course, shift back and forth to serial processing. More important, a very large number of cross-connections in the parallel channels are available. In the cerebellum, for example, which, as we shall see, is the primary coordinating point for movement and sound in the lower centers (the hindbrain), there can be as many as 2,000 synapses per cell.

This fundamental difference in the operations of the human nervous system as compared with the computer is most easily dramatized by realizing that a single error in a computer program reduces the results to garbage. On the other hand, the remarkable degree of redundancy built into the organism means that there are all sorts of restorative channels available to minimize difficulties. I am reminded of a common judgment made about English statesmen (at least some of them) in the last century. It was often remarked that X's knowledge of the facts was almost nonexistent; his reasons for making a decision were almost always wrong, yet by means of some deep process going on which neither the statesman nor the observer understood, he almost always came up with the right decision.

(3) Of equal importance is another consequence of this redundancy, namely that the CNS operates at very low precision. Its pulse train intensities are on the order of 50 to 250 cycles per second, whereas computers use equivalent trains of from 10^{-10} to 10^{-12}. Part of the reason for such computer requirements, the ranges of which are being continuously increased, stems from the arithmetic or mathematical part. To handle complicated tasks as the nervous system obviously does, a computer requires great precision because when long calculations are made, errors cumulate and amplify early errors as the calculations continue. The nervous system, on the other hand, uses periodic or nearly periodic trains of pulses, a kind of frequency modulation, intensity transformed into frequencies. Von Neumann points out that no known computer can operate reliably within these limits. Apart from the properties of arithmetic, computers also require a language or statement of logics which is, after all, derived from our everyday language. It is clear that this language cannot be the language of the central nervous system, nor can its "arithmetic" either.

(4) Now the significance of what von Neumann had to say was first pointed out, as far as I know, by the composer, George Rochberg (1972). He made the point:

> Quite obviously, music has the structured capability of being both highly parallel and completely serial. All harmonic and polyphonic structures embody parallel, i. e. simultaneous, streams of pitch relations. The continuous flow of their temporal movement— even where breaks in the form of silence or rests occur—embodies serial succession. Only in the instance of monophony, i. e. unaccompanied single-voiced melodic structures, is the parallel mode suppressed and temporarily successive pitch relations, i.e. serial,

define the mode of projection. Given the essentially parallel structure of the human nervous system, i. e. its ability to deal with many things at once or many things together in what I shall call an "ensemble" relationship, it is apparent that the natural structure of the central nervous system, the human brain, is adapted to receiving parallel musical structures, i. e. ensembles of simultaneously organized levels of pitch and rhythmic relationships, directly and without the aid of inter- mediary functions. The central nervous system is also capable of receiving any order of successive serial events organized on the melodic plane. (pp. 80–81)

After discussing in these terms the reasons why the music of the past is so meaningful to us, he goes on to say, in partial summary:

It seems to me that where what is received activates and animates the human nervous system *corresponds* to its natural order or functions (parallel/serial) there we should expect to find the highest degree and most synchronized release of energy—and therefore flow of communication, uninhibited and undisturbed, be- tween the source of the stimulus, in this case music, and the receiving, responding system (human nervous system). Conversely, therefore, where what is received disturbs and inhibits this flow of communication, i. e., taking in, organizing sense impressions of external phenomena and registering them in forms of logical response, and synchronization of energy release, does not correspond sufficiently or at all with the natural order of the central nervous system's functioning, the chances are very good, indeed excellent, that the central nervous system is likely to suffer temporary "breakdown," i. e. inability to relate to the musical messages streaming into it from outside. In short, as the saying goes: "we don't get it." (p. 82)

Finally, by way of conclusion, after quoting the last part of von Neumann's final chapter, Rochberg says:

I think it a reasonable assumption to make that music is a secondary "language" system whose logic is closely related to the primary, alpha logic of the central nervous system itself, i. e. of the human body. If I am right, then it follows that the perception of music is simply the process reverse; i. e. we listen with our bodies, with our nervous system and their primary interacting parallel/skeletal and memory functions. The potential perceptual meaning for each of us individually of musical stimuli, i. e. message systems, increases with the increase of conscious attentive awareness. If this is true—the question is how to corroborate it—the implications are very great and far reaching. At the very least, the pulse-trains which transmit messages in the nervous system suggest a direct correspondence with the logic of musical events characterized by structural continuity based on self-perpetuating forms of repetition and recall. The fact that these pulse-trains function periodically suggests that music itself may be or is a direct expression or reflection of the fundamental language of the human nervous system. (p. 88)[1]

What is essential, I think, in understanding the fundamental properties of interaction rhythms, is to recognize that we have to expand Rochberg's thesis to sound *and* movement, to recognize that these together make up the total response patterns of the individual and that those parallel chains in all their complexity of input and processing comprise integral configurations on which interaction rhythms are built. We hear with our bodies, we make music with our bodies, and we use our bodies as

[1] Curiously, Rochberg was using von Neumann as a means of attacking the so-called aleatory composers who start off with stochastic or numerological combinations to construct highly artificial music. He used von Neumann's book and his own gloss upon it to prove that they were violating the properties and limitations of the CNS. As a subtheme, he attacked science and technology as creators of this "rational madness," apparently able to block out from his consciousness that von Neumann was, after all, a mathematician-scientist (there was Los Alamos, there were computers, and there were neurophysiologists on whom von Neumann based much of his book).

instruments through which we intensify the meanings of which it is capable, and by which we set in motion similar patterns in the bodies of others. Parenthetically, I should point out that, though Rochberg saw the significance of von Neumann's analysis, it should not be thought that he is alone in understanding the primacy of the body in the arts. I need only mention Stanley Burnshaw, Suzanne Langer, André Spire, Ortega y Gasset, and, for that matter, Mr. Justice Holmes (see References).[2]

To investigate the properties of interaction rhythms, verbal and nonverbal, thus requires bringing together all forms of the expressive and performing arts—music, dance, theater—as well as the interactional events of everyday life. Nor must we forget that these, by necessity (and by choice for the scientist), include the rites and ceremonies performed in periods of crisis of the individual or the group, the latter expanding to the whole society. Further, by contrast to many classifications, we cannot exclude all those formal and informal ritualized performances so evident in sports, in political gatherings, in meetings of business or governmental groups—the list is endless (Chapple & Coon, 1978). Not only are these made up of the rhythmic interactions between the participants, but the variations within a semiformalized framework provide great opportunities for highly individualized performances of expressive rhythms.

Given all these systems of interactional forms and their organization into complex architectonic structures, we need to begin by asking how biological rhythms gain their expression. Most of us have read about the pervasive influence of the circadian rhythms found at every level of the organism—from DNA and RNA metabolism, cell division, up through the integrative systems of the CNS to the patterns of activity and inactivity of the total organism. I suspect that what we primarily remember is how it affects us in jet travel across several time

---

[2] Holmes, Oliver W., Jr., see *inter alia* his comments in letter to Harold Laski, in *Holmes-Laski Letters*, New York: Atheneum, 1963, pp. 306, 357 in Vol. 1. There are many other such comments, e. g., Vol. 2, p. 11, "Sound [of a writing] is the half of immortality."

zones. So profound is the discomfort produced by what the biologists call the uncoupling of the rhythms, their loss of synchronization, that manuals are now available which tell you how to prepare yourself for such long trips and what body systems take the longest time to get back into synchrony. Since flying east is the most disturbing—your clock time telling you it is early morning when in fact those living there are in their afternoons—you need to preadjust your schedule before you leave, to shift your clock ahead. Flying west, the clocks need to be slowed down, and, we are told, the wise traveler will have cocktails on a westbound trip (alcohol slowing down body functions), but is urged to avoid them going east.

There are two fundamental hypotheses relevant for all rhythms systems in the body, about which we are usually uninformed.

(1) Our biological clocks are what are technically known as relaxation oscillators of the van der Pol type. Van der Pol initially developed the equations we and others use and have expanded to describe the beating of the heart. Quite in contrast to other periodic functions, biological oscillators are not of the harmonic pendulum type; they are also nonstationary, nonlinear, and nonconservative (Chapple, 1971, 1979). What this means is that, unlike pendulums or other familiar periodic functions, they can shift their values radically from one "beat" period to the next, a characteristic obvious in music, dance, and interaction patterns generally. Moreover, oscillators are driven by an alternating sequence made up of buildup of energy (inaction) and then its discharge (action), the properties evidenced being under the control of the CNS. A capacitor in an electrical current or, of course, the neuron is a familiar example of the physical model.

Most science writing has concentrated on the circadian rhythms, the more or less 24-hour cycle best illustrated in the animal's being active (and awake), being inactive (and usually asleep). But the fact is that such oscillators characterize all the rhythms of the body, from very fast, on the order of fractions of seconds—muscle fibers discharge at 20 per second; motor patterns at 6 per second out of which interaction is built together with respiration at a rate of 16 per minute; heart 72 per minute—to very long, even up to year-long, circannual cycles, typifying migrating animals (Iberall & Cardon, 1964). Before discussing these within the framework of interaction rhythms, a second point needs to be made.

(2) What should be obvious, but apparently is not, is that since biological oscillators drive all levels of the body, the rhythms they exhibit are endogenous. In the old language of general physiology, they are spontaneous and continuous, usually coterminous with living. This does not mean, of course, that they operate independently of one another; on the contrary, they are parts of highly complex interrelated systems whose resultants, consequent on the ongoing interplay of genotype and environment, modify, inhibit, or maximize their expression in the phenotype of the genetic potentialities (Chapple, 1979).

My reasons for emphasizing these properties of the constituents of the total organism (and its individuality) are that the basic neuroendocrinological, more generally, neurobiological properties (particularly those of the somatic nervous system) cannot be described within the severe limitations of a stimulus-response system. The organism is no Lockean *tabula rasa*, to be regarded in today's belief as a passive animal, waiting and needing a stimulus before beginning a response, a notion popularized by B. F. Skinner. Perhaps its wide acceptance is due to the American glorification of learning as the all-encompassing process which attributes to environmental influences alone the shaping of our individualities, ignoring biological realities.

If we are to obtain measurements of interaction rhythms with any accuracy, without which we will be unable to differentiate rhythms and their variations from one another, we need criteria for endpoints for each action and each inaction. An action begins when the muscle systems selected for observation contract; it ends when they reach a state of relaxation. These alternate states are easy to observe; they can be substantiated by the electromyograph, since absence of electrical current indicates relaxation is present. Most contacts between people involve conversation or more formal types of interchange. In these situations, the muscle systems are primarily those of the face and the head, particularly of the mouth (sound if muscle movement is not apparent), and gestures of the hands, arms and shoulders. Gestural movement and speech are interdependent. They may substitute for each other in a single action due to cultural and idiosyncratic differences among the individuals taking part. The action phase thus consists of the total response of the person, and equivalent criteria are necessary where the interaction involves body movement, locomotor action in spacing, and directional orientation.

Regarded as an oscillator, we identify the frequency with which action begins and the durations of the phase states for each period (of the frequency). In free-running or basal states, where there is no disturbance of the rhythm (by another person), the rhythm is ordinarily regular. Given another person, however, the situation changes since the coupling of the rhythms sets in motion an entrainment process where perturbations occur until some kind of stability in their frequencies occurs, approaching equality of sub- or superharmonics of them. The phase differences are close to 180°, since the sum of the action and inaction of each person equals the 360°-cycle. If synchronization does not occur, then the degrees of arc of difference are positive or negative (clockwise or counterclockwise). Positive degrees indicate an overlap of their actions; negative their inactions ("silences" if understood to mean absence of sound or expressive movement) (Chapple, 1971).

Where asynchrony occurs during this process of entrainment, as it almost always does, it may be sufficiently small to be below the threshold level of the individual, for that type of asynchrony.

When the magnitude of the interaction stress (asynchrony) is above the threshold, a disturbance of the rhythm of the individual's basic oscillator occurs. This involves positive or negative changes in frequency. The phase difference, following the terminology of electrical engineering (and biology), is called a transient. In the simplest case, where only a single pattern of stress occurs, usually repetitively, and as we do experimentally, the shift in the values of the oscillator during the stress does not mean an immediate return to the basal level when the asynchronous stress is ended. What happens is that the immediate reaction to the stress is triggered off by neuronal activation and the beginning of the release of hormones into the body system. When the stress ends, the hormones are still present and cumulating. Thus, the chemical reactions continue until they have been absorbed, structurally modified by a chemical antagonist, or otherwise undergo change which reduces their activity below threshold levels (Chapple, 1979).

Even to give you the briefest summary of the regulatory systems of the CNS, directly bearing on interaction rhythms, is far beyond the scope of this lecture. [And even a book, such as the one I am writing on the neurobiological foundations of violence can treat only a small fraction of the total system (Chapple, 1970; Chapple, *in preparation*).] But several points are worth making.

(1) The interaction rhythm we have begun to discuss represents the resultant of complex systems of populations of mutually coupled oscillators; each population through that coupling becomes a monofrequency oscillator. At each hierarchical level of such monofrequency oscillators, they in turn can be, and usually are, mutually coupled to form a higher order monofrequency oscillator, the whole animal being the ultimate synthesis.

When interactional stress occurs, this compounded oscillator is subject to rhythm splitting, that is, to the loss of
synchrony (and coupling) between two or more sub-
oscillators. What this means is a shift in thresholds, in
the intensity of a given transient to a particular stress; in
fact, to the disparities and deviations (and pathology)
which accentuates the differences already existing between one individual and another.

(2) Although other oscillators regulating other components
of the body contribute significantly to the final resultant
monofrequency oscillator of the action-inaction sequencing of the total organism, the basal or fundamental
oscillatory system on which the interaction rhythms are
developed is located in the vital centers of the medulla
oblongata. Without going too much into anatomy, this
body is directly above the spinal cord and contains the
vital centers for respiration *and* activity, heart rate and
circulation. Immediately above the medulla is the pons,
which modifies these inputs; it also receives and transmits data on sound to the auditory cortex. Finally,
(almost omitting the 4th ventricle) as integrator of this
so-called hind-brain system, the cerebellum serves to
manage posture, movement equilibrium, and finely
coordinated motor skills including speech. Consider its
relevance to our present concerns. This whole hind-
brain system is interconnected by the reticular formation internally and externally to higher and lower levels
of the CNS. It also maintains wakefulness, and when
the frequency of impulses it transmits to the cerebral
cortex decreases, it facilitates sleep.

(3) Though the cerebral cortex is supposedly the triumphant
achievement of the evolutionary process, what makes
Johnny run is at the subcerebral level, a configuration
of neural and chemical transmitters—hypothalamus,
pituitary, pineal gland, and limbic system through
which the somatic, autonomic, and endocrine systems

are regulated. This is the system, coordinated by the inhibiting and releasing hormones of the hypothalamus, which manages the internal environment and activates the reaction of the organism to external stress. It is convenient to differentiate its operation (including what happens at the hind-brain level) into sympathetic and parasympathetic functions (which are, in fact, the traditional anatomical divisions of the autonomic nervous system). I say traditional, because the situation is more complex. The sympathetic (usually referred to as producing the adrenergic state) is responsible for alerting the body to danger—fight or flight, anger or fear— while the parasympathetic (called cholinergic for acetylcholine, a neural activator) acts directly on separate organs and, under medium stimulation, it produces feelings of pleasure, affection, love. When stresses become severe, both combine, intensify, and radically change the reactions beyond their low-level activation patterns. It is from this whole conjoint system that all the shadings of interaction rhythms which differentiate one state from another arise. It is here that reaction and action are triggered off.

Thus if we begin to look for the roots of the musical language of body rhythms, it is here that we have to begin. But something more has to be taken into account before our picture can become clear.

Two people in interaction, whatever the form of their duet, however varied their synchrony or the stresses they impose on one another, hardly provide us with the whole framework we need if we are to incorporate the performing arts and their not so artistic variants into the total design. These can only occur where more than two people, often many people, are in interaction. We may think that a solitary performer, alone upon the stage, can provide us with evidence of a free-running oscillator without perturbations of any sort to interfere. But out there, as every performer knows, is that multiheaded creature, the audience, unsynchronized, too often asynchronous and unresponsive. There is no directional order, no polarity, when two people interact. Though entrainment may develop, the stability of synchronization is at the mercy of other pairs with whom each also interacts, where the coupling coefficients may shift in magnitude as time goes on.

But where one person is the pacemaker, the initiator, for others to respond to, all the oscillators of the individuals participating can be attuned (entrained) to become a monofrequency oscillator (Chapple & Lui, 1976). These are set or group events, the primary means by which the performing arts secure their effects. Thus, the person as pacemaker is aware from moment to moment, or should be, of the degree to which the members of the audience are responding in synchrony at the frequencies set and in the phase relationships intended.[3] We all know to what lengths a performer will go to try to get them ''up'' to the rhythm he or she is trying to establish and the impact that failure to achieve and sustain that synchrony can also create. But we don't have to use the theater and the performing arts as illustration. The success of every group, every meeting, every political campaign—the dynamics of every organizational system—depends on the degree to which this polarization takes place and is maintained. And this is true for that chaotic lack of organization a mob illustrates. Yet in a few moments, some individuals, call them leaders or demagogues, can rouse them and weld them into a cohering group capable of victory.

Moreover, in *Principles of Anthropology* (Chapple & Coon, 1978), these set or group events and their structural forms, there called a set (now better called an interactional set), were applied by us to the analysis of simple and complex organizations and their mutual relations. By definition, an interac-

[3] See my quotation from Mark Twain's account of how carefully controlled the timing of a pause has to be in getting the maximum response in telling a ghost story in *Principles of Anthropology*, 1978.

tional set is a unidirectional array in which individual A initiates action to a number of persons, B 1, B 2, B 3 . . . B n. They are, therefore, mutually entrained to the pacemaker oscillator, in this example, individual A. This array becomes polarized directionally when the B's initiate in set events to a series of C's. A will also initiate to them, and, sometimes, all the B's and C's will respond together. Most important, the reverse order in set events for that array running counter to the direction established does not occur. We also showed how complex organizations were (and are) built out of interactional sets following different directional flows—like work flow, staff-line as well as supervisory orders.

What is important, however, is why does it work, what makes such interactional sets so powerful, and how does it fit the theory of biological organisms as oscillators? Part of the answer came from Norbert Wiener who had shown that mutual entrainment is only possible if the component individual oscillators are nonlinear (Wiener, 1958). Several biologists, interested in biological (interactional) rhythms, called his attention to a species of firefly in Malaysia where, beginning erratically, mutual entrainment develops until all the fireflies are flashing in synchrony. Wiener pointed out that a population of uncoupled oscillators has a normal frequency spectrum. When mutually coupled, the spectrum peaks and generates a narrow frequency band. By the ergodic theorem, a measurement over a population ensemble is equivalent to a measurement over time (Barlow, 1960). Thus the greater the number of individuals mutually coupled, the greater the stability of the ensuing oscillator, because the frequencies of response of all the participants are maximally synchronized.

Consider then the development of an interactional set organizing a large number of persons. The pacemaker, individual A, establishes the frequency for all the participants, but there is a systematic phase difference from that of the pacemaker, following the direction of the polarity. (In simple words, he talks most of the time and sets the rhythms by momentary pauses for them to respond.) Moreover, spatial distribution and relative position will also filter out. Those at the bottom of the array will be separated by the longest distance from the pacemaker (our leader). Thus, this interactional set of relationships acquires a common oscillatory rhythm with the pacemaker A, who has the fastest oscillator and the greatest coupling strength (through dominance). This polarity is a property of the *whole* interactional set and is characterized by a frequency gradient from fastest to slowest. If the gradient falls off too steeply, the number of levels of the hierarchy decreases.

Without elaborating on the mathematics, one point is essential, apart from the properties of the polarity itself. That is, the equation requires and includes a spatial parameter for the distance from the pacemaker to persons in stage 1, to stage 2, etc. This is a function of perceptual (visual) input, is nonlinear, and is used in equations which enable us to define the critical size of a group, beyond which it will begin to break down (Chapple & Lui, 1976).

Now the utility of this kind of analysis, which I have developed elsewhere, lies in the fact that it becomes possible to bring together the architectonic structure of individuals as oscillators as they become involved in space-time configurations of interaction rhythms. As the number of individuals included grows, the power of attraction upon them sharply increases since the rhythmic and synchronous reactions are perceptually observed, even where the participants are not directly aware of the synchrony of the sensory inputs. Thus the CNS rhythms, modified directly by the somatic nervous system, become closely coupled. Autonomic and endocrine nervous system activation is as one with the somatic whose rhythm we observe in skeletal muscle patterning. The great rites and ceremonies, the control which the leader exercises over his followers, are thus capable of analysis and prediction (Chapple & Coon, 1978). More important, perhaps, is what this tells us about the direct impact on us of the language of rhythm derived from the biological oscillators of the human body, not merely in the performing arts and politics, but in those other language rhythms which directly affect us. John Donne said, "The Body Makes The Minde," and it is this quotation which is symbolic of much of the work of Suzanne Langer, Stanley Burnshaw, and Ortega y Gasset (see References).

Each of these languages (rhythmic modalities) is characterized by its capacity to elicit responses from the largest number of uncoupled oscillators possible and entrain them, rapidly and with intensity, so that the responses of the constituent individuals become synchronized and their polarities established and maintained. So the rhythms become musical, not in the restricted literal sense always, but in spacing individuals in places relative to one another and in combining their movements in space with their responses or nonresponses as they act as the oscillators require. The language of music utilizes the infinite variations which the rhythm timing provides, shifting the volume to accentuate the melodic contrasts mediated by pitch changes. And all this is patterned neurobiologically by the divergent directions of the acoustical frequencies of the major and minor systems which appear clinically, at least, to represent sympathetic and parasympathetic configurations. Not too much investigation has been done in identifying the paths in the CNS which make us respond so differently, but it is reasonably clear of what they probably consist and how one could go about the analysis. Moreover, similar contrasts are identifiable in dance and other forms of expressive movement, and here we have a background of muscle-system inquiry dating back considerably before Darwin's *The Expression of the Emotions in Man and Animals* (1872) to the almost forgotten anatomical-physiological work of the great French neurologist, Duchenne, who is primarily remembered for his identification and description of locomotor ataxia, multiple sclerosis, and bulbar paralysis (Duchenne, 1867).

For, if we accept the view that the arts of apprehending through interacting and performing comprise a unified system (not quite a "seamless web" in Stanley Burnshaw's sense), since we can isolate and identify the musical language which results, even while recognizing its coherence as *form*, then it should follow that this is the primary language, one step removed from the body's oscillators, representing a true first-order abstraction. Moreover, learning the tertiary languages we have hitherto regarded as of primary or basic importance, the "three r's," depends on the skill with which we use the expressive arts of interactional movement within rhythms (of music) to give reality to the perceptual and cognitive skills that hitherto we have assumed were the basics. I do not say this lightly, since already there is much evidence that this is the way to break through the cognitive barriers which seem to puzzle so many people.[4]

I do not mean to imply that such a conclusion is intended to

[4] A remarkable but neglected series of studies was carried on by Richard Dean Weber, in the 1950s and 1960s, described in many published popular reviews and in his Ed. D. thesis, done at Teachers College, Columbia University, *An Approach To The Use of Musical Instruments In The Education of The "Trainable" Mentally Retarded*, 1966. He taught the use of musical instruments to the mentally retarded, including those with Down's syndrome, to the autistic, and to those with various forms of behavior disorders. Without being familiar with work done in interaction measurement, he prescribed interactional patterns (movement and timing) on a one-to-one basis, following sequential order in the acquisition of performance skill and pointing recurrently to lettered keys. In developing his technique, he found it essential to break down the letters into geometrically separate and identifiable parts since all of the instances of dyslexia he found, whatever their form, turned out to be due to the perceptual confusions preventing unerring differentiation between the letters of ordinary print.

Over many years and with a large number of young people, his most important finding was the universality of success, the surprising speed with which it occurred, and the carry-over in major improvement in reading and in speaking, outside of instrument performance. He describes autistic young people who hadn't spoken in years who began to talk, etc. Most of the retarded had WISC scores of 25 or less, ordinarily regarded as unreachable, yet they were able to play well; even more encouraging, to perform in public. In fact, a concert was put on at Carnegie Hall by some of these young people, reported enthusiastically in the *New York Times* (Jaffe, Natalie, "Retarded Learn A Matching Game: 'Unteachables' Are Taught Alphabet With Music," *New York Times*, July 24, 1965, p. 13).

justify turning our efforts to therapeutic or educational endeavors. As a byproduct, yes; but I would hope the primary emphasis of those concentrating on nonverbal communication research would be to put all the pieces together. Then it would become clear to everyone that there is indeed a seamless web of movements and sounds in interactional rhythms whose significance has too frequently been frittered away be well-meant, but secondary, examinations into surface phenomena.

For though communication is an "in" word today, it is an inappropriate description of our primary concerns. Yet many have been intrigued by a lexicological approach, translating movement into signs and symbols, presumed equivalent to verbal forms. In my view, this is a futile exercise. Direct impact, yes; linguistics, no.

Consider the enormous range of biological rhythms in the human body, fast and slow, transmuted and integrated by the complex interdependence of the somatic, autonomic, and endocrine nervous systems. The results of this synthesis of movement and sound act directly on us, spatially and temporally differentiating our interactional patterns. It is this body language which primarily expresses the functioning of the CNS. What we call language (verbal and nonverbal) is a cultural derivative, secondary to the cultural shaping of body language itself.

REFERENCES

Barlow, J. S. *Cold spring symposia on quantitative biology.* 1960, *25*, p. 54 (New York: Long Island Biological Association).

Burnshaw, S. *The seamless web.* New York: Braziller, 1970.

Chapple, E. D. "Understanding" is not enough. *Human Organization,* 1949, *8.*

Chapple, E. D. Toward a mathematical model of interaction: some preliminary considerations. In P. Kay (Ed.), *Explorations in mathematical anthropology.* Cambridge, Massachusetts: MIT Press, 1971.

Chapple, E. D. and Lui, Y. Y. Populations of coupled non-linear oscillators in anthropological biology systems. In *Systems, man and cybernetic society conference proceedings.* Washington, D. C.: The Institute of Electrical and Electronic Engineers, Inc., 1976.

Chapple, E. D. and Coon, C. S. *Principles of anthropology* (Rev. ed.). Huntington, N. Y.: Robert Krieger Co., Inc., 1978.

Chapple, E. D. *The biological foundations of individuality and culture.* Huntington, N. Y.: Robert Krieger Co., Inc., 1979. (Originally published as *Culture and biological man.* New York: Holt, Rinehart and Winston, 1970.)

Chapple, E. D. *Violence: Biological realities and criminological myths, in preparation.*

Darwin, C. *The expression of the emotions in man and animals.* Chicago: University of Chicago Press, 1965. (Originally published, 1872.)

Duchenne, G. B. *Physiology of motion.* E. B. Kaplan (Ed. and trans.) Philadelphia: W. B. Saunders Co., 1959. (Originally published as *Physiologic des mouvements,* Paris, 1867.)

Guillemin, R. Biochemical and physiological correlates of hypothalamus peptides. The new endocrinology of the neuron. In S. Reichlin, R. J. Baldessarini, and J. B. Martin (Eds.), *The hypothalamus.* New York: Raven Press, 1978, pp. 155–194.

Holmes, O. W. *Holmes-Laski letters.* New York: Atheneum, 1963, pp. 306, 357 in Vol. 1.

Iberall, A. S. and Cardon, S. Z. Control in biological systems: a physical review. *Annals of the New York Academy of Sciences,* 1964, *117,* pp. 445–518.

Langer, S. K. *Mind: An essay on human feeling.* Baltimore: Johns Hopkins, 1967.

Ortega y Gasset, J. *Man and people* (W. R. Trask, trans.). New York: Norton, 1957.

Pearse, A. G. E. Common cytochemical and ultra-structural characteristics of cell producing polypeptide hormones (the APUD series) and their relevance to thyroid and ultimo branchial C cells and calcitronin. *Proceedings of the Royal Society of London (Biology),* 1968, *170,* pp. 71–80.

Pearse, A. G. E. and Takor, T. Neuroendocrine embryology and the APUD concept. *Clinical Endocrinology,* 1976, *5,* pp. 229s–244s.

Rochberg, G. The avant-garde and the aesthetics of survival. *New Literary History,* 1971, *3,* pp. 71–92.

Spire, A. *Plaisir póetique et plaisir musculaire.* Paris: Vanni, 1949.

von Neumann, J. *The computer and the brain.* New Haven: Yale University Press, 1958.

Weiner, N. *Non-linear problems in random theory.* Cambridge, Massachusetts: John Wiley and MIT Press, 1958.

Chapter 2

CULTURAL MICRORHYTHMS [1]

William S. Condon

INTERACTIONAL AND SELF-SYNCHRONY

I see myself as a neophyte student of human behavior and interaction, perhaps somewhat similar to the early Sanskrit scholars in studying linguistics. I spend hours and hours just trying to see what's happening in individual behavior or between people during conversation.

At first I became interested in gesture. Two very great people in my life, and there have been many, but two particularly, Ray Birdwhistell and Albert Scheflen, influenced me a great deal. I think they're geniuses in this area and have involved many students in it. The development of this research stems in great part from Eliot Chapple, Birdwhistell, and Scheflen. When I started studying gesture in 1962, Ray sent an old film to a group of us in Pittsburgh, and we were looking at it and couldn't get

[1] This chapter was edited from a transcript of the lecture, and the informal tone has been preserved. [Ed.]

anywhere. We had the naive view that all you have to do is look at a sound film and see how people behave, see what the units of the behavior are, and lo and behold you'll understand communication. But the people in the film refused to cooperate. There was never any noncommunication. There were many, many levels of interaction going on simultaneously. Below the gesture level I was always seeing body motion; the head going, the hands going, the legs going, trunk going.

What is a unit in all of this? How can you begin to study this? I started studying it at the micro level, frame-by-frame. Down there I began to see that the body motions occur in bundles; that, as a person is talking, there's a changing and moving together of the body parts which are precisely synchronized with the articulatory structure of his or her speech. The normal person is self-synchronous with himself and his speech. This is illustrated in Fig. 2-1. You can't break out of this no matter what you do. It even covers higher levels such as a phrase (Fig. 2-7 on p.65 contains notation charts for figures.)

A major problem in this research is determining how one can segment some thing that is relatively continuous. How do you find the discrete-like within it? The concept of self-synchrony emerged, including the view that behavior is both discrete-like and continuous.

Further intensive study led to the startling observation that listeners move synchronously (entrain) with the articulatory structure of the speaker's speech. I was looking at the 4½-second segment from one of the films that Gregory Bateson had made on the West Coast. It was a woman, her husband, and their son eating dinner. I will remember what she says as long as I live. She says, "You all should come around every night. We never have had a dinner time like this in months." To carefully study the organization and sequence of this, the approach must be naturalistic or ethological. You just sit and look and look and look for thousands of hours until the order in the material begins to emerge. It's like sculpturing. Everything I've talked and written about before is only partially correct, because continued study reveals further order. When I was looking at this film over and over again, I had an erroneous view of the universe that communication takes place *between* people. Somehow this was the model. You send the message, somebody sends a message back. The messages go here and there and everywhere. But something was funny about this. I went through 130 copies of the 4½-second segment of this film. Going through each copy 100,000 times, I wore out 130 copies. I spent a year and a half studying 4½-seconds four or five hours a day, before I could see interactional synchrony.

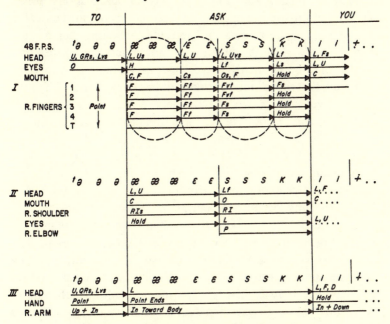

Figure 2-1: Self-Synchrony. The hierarchic synchronizing of the speaker's body with his own speech. There are sustained relationships of movement of the body motion bundles, which occur isomorphically with the articulatory "units" of speech. The analysis is of the body motion of one psychiatrist saying to another, "I was gonna ask you ... why do you ... um ... have difficulty with your late appointments?" (See Fig. 2-7) for explanation of the notations on each figure.)

Such an experience has taught me that we must be very, very careful about all of the mythologies we have about the universe. Maybe 95 percent of reality for us is mythological, and it behooves us to begin to look *at* the universe itself and let it speak and talk. It takes a long time to see things. I think for us to learn we've got to go through the fatigue of giving up prior positions, prior sets, such things as, for example, consonants and vowels. Everyone knows what they are. Really? Try listening and looking at a film to determine in reality what a consonant and a vowel are; you won't have the textbook definition. We have to relinquish something and pay an observational price. Today I'm illustrating patterns that seem very obvious now, but it took 16 hard, long years and thousands of hours to begin to see them. Why? Because our view of the universe in a sense precluded their being seen. The very picture we had of the universe was such that these kinds of things didn't even fit in it. All of the things I've hypothesized have emerged from looking at films over and over. I could never have dreamed up such a thing as interactional synchrony in advance. It would never have occurred to me. But it emerged in a sense out of the materials like a sculpturing process over time in which order slowly emerges.

After a year of continually looking at the Bateson film, I began (I think because of peripheral vision) to see the wife turning her head exactly as the husband's hands came up, and this occurred over and over again with other behavior. So I began to look at ostensible or "relative" simultaneity and saw that the speaker was moving in organization of change of the body which were precisely synchronous with the articulatory structure of his own speech; that is, the body frequency-modulates in a sense to its own speech. The listener's body also frequency-modulates, at least within 50 milliseconds, to the incoming sound structure of the speaker's speech. Figure 2-2 shows the synchronization or entrainment of the organization of the listener's body with the speaker's speech. It also occurs in infants as seen in Fig. 2-3. The whole concept of self-synchrony and interactional synchrony more and more had to be modified. It turns out that interactional synchrony really is an early phase in the auditory perceptual process, that most organisms do this in relation to hearing.

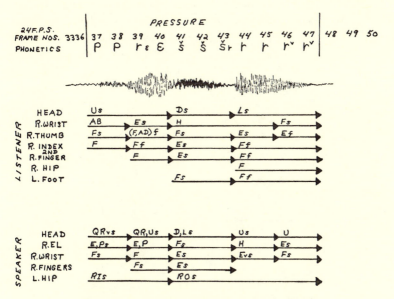

Figure 2-2: Interactional Synchrony. The synchronization of the listener's body with the speech of the speaker. The speech segmentation is based on an oscilloscopic display of the speech. As in the case of the speaker's body, there are body motion bundles in the listener's body which parallel the emerging units of the speaker's speech.

We entrain and lock in even with inanimate sounds within 50 milliseconds. You can get a myogenic (muscle) response within 10 to 50 milliseconds. These muscle or myogenic responses depend on the time-locking of ongoing tonic activity in muscles to acoustic stimuli, usually loud clicks. The responses are strongest when an electrode is placed near an active muscle (Davis, 1973). Since ongoing muscle activity can synchronize with click sounds as early as 10 to 50 milliseconds, it is not too difficult to conceive that muscle activity could be modulated in

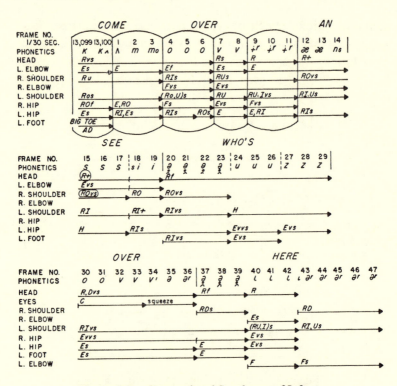

Figure 2-3:   Interactional Synchrony of Infant.
This figure shows the synchronization of the body
motion of a two-day-old infant with the speech of the
male physician talking to him. The infant was awake
and alert and looking away from the speaker. Infants
synchronized in the same way to tape-recorded speech.

relation to the structure of incoming speech within the same 10
to 50 millisecond interval. This is a possible test for deafness. If
muscles can move at 10 milliseconds or so, time-locked to
sound, the person can hear. What I am trying to clarify now is
that interactional synchrony is really a primary phase of the
perceptual process. In a sense, all of these thousands of years
our sensory processes are geared in to reflect the world adequately, and one of the first levels of this is the body's organized
response to the incoming sound signal.

There also appears to be a 1-second rhythm cycle in speaker

behavior. In Fig. 2-4, the phrases and body motion can be seen to occur at approximately 1-second intervals.

When I report this work to an audience, I can't present 50 films and 500,000 hours of analysis in 30 minutes. What I can do is pull out a segment of film and illustrate the phenomenon with it. Some may say, "Well you've only shown it there. What about all the rest?" But they don't realize that I've looked at

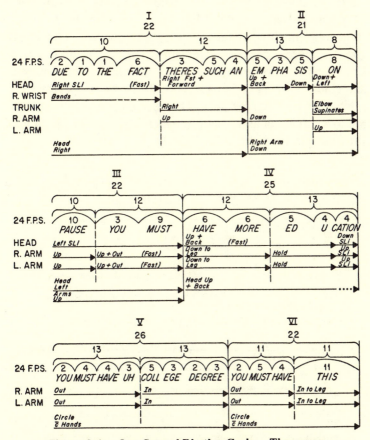

Figure 2-4:   One-Second Rhythm Cycle.   The roman numerals mark six phrases, each lasting approximately one second. The average time of excursion of the body parts is approximately 1 second. These tend to coincide with phrases. There seems to be a clear 1-second rhythm in human behavior.

another hundred films all the way through, and it's there most of the time.

I am in the process of conducting intensive reliability studies to support the hypothesis of self- and interactional synchrony, and a paper is planned. For example, an earlier intensive analysis of body motion (kinesics) by two independent judges was remarkably reliable. Marianne LaFrance and I independently analyzed several seconds of a listener's body motion from a 24-frame-per-second (fps) film. The listener's body was in constant motion. Several seconds may seem a small amount, but there is a great deal of movement occurring during that time. Decisions had to be made at each film frame concerning all detectably moving body parts. The Pearson and Spearman correlations were both $p < .001$. The Pearson correlation is preferred to a percent of agreement statement (Ebel, 1951). Figure 2-5 shows a sample of this reliability study.

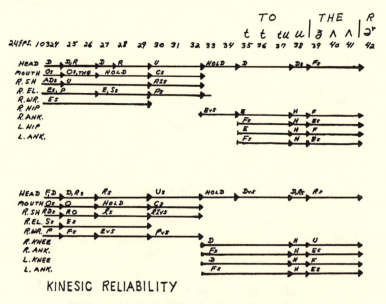

KINESIC RELIABILITY

Figure 2-5:   Reliability Study.   This is a brief
segment comparing the kinesic segmentation of
two independent judges to illustrate the accuracy.
Judge one is above, and judge two below.

Dr. LaFrance and I then independently analyzed several seconds of a speaker's kinesics, as a replication study, using 48 fps film. As before, there was constant ongoing movement. Again the reliability was $p < .001$. This study also supports the concept of body motion as formed of "process units" or bundles of movement, where the body parts change and sustain motion together. It also provides support for the nature of the basic units of kinesics. These were very careful and arduous studies. I trained Marianne carefully for six months prior to the studies. The finding is clearly that well-trained kinesicists *can* segment body motion at the microlevel with high reliability. A variety of other studies have been and are being conducted; and all have, thus far, supported the hypotheses of self- and interactional synchrony. Time does not permit a detailed exposition of them here.

ASYNCHRONY AND PATHOLOGY

What also helps clarify the study of synchrony is the study of pathology, because pathology is asynchronous. People with severe psychopathology or communication disorders are self-asynchronous and also interactionally asynchronous. If all there is is self-synchrony and interactional synchrony, how do you find the negative, how do you disprove it? In pathology you find a breakdown of the synchrony. The first time I studied this was while looking at a film of Eve Black, the woman portrayed in *The Three Faces of Eve*. I thought that she was faking and was interested in seeing the original film of Eve in her three different phases, to study it very carefully and try to find the differences. I spent three months studying Eve Black (as you may remember, there is Eve White, Eve Black, and Jane, the later normal personality), and, after three months of this, I began to see a strange asynchrony.

I can look at film four or five hours a day without much trouble, but if I start looking at film and after about an hour I have to go to sleep, something is happening dynamically between me and the data. Something new is starting to emerge. I suddenly began to see that, as she smiled and talked, one eye shifted over to the camera, while the other stayed on the psychiatrist. Then the first eye came back; they both went out; they came in again in an asynchronous pattern of behavior.

I've studied a lot of dyslexic and learning-disabled children, as well as autistic children and schizophrenic adults—and all of them are asynchronous. You'll see one side of the face go out of phase, one eye out of phase, one eyelid out of phase. I looked at an anoxic infant eight days old, and at one point one eyelid was going down and the other one was going up. We are fused at the midline, and damage in the brain throws one side out vis-a-vis the other, so self-synchrony gets broken up. The point is, however, one's world breaks up, and this can be slight or very severe. Rhythm is a key aspect of this. The energies are in a rhythmic distribution and a hierarchy of rhythmic distributions, so that if you get energy coming in in the wrong place, it throws the whole system out.

In dyslexia, I think the eyes are out of phase with the auditory system, so that, when the person is reading, he is not locking in and hearing what he's reading; he's clumping it wrong. He can take the last two words of one sentence and the first two words of the next sentence and put them into a unity that doesn't make sense.

In severe autism there appears to be a multiple response to sound. These children are entraining at precise intervals following a sound as if their body is getting a reverberation of sounds. The severely autistic child looks around multiple times as well. In other words, these children are interactionally synchronizing or entraining to sounds that aren't there. The precision of this pathological late entraining provides further support for the hypothesis of interactional synchrony.

THE CVC PATTERN

What has emerged that is new and very exciting to me is that the normal-speaking person seems to be following a consonant-vowel-consonant (CVC) format in his body motion.

The CVC distinction is a fundamental aspect of speech. When a speaker articulates a word, for example, there is an initial onset or releasing sound which rises in intensity and then falls to an arresting sound form, ending the word. This appears to be a feature of all the spoken languages of the world. Stetson presented this pulse-like view of the ongoing speech stream (Stetson, 1951). For any word like "dog," "cat," or "sat" there is an onset sound, a louder sonorous sound and an arresting sound. In "sat" one can distinguish aspects within this continuous flow as an initial consonant /s/, the vowel /a/, and a terminal consonant /t/. In speech there is a continuous flow of CVCs, some louder, some softer, but ongoing. What is emerging is that the body is precisely locked in and integrated with this flow so that the body will hold quietly on a consonant and speed up on a vowel. You can't see it, it's so fast, but at least 80 percent of the time it looks like this is happening. The body is slightly slow, speeds up on the vowel pulse, then damps down, and this rhythm occurs within other rhythms, resulting in a wider 1-second rhythm. Speech and body motion are a unity. This CVC pattern can be seen in Fig. 2-6. I have looked through 15 films in the last three or four weeks intensively and seen the CVC pattern through all of them.

In the film example of a black man and white man talking, which I studied in depth, they had never met prior to the filming. There is tremendous interactional synchrony going on even though these two males are in a dominance-submission interchange. To digress, with males talking to each other, one often sees pointing, jabbing, a smile that is not a smile, and so on, i. e., covert aggressive actions.

However, we can see the black man talking and note the self-synchrony within the CVC structure (see Fig. 2-6). The black exhibits the CVC pattern in both his speech and body, but in a manner differing from that of whites. His behavior emerges in a beautifully syncopated and self-synchronous pattern. One part of the body, particularly the hand, will move slowly in synchrony with the occurrence of the initial consonant, then the other hand will move rapidly in synchrony with the occurrence of the

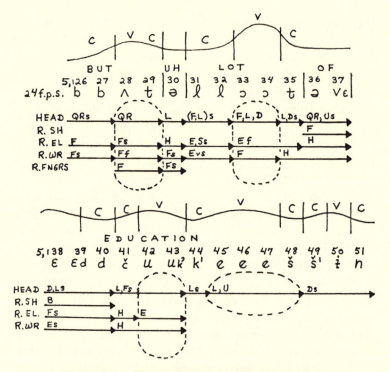

**Figure 2-6:   The CVC Pattern in the Body Motion
of a Speaker.   There are variations in the body motion
which parallel the emergent CVC forms of speech.**

vowel, and finally there appears to be a slowing of both hands across the terminal consonant. Or the head may move slowly across the consonant and the shoulder may speed up across the vowel, etc. The nature of the body motion across the terminal portion must be investigated further. White behavior lacks this sense of syncopation, displaying less infra-articulatory body motion contrast. It appears that the white will usually carry the CVC pattern in his body with the same body part. For example, if he is moving his arm while articulating, it will move slowly across the initial consonant, speed up across the vowel, and slow again across the terminal consonant. The white does not tend to

Figure 2-7   Notation Chart for Figures

Q = incline L or R	O = open (mouth)
F = forward if for head;	C = close (mouth)
flex if for joint	RI = rotate inward
L = left	RO = rotate outward
R = right	RU = rotate up
D = down	
U = up	*Subscripts*
E = extend	VS = very slight
S = supinate	S = slight
P = pronate	*No Subscript* = medium velocity
AD = adduct	f = fast
AB = abduct	
H = hold (no movement)	
B = back	

use one body part in relation to the consonant and another for the vowel, although this does occur occasionally. It is the proportion of time that is important. If he is using both arms, both of them will follow the CVC contour together rather than each one covering different aspects as in black self-synchrony.

The listener's body also seems highly tuned to the speaker's CVC rhythm contour. He/she will often speed up and slow down synchronously with these ongoing variations of the speech stream. Frequently, major onset movements will occur in concert with vowel onset. This CVC pattern appears to be a fundamental feature of human speaking and listening behavior and probably has neurological correlates.

However, a poignant difference can occur in schizophrenic behavior. In at least two schizophrenic patients I have looked at, they're out of phase with themselves in terms of the speech stress pattern. If I say, "I went to the *store*," the word store is loud, and my body speeds up with the word. If a schizophrenic says it, he might also say, "I went to the *store*." But the gesture is delayed. His body motion is delayed in its intensities and systematically behind his articulation. It is very threatening because, if one is talking to him and he's coming in with fast movements when his speech intensity drops down, it is disconcerting. It is out of phase with the articulatory rhythm.

CULTURAL MICRORHYTHM DIFFERENCES

In all the cultures I have looked at (West Indians, Kung Bushmen, Mayan Indians, Chinese, French) the same CVC phenomenon is there. As I indicated, I have also focused on black/white interaction patterns. I think the dance between members of the same culture is perhaps a little better and a little more precise than, let's say, the dance between two people from different cultures.

As a white, middle-class male, I'm on a 4/4 type of pattern. If I say the word "because" both my hands may extend exactly together. In black behavior, however, the right hand may begin to extend with the "be" portion slightly ahead of the left hand and the left hand will extend rapidly across the "cause" portion. This creates the syncopation, mentioned before, which can appear anywhere in the body. A person moves in the rhythm and timing of his or her culture, and this rhythm is in the whole body. Furthermore, the timing dimensions of the language are being manifested. People are neurologically unified organisms.

In some black speakers more body parts are involved with greater intensities which I think can be frightening to whites. These sudden movements are innocuous but seem disturbing to those of a different culture. It may be that those having different cultural rhythms are unable to really "synch-in" fully with each other. I don't know this, but rhythm is a very subtle and delicate presence across multiple dimensions of interaction.

I think that infants from the first moment of life and even in the womb are getting the rhythm and structure and style of sound, the rhythms of their culture, so that they imprint to them and the rhythms become part of their very being. When they say the baby will babble French or babble Chinese, this may mean that the predominant rhythms are already laid into the neurological system, so that, when the child starts to talk, he incorporates the lexical items of the system right into these rhythms. You know, I find more and more a sense of the sacred about human beings. I am far, far more impressed with human beings now than I ever was before studying human communication.

For me all human behavior now is more and more beautiful. I find there's a tremendous aesthetic dimension to the study of behavior and communication. I also think there is a profound ethical dimension that we need to begin to deal with. Communication does not just go out and stop and drop dead. Human communication affects the inner being of others. Even some of the out-of-awareness, nonverbal posture sharings, or movement ensemble patterns affect the inner life of people. It is not a game. We're holistically involved. The more I see, particularly in my studies of cross-cultural behavior, the more I realize that we're more alike than we are different. Each culture to me is very, very beautiful. The black syncopated rhythm is a very beautiful thing. Some of the most beautiful movement I've seen is in French behavior. It looks like ballet at the microlevel.

The pursuit of knowledge about human communication and the human inner life, apart from the pursuit of happiness and a heightening of the ability of human beings from all cultures to interact meaningfully, is ultimately meaningless. The purpose of life is not to find an ultimate secret about existence but to create the kind of human dignity our reason can enable us to achieve.

DISCUSSION

Participant: What implications are there for treatment in the work you have reported?

William
Condon: Well, with the autistic we hope to map their distorted world and create instrumentation

which will compensate in some way, such as delaying one ear vis-a-vis the other. If you put yourself under delayed auditory feedback, you become literally aphasic. Your body goes out of phase. The whole rhythm and timing which is so critical is disturbed. You are getting your consonant back just as you are saying your vowels. This overloads the vowels, so that you get too much energy, and it just disrupts your entire ability to talk.

Participant:
Could you say something about these patterns in someone who is bilingual?

William Condon:
This is a real problem. Laurence Wylie and I are now studying some bilingual people, and one has a multiple response to sound. He has jumps and jerks. He is out of phase. That may be because he has a slight learning disability and may not know it or it may be that, if you make somebody bilingual, you are causing troubles in rhythms. You are giving him double rhythm structuring. For example, the black child in the ghetto learns the black rhythm and speech at home and then goes to school and they are trying to impose a white kind of rhythm on him. There are many more differences than I have pointed out, of course, very subtle ones. I think what people do very often is to react and be put off by the differences rather than seeing how beautiful and necessary they are.

Participant:
Are there individual styles of motion?

William Condon:
Do you mean, for example, would an obsessional move obsessively? I don't know for sure. I do know that in psychotherapy patients will present themselves nonverbally in ways that reflect their dynamics. One woman we

studied who had been abandoned when she was three by her mother had a kind of withdrawn manner. Her whole presentation was one of of distrust of herself and others, and this was coming through in her mobility.

Aron Siegman: I have been watching many interviews, and there are tremendous individual differences. I have seen people like yourself who are extremely expressive with tremendous mobility. But there are others who talk for half an hour and there are not any movements at all.

William
Condon: Yes, this immobility can be seen in schizophrenics a lot. But there must be micromovements of some order. They are very still, but there are probably some movements.

Daniel Stern: I would like to bring up what for me is an important point regarding Bill Condon's findings about interactional synchrony. It strikes me that it is very hard after seeing those films not to feel that that is sort of the atomic unit, so to speak, upon which all later rhythms are going to get built, and, because I see it as having the importance, and I do not mean the predominant importance, but simply the importance of being the smallest unit we have talked about, the one that is closest to biology which we assume is more universal, I would like to say a word about it. Adam Kendon did mention that there are two models of how one can get into synchrony. The one that I think Bill Condon uses (and I might add I am in a good position to take some difference with Bill since he taught me how to do frame analysis) is the driving model, one

---

[2] The discussion which follows was part of a panel discussion. Dr. Condon elaborated on his answers during the editing of this paper. [Ed.]

driving the other. The other model assumes one learns somebody else's program and sort of latches onto it. I think that this is an extremely important issue at the smallest level because the issue of synchrony, as defined by Bill, is that people will start, stop, or change at the precise moment, 1/48th of a second, or within 50 milliseconds. Operationally speaking, interactional synchrony is seen within 1/24th and 1/48th of a second on the film.

My point is this. For most of the rhythms at a higher level that we are talking about, such as posture-sharing patterns, one doesn't need to start or stop exactly at the same point as long as you are roughly doing things together at the same time. But the issue of starting or stopping within such a small unit of time becomes of enormous biological importance to those of us who are dealing at the biological level, and that is why I am paying attention to it. It may not be important at the other levels. For people to match their behaviors within 50 milliseconds requires some mechanism unknown to man. Now, I find that very exciting, and I think Bill Condon does, too. I think the burden when you have a mind-boggling phenomenon in your hands—and this is a mind-boggling phenomenon—rests very heavily on those who found it, to find a mechanism whereby it can be explained or at least to make very sure that it is there and robustly there.

Now it is impossible for me to imagine how it would work in the Condon model because of reaction time. Actually it is impossible for me to imagine how it would work with the model of mine that Adam Kendon talked about, since one can only "latch on" to somebody's rhythm for a few phrases or for a short period of time. At those times I agree with Bill completely, it really happens, and it is fabulous, and it may be a high point as far as emotional and other things concerned, but for the rest of the time I can't imagine it happening.

I would like to point out that there is a real methodological problem that becomes obvious when you get into this work, such as Beatrice Beebe and I have done, and I know Bill has struggled with this too. Namely, the appearance that things happen synchronously may be more in the perceiver's eye than in the world out there. We may organize events such that they look as if they are happening all at the same time. What is required that has not been done, and actually I have been urging Bill to do for two years, is to have an independent analysis of the voice, of the separate limb movements, and of the separate people so they can be analyzed at different times in different places by different people and then put together.

I am saying this because I feel interactional synchrony is one of the most striking, extraordinary, and important psychobiological phenomenon that anybody has come across for an awfully long time, and it is everybody's duty to knock it home, especially if we are going to give it the status of an underpinning unit in the hierarchical levels of interaction.

William Condon: From the manner in which I have tentatively formulated the phenomenon of interactional synchrony, it would seem to appear that I have adopted a drive model. However, I have not explicitly formulated a model for myself. The resolution of the question will require much further research. A model may emerge which incorporates aspects of both drive and rhythm models without contradiction. What could be rhythmic at a very microlevel might appear like drive at a higher level. The omnipresence of rhythm in nature would suggest that some rhythmic factors are inevitably involved in interactional synchrony.

I do feel that interactional synchrony or entrainment, however it is mediated, is occuring most of the time when a listener is listening to a speaker. As I stated earlier, I feel it is a basic reflection of the auditory perceptual process. I do not mean that the body of the listener must move in isomorphic configurations with the articulatory structure of the speaker's speech for hearing to take place. I see the synchronization of the listener's body as a motoric reflection of the hearing process.

I suspect that there may be very rapid neural processes which have not been fully elaborated as yet. It would seem that we must have some mechanisms for tracking the very rapid and varying transformations of a person's speech. Some linguists postulate a tracking process similar to my own. A speaker's phone types can last as briefly as 40 milliseconds, and I understand that interaural time discrimination can occur very rapidly. For example, the brain can detect a 6- to 9-microsecond (1 millionth of a second) interaural time disparity for a variety of signals, i. e., the smallest time that is perceptible as different from zero. As with interactional synchrony this leads to a mystery. How can the brain detect an interaural 6- to 9-microsecond difference when the average synaptic latency is about 1 msec (1,000 microseconds)? This 6- to 9-microsecond difference is apparently a simple measurement and is well-established. They know it happens but can't explain it. The point in alluding to this is that there may be many levels of rapidity of information processing which are summated into higher-order unities.

I recently slowed down a tape recording of a vowel sound /a/ many times, and, when it slowed, it sounded like a series of slow clicks of tapping sounds. It would appear that the brain could quite easily discriminate these clicks and their interinterval variations which help compose the vowel sound, although at our level of conscious perception this would be utterly impossible. I have no difficulty imagining that some aspects of summated information detectable at 6 to 9 microseconds could be transmitted to motor areas by 10 msec which is a far longer time interval. Tobias (1972), who wrote about the microsecond interaural time disparity above, also feels that some form of neural synchronization is involved in it as well as in the periodicity-pitch tracking. He says, "This same simple threshold measurement leads to another kind of conclusion about the neurophysiology underlying auditory processing. The kinds of neural activity that would allow an interaural-time-disparity threshold to exist are all associated with a counting (a periodicity) function. Because the threshold improves with frequency up to about 1,000 Hz, then worsens until, by 1,500 Hz, it is unmeasurable, one may conclude, that periodicity, in the form of neural synchrony with the signal, likewise changes with frequency in the same way. And, in fact, both periodicity-pitch students (Small, 1970) and localization students reach similar conclusions'' (Tobias, 1972, p. 475). There is, then, emerging evidence to suggest very rapid discrimination and also a model of neural synchronization with sound structure.

I didn't particularly relish the concept of interactional synchrony. I think it was forced on me from the observations. Reaction time seems to be within the boundaries I mentioned. We are, in a sense in an ocean of interconnections, and, as I say something, sound waves go out, and they hit the tympanum of the listener's ear and it vibrates and oscillates in perfect synchrony with that sound, and then to the ossicular chain, and then into the cochlea, and then into neural pathways. I think interactional synchrony may be mediated in the brain stem. Now, I understand that auditory signals can go in and be all the way up to the inferior colliculus in 10 milliseconds. There can be muscle responses within 10 milliseconds. In other words, there can be muscular responses to auditory stimuli within 10 milliseconds, as I mentioned in the lecture. I have been checking into this because obviously I have put forth a very difficult hypothesis.

Also, how can we account for multiple entrainment in autism? I can synchronize an autistic child to sounds that are not there, that are systematically delayed. Also, if there is a normal, wide awake infant, and the infant is looking away, and you are behind it, when you slap your hands, the infant will startle within two frames on the film. Now that's in 60 milliseconds, and there is no question about that, Dan. And the infant's hands and feet start at the same moment. The way he goes into the Moro reflex is total.

The preceding material is relevant to the concept of response. I am not at all clear what Dr. Stern means by a response or reaction time. What constitutes a "response" is a relative matter depending on what is being measured and how. For example, there is a cochlear microphonic "response" of the ear which is measured by an electrode placed near the round window. This occurs in 1 to 4 msec. The "response" of the listener in interactional synchrony is a motoric change in the ongoing organizational flow pattern of the body in relation to various features in the structure of auditory input. I do not mean response in the sense of how fast a subject can press a button after a sound occurs. That may take 200 msec or longer. If Dr. Stern means this latter sense of response, it would obviously be impossible for interactional synchrony to occur within 50 msec.

He is correct in that I did suggest that interactional synchrony might be occurring as fast as 1/48th of a second (21 msec), and at the time I felt this might be the case. I may well be mistaken about that figure, but I do adhere to the hypothesis that interactional synchrony is occurring within 50 msec. Interactional synchrony is not so much a stopping and starting together as it is an ongoing modulation, like a car following a road rather than a car starting up and stopping at intersections. I do plan to do the kinds of studies Dr. Stern wisely suggests. I think his point is a very serious one, and I utterly agree that much more work has to be done. If the phenomenon is not there, I would be the first to want to know about it.

Alan Lomax: I think it is time to raise the question of level of operations. I think that what Bill Condon shows us with his magic wrist is real and true, but there are an awful lot of other things that have gone on in those frames that he doesn't talk about. He picks out the things that deal with synchrony, and he has, I think, the beginning of a good theory about them. But he has his cut-off point because he is interested in looking at human behavior at 1/48th of a second or wherever he decides to cut it, and at that level he has found something like biological interactions system.

However, Birdwhistell, who worked at another level, chose the time-cut that he chose in order to study language, the nonverbal lexication system, and he worked around until he found the right level of observation for that. Other people have chosen other levels of cut because they wanted to look at a certain kind of phenomenon, and then, when they chose that cut, they made perfectly arbitrary classification systems inside of that level and tried them out and, if they worked, good. If they didn't work, they threw them away and tried something new until they got a set of operations that would work and that took care of most of the information. That is what we are doing. We are not talking about reality here. We are talking about dealing with a series of operations that we can actually write on paper and share with each other.

Because a unit is small doesn't make it any more serious than one that takes a hundred years. It depends on what you are interested in finding out, and that is an arbitrary decision of science, right?

William
Condon:

I agree wholeheartedly with Alan, there is no privileged position in describing the rhythms and organizations of rhythms which pervade existence. That there is no such privileged position is at the heart of a holistic, organizational view of nature. In that sense, no organizations are more important than any other or can exist in total isolation from any other. It may be arbitrary at what level a person decides to focus (I have some doubts about that), but, if that person diligently studies that level, the order he or she detects is not arbitrary.

REFERENCES

Condon, W. S. Neonate movement is synchronized with adult speech: interactional participation and language acquisition. *Science*, 1974, *183*, 99–101.

Condon, W. S. Neonatal entrainment and enculturation. In M. Bullowa (Ed.), Before speech: The beginnings of human communication. London: Cambridge University Press, 1979.

Davis, H. Classes of auditory evoked responses. *Audiology*, 1973, *12*, 464–469.

Ebel, R. L. Estimation of the reliability of ratings. *Psychometrika*, 1951, *16*.

Stetson, R. H. *Motor phonetics*. Amsterdam: North Holland Publishing Co., 1951.

Tobias, J. V. Curious binaural phenomena. In J. V. Tobias (Ed.), *Foundations of modern auditory theory*. New York: Academic Press, 1972.

Chapter 3

RHYTHMIC COMMUNICATION IN THE MOTHER-INFANT DYAD

**Beatrice Beebe, Louis Gerstman,
Beatrice Carson, Merelyn Dolins,
April Zigman, Hetty Rosensweig,
Kathryn Faughey, Myron Korman**

This study addresses the issue of how maternal rhythm may affect the four-month-old infant's negotiation of the face-to-face encounter. This negotiation is described in terms of infant "levels of engagement," defined as particular combinations of orientation, gaze, and facial expression. We will argue that various conditions of maternal rhythm influence the infant's level of engagement.

The importance of rhythm in primitive perception has been stressed by previous authors concerned with the nature of pre-verbal experience (Church, 1961; Schilder, 1964; Werner, 1948; Wolff, 1967). The infant's perception of the caretaker's rhythm (Brazelton, Kozlowski, & Main, 1974), as well as the rhythmic regulation of the infant's own behaviors (Wolff, 1967), have been considered to play important roles in the infant's development.

"Macrorhythms" of lower frequency periodicities, such as the sleep-wake cycle (Sander, 1977; Sollgerber, 1963), have received most attention, to the relative neglect of "microrhythms" of high-frequency cycles lasting seconds or fractions of seconds, as Wolff (1967) has noted. Rather than the global descriptions of most reports, Wolff (1967) advocates careful quantitative analysis of microrhythms in a developmental context. Not only is much of the infant's behavior organized at the level of microrhythms, but it is also at the microlevel that crucial aspects of social interactive regulation occur (Stern, 1971; Beebe & Stern, 1977). Wolff's own work measures the microrhythms of two infant behaviors, sucking and crying, in a noninteractive context. The present investigation measures the mother's microrhythms, in an interaction with her infant.

Whereas most work examines the nature of the infant's rhythms (Ashton, 1976; Wolff, 1967), increasingly the literature on mother-infant interaction suggests that maternal rhythms may play a central role in the organization of the face-to-face encounter. Yet in most of the work to date, the maternal rhythm itself was not carefully examined (e. g., Brazelton et al., 1974; Stern, 1974). The recent work has rather focused on the mother's capacity to attune herself to the infant's rhythms, such as Brazelton et al.'s (1974) demonstration of the necessity of the mother's respect for the infant's attention-nonattention cycles, or Sander's (1977) finding of the importance of the mother's capacity to follow the infant's initial macrorhythms of sleeping and feeding.

The work that has most closely measured maternal microrhythms in an interactive context is that of Stern (Stern, Beebe, Jaffe, & Bennett, 1977; Stern & Gibbon, 1978). Stern et al. (1977) showed the regularity of mother's rhythm during an "episode of maintained engagement," and the mother's tendency to change her "beat" from one episode to the next, presumably to initiate and maintain an optimal infant affect range. However, these studies fail to address the influence of maternal rhythm on the organization of the interaction, or the degree and quality of the infant's engagement.

Rather, Stern has focused on the importance of maternal rhythms as a cognitive event, and as a timing mechanism, whereby the infant can form a temporal expectancy of when the next maternal event is likely to occur (Stern & Gibbon, 1978). Not only may maternal rhythms contribute to the organization of infant cognition (Lewis & Goldberg, 1969; Stern et al., 1977; Stern & Gibbon, 1978), but they may also be important in the organization of infant affect. Stern (1974, 1977) has hypothesized, but never actually demonstrated, that changes in content or tempo of maternal rhythm may be used by the mother to "fine-tune" her behavior to maintain an optimum level of attention, arousal, and positive affect in the infant.

In order to examine the maternal rhythm per se, as well as its role in the organization of the level of engagement in the face-to-face encounter, a stretch of interaction in one mother-infant pair was chosen for analysis, during which a dramatic increase in the level of engagement occurred when the mother introduced obvious rhythmic behavior, swinging the infant's hands in her own. Until the introduction of the hand-swing rhythms, this mother had consistent difficulty in engaging her infant, as demonstrated in a previous analysis of this pair, where they were locked in a "chase and dodge" struggle, in which the infant had virtual veto power in avoiding a posturally oriented, visually engaged encounter (Beebe & Stern, 1977).

By no means an extensive analysis of the kinds and uses of maternal rhythm, this study examines one range of maternal rhythms used in subtle but important modulations of face-to-face play in one mother-infant pair at four months.

METHOD

The subjects were an upper-middle class mother and her first-born four-month-old boy, of normal delivery and developmental course. The study was described as a study of the social development of normal babies, and after being familiarized with the experimenter and procedure, the mother was told that her only task would be to play with the baby as she would at home.

In an otherwise vacant room, mother and infant were seated opposite each other in the same plane, the infant in an infant seat. Data were collected by videotape, with two cameras, one on each partner's face and upper torso, which a special-effects generator combined into one split-screen view (see Beebe & Stern, 1977, for details).

A sample of approximately 2 minutes (1 minute, 55 seconds) was chosen for analysis due to the obviously rhythmic nature of the maternal stimulation, beginning as the mother took the infant's hands in her own and swung them to and from midline, on a horizontal plane. The purpose of the analysis was not to generalize as to what might be characteristic for their relationship, but rather to delineate organization of behavior in this particular sample. For data reduction, the videotape sample was converted to 16 mm film, and consecutive numbers were printed on each frame of the film.

Method of Frame-by-Frame Analysis of Film

This method has been developed by Birdwhistell (1970), Condon (Ch. 2), Stern (1971), and Beebe (1973). Films are viewed on a hand-crank movie-viewer (Craig Projecto-Editor), so that the investigator can go back and forth over any number of frames in slow motion to determine the exact frame a movement begins and ends, to the nearest 1/24th of a second. The user of the movie-viewer, which operates without sound, limited the analysis to kinesics (body motion) and omitted analysis of vocalization. Units of behavior were defined as movements in process of transformation, from the beginning to the end of ongoing action. The movement was defined as having ceased when a steady posture was held. The steady posture was termed a behavioral "hold," analogous to a pause in speech, during which time no movement occurred. For example, the process of the head going up was defined as a unit of movement. Once the head was in a steady "up posture," it was not scored as a movement, but rather a "hold." A movement and an ensuing steady-state posture comprise a "movement-hold cycle."

Criteria of Maternal Rhythmicity

Examination of the mother's hand movements while swinging the infant's hands in her own yielded the discrimination of three modes of maternal rhythm, labeled "games," "transitions," and "hand pauses," according to the following criteria:

Games were kinesically tightly regular repetitions of handswings, with the criterion of a "run" of four or more repeating movement-hold cycles of identical kinesic pattern of excursion in space. Three distinctly different kinesic patterns of degree of excursion were discerned: "full-out," which swings the infant's hands out to a full degree of excursion (cycle $\dot{x}$ = .64 sec., S. D. = .20 sec.); "half-out," which swings the infant's hands halfway out (cycle $\dot{x}$ = .28 sec., S. D. = .11 sec.); and "short-out," which swings the infant's hands a very short degree of excursion, often a somewhat circular motion (cycle $\dot{x}$ = .15 sec., S. D. = .02 sec.).

Transitions were kinesically *irregular* occurrences of handswings, with the criteria of either (a) two or fewer movement-hold cycles of identical kinesics; or (b) kinesically *varied* movement-hold cycles of any number (e. g., mixtures of full-out, half-out, or short-out).

Hand pauses were periods when the mother's hands were at rest.

Behaviors Coded for Infant Engagement Scale

Table 3.1 defines the behaviors coded for infant engagement. Each kind of behavior, e. g., orientation, gaze, and facial movement was separately assessed by frame-by-frame analysis throughout the data base. The coding of behavior was done by the first author, who has extensive experience with this method and whose record was used as the standard for comparison in assessment of reliability. Reliability did not fall below 94 percent agreement with an independent coder regarding the judgment that a particular behavior occurred. Reliability was 90 percent agreement for those infant facial behaviors requiring a discrimination of degree of display (e. g., mouth open, mouth widen, or "bow"—curvature of the outer corners of the mouth). Regarding the judgment of the exact frame in which a movement began or ended, coding was reliable to the nearest 1/12th of a second.

Infant Face-to-Face Engagement Scale

Following the coding of individual behaviors, the entire record was then recoded into an engagement scale, presented in

Table 3.1   Behaviors Coded for Infant Engagement Scale

Behavior	Definition
Orientation	
(a) Horizontal plane:	Head center at midline, oriented directly toward partner; vs. head rotated from 2° to 90° away from midline. Body vis-á-vis or rotated.
(b) Vertical plane:	Head up or down.
(c) Sagittal plane:	Head and/or body forward toward partner vs. pulled back away from partner.
(d) Limp head hang:	Described previously (Beebe & Stern, 1977) as "inhibition of responsivity": sudden cessation of activity to a motionless, limp state.
Visual Attention	Infant looking at face of mother.
Facial Expressive Display	
(a) Degree mouth open:	Distinctions of 4° of display, from lips slightly parted to a fully opened mouth. (See photo illustrations, Fig. 3-1.)
(b) Degree mouth widen:	3° of mouth widen (without bowing). (See photo illustrations, Fig. 3-1.)
(c) Bowing:	Mouth widening involving upward curvature of outer corners of mouth.
(d) "Negative" displays:	Grimace, frown, "line-mouth" (pulling in of the lips, pressing into a "line-like" expression.)

Table 3.2. The scale is based on particular combinations of orientation, visual attention, and facial expressive display, as defined by the criteria in Table 3.2. The infant engagement scale was previously conceptualized by Beebe & Stern (1977), and the upper half of the infant scale was previously defined by Beebe (1973). The levels of engagement were heuristically ordered into an ordinal scale, where a higher number was taken to represent a more engaged state than a lower number. The reader may form an independent judgment of the scale's ordinality by examining Fig. 3-1, where sample photographs illustrate the scale. The lowest level of the scale is depicted by two photographs, since inhibition of responsibility spans a range of frames.

This infant engagement scale provides an ordinal system of quantification of interactional behavior which can be tracked as a function of time. It can be conceptualized as operating within an "engagement-desengagement spectrum" (see Beebe & Stern, 1977), which comprises a continuum of sustaining and disrupting the face-to-face encounter. The levels not only imply "magnitudes" of relatedness, but are better formulated as complex "modes" of interpersonal relatedness across a continuum from high positive engagement to an inhibition of responsivity altogether (Beebe & Gerstman, 1980).

The upper and lower halves of the scale (with neutral the midpoint) can be conceptualized somewhat differently. The upper half of the scale is simpler, in that vis-a-vis orientation and gaze at mother remain constant, and the differentiations among levels are based on subtle differences in presence and degree of display of mouth opening, mouth widening, and bowing. In the lower half of the scale, all of the criteria of the scale (orientation, visual attention, and facial expression) are subject to change. As the scale descends below neutral, the levels are more clearly increasing "compromises" in the degree of engagement (see Beebe & Stern, 1977).

Table 3.2 Infant Engagement Level Scale

Level	Attention	Orientation	Degree mouth open (M.O.)	Facial Expressivity Degree mouth widen (M.W.)	Other
90 High positive	Look	Vis-à-vis	M.O. 4	Bowing	
85 Medium high pos.	Look	Vis-à-vis	M.O. 3	Bowing	
80 Medium positive	Look	Vis-à-vis	M.O. 2	M.W. 2 or 1	
70 Low attention	Look	Vis-à-vis	(a) M.O. 1 or (b) M.O. 0	M.W. 0 M.W. slight	
60 Positive attention	Look	Vis-à-vis	(a) M.O. 1 or 2 or (b) M.O. 0	M.W. 0	
50 Neutral	Look	Vis-à-vis	M.O. 0	M.W. 0	
40 Negative attention	Look	Vis-à-vis			Grimace or "line mo." or frown
30 Oriented, not look	Look away	Vis-à-vis	M.O. 0	M.W. 0 or	Negative
20 Avert	Look away	Orient away	M.O. 0	M.W. 0 or	Negative
10 Inhibition of responsivity	Look away or eyes closed	Vis-à-vis or away: Body limp	M.O. 0	M.W. 0	

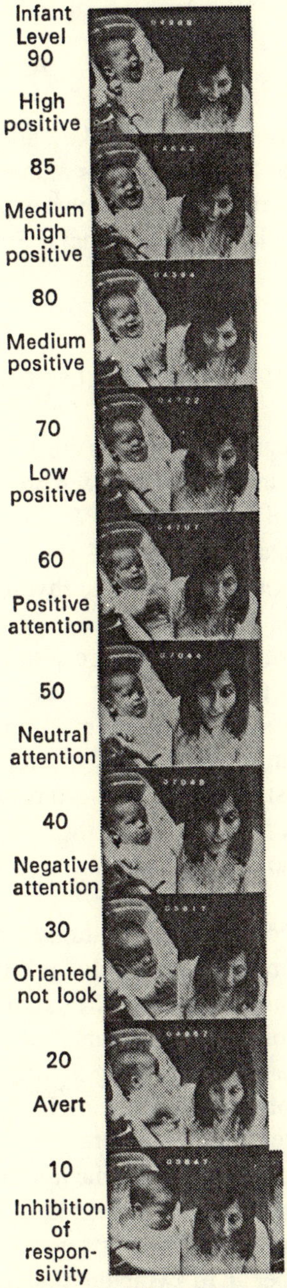

Infant
Level
90

High
positive

85

Medium
high
positive

80

Medium
positive

70

Low
positive

60

Positive
attention

50

Neutral
attention

40

Negative
attention

30

Oriented,
not look

20

Avert

10

Inhibition
of
respon-
sivity

**Figure 3–1:   Infant Engagement Scale (Reprinted in part
from Merrill-Palmer Quarterly)**

Data Processing

The data base for this study was key-punched with one card for each frame of the 2,729 frames or almost 2-minute sample, and the cards were processed by the library programs contained in the Statistical Package for the Social Sciences (Nie et al., 1975).

RESULTS AND DISCUSSION

That repetition and microrhythms are characteristic of maternal stimulation to young infants has been previously documented by Stern (Stern et al., 1977; Stern & Gibbon, 1978), in the modalities of vocal and facial-head rhythms, and was again found here, in the modality of kinesic rhythms of hand swings. Although gesture has been considered to be a relatively continuous phenomenon, rather than a more discrete, on-off system, such as speech units (see Oliva, *this volume*), frame-by-frame analysis of film is a sufficiently precise tool to allow the possibility of segmenting gesture into discrete units. With this method we have construed maternal gesture to be a more digital, on-off phenomenon, by considering the movement and its hold in a particular position as analogous to a speech phrase and its ensuing vocal pause.

Prior to the introduction of rhythmic "hand games," this infant was involved in a "chase and dodge" interaction with the mother. To every maternal overture, this infant used a remarkable repetoire of avoidance behaviors, essentially "dodging" every maternal "chase," exercising a virtual veto power over the mother's attempts to engage him in a visually attentive face-to-face encounter (Beebe & Stern, 1977).

There was a dramatic effect of the introduction of maternal hand-games on the infant's engagement level. Immediately prior to this moment, the infant was at level "avert" (20). The moment the mother began to swing the infant's hands rhythmically, the infant oriented to her and looked at her, at first sober-faced, and then showing increasingly positive expressiveness. This sequence is illustrated photographically in Fig. 3-2, which begins while the infant is still in "avert," 4½ seconds prior to the introduction of maternal hand rhythms, and shows the infant's immediate increase in engagement level after the mother begins rhythmic hand games (Beebe & Gerstman, 1980).

As can be seen in Table 3.3 significant differences were found in median infant engagement level as a function of the maternal rhythmic conditions. Kruskal-Wallis analyses of variance of infant engagement level were highly significant ($x^2 = 466$, $p < .001$), and retrospective Mann-Whitney U contrasts of infant engagement were significant for the following adjacent pairs: half-out games vs. transitions ($Z = 10.98$), transitions vs. hand pauses ($Z = 6.37$), both $p < .001$; and not significant for full-out vs. half-out games ($Z = 1.00$), and hand pauses vs. short-out games ($Z = 0.26$) (Beebe & Gerstman, 1980).

There is a strong hierarchical relationship, so that in general regular rhythmic games are associated with highest positive infant engagement level ("medium high"), transitions with an intermediate level, only very slightly positive ("positive attention"), and hand pauses with the lowest infant engagement level ("neutral attention"). These findings confirm the importance of expectable, rhythmic sequences for positive infant affect, hypothesized but not previously demonstrated by other authors (Brazelton et al., 1974; Stern et al., 1977). When mother becomes irregular in tempo and kinesics or does not sustain repetitions, as in transitions, the infant's engagement significantly decreases, presumably because the infant has more difficulty predicting mother's behavior.

There is one exception to this general picture. Within the highly rhythmic games, there are variations in the particular kinesics (full-out, half-out, short-out), which are associated with characteristic mean tempos (2/3 second, 1/4 second, and 1/8 second mean cycle, respectively) and cycle variabilities (S. D. = .20, .11, and .02 seconds, respectively). Some of these

Frame	Time (Sec.)	(Infant Level)		(Maternal Level)
4179	— 4.54	20		50
4193	— 3.96	20		70

4288		0.1
Initiation of Maternal Hand Rhythm Start Game 1		→

Frame	Time	Infant		Maternal
4293	0.21	30		60
4310	0.92	50		60
4328	1.67	70		60
4343	2.29	80		70
4356	2.83	80		70

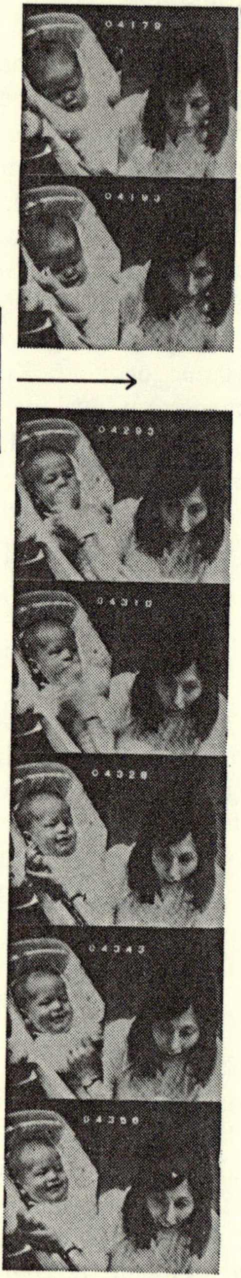

Figure 3–2: Effect of Maternal Initiation Engagement Level of Rhythm on Infant (Reprinted from Merrill-Palmer Quarterly)

**Table 3.3 Mother Infant Engagement Levels for
Five Maternal Kinesic-Rhythm Conditions**

Maternal Condition	Number of Frames	Infant Engagement Level
Full-out Games	707	80
Half-out Games	473	78
Transitions	548	60
Hand-Pauses	300	50
Short-out Games	192	52

Note: Braces connect non-discriminable conditions. Otherwise adjacent conditions significantly differ, p < .001.

Reprinted from: Beebe, B. & Gerstman, L. The "packaging" of maternal stimulation in relation to infant facial-visual engagement: A case study at four months. *Merrill-Palmer Quarterly*, 1980, Vol. 26, no. 4, 321–339.

variations in the rhythmic games are associated with significant differences in infant engagement.

When mother changes from full-out to half-out games, the tempo (mean cycle duration) quickens, the variance around the cycle mean does not change significantly,[1] and as can be seen in Table 3.3, this maternal change does not make a significant difference for the infant. However, when mother changes from full-out or half-out games to short-out games, the tempo is even more rapid, the cycle variance *is* significantly less,[1] and the change does make a significant difference in a lowered infant engagement level (which is not discriminable from infant's engagement during hand pauses).

If it is the very rapid tempo which is the critical variable in

[1]The variabilities around cycle means for the full-out vs. half-out games were not distinguishable (U = 13, p < .10). However, when the variabilities for the full-out and half-out games combined were contrasted with those of the short-out games, there was a significant difference (U = 3.5, p < .01).

the infant's lowered engagement in short-out games, it lends weight to Tronick et al.'s (1979) suggestion that slower maternal tempos appear to achieve a higher affective involvement in the infant. If it is the minimal variance around the cycle mean which is the important variable, it lends weight to Stern's (Stern et al. 1977) concept that it is repetition and rhythmicity within an optimal range of variability, neither excessive nor insufficient, which is ideally suited to getting and holding the infant's attention during the face-to-face encounter.

In either case, the exception of lowered infant engagement during short-out games, within the larger picture of the association of maternal microrhythms with high positive infant engagement, suggests that rhythmicity alone is not a sufficiently differentiated concept when considering its role in infant affect. Both the particular tempo and the degree of variance are relevant in assessing the relationship between maternal rhythm and infant affective involvement.[2]

Several studies show rates of maternal rhythms varying from approximately ½-second mean cycles to 2-second mean cycles. Stern et al. (1977), in examining free-play with three- to four-month-old infants, found cycles of maternal vocal rhythms to be 1.38 seconds, and cycles of maternal kinesic (head-face) rhythms to be 1.88 seconds. Stern & Gibbon (1978) with the same method found maternal vocal rhythms to vary from 1- to 2-second cycles. These rates, together with the range of rates found in the current report (1/4- and 2/3-second mean cycles), correspond roughly to the 1 cycle per second optimum used in studies of soothing with neonates (Ambrose, 1969; Salk, 1962). Although soothing rhythms for neonates differ from free-play "arousing" rhythms for three to four month olds, it is striking

---

[2] Although a definitive study was not done, at various other points during this videotape session the mother touched the infant or held the infant's hands, but without rhythmic stimulation, and she did not succeed in engaging the infant. We therefore assume that it is the rhythm, not the fact of touch per se or holding the infant's hands bilaterally, that is a relevant variable in engaging this infant in this sample of data.

that the range of tempos is so similar. This range, from approximately ¼-second cycles to 2-second cycles, is probably the "ballpark" of the infant's early temporal world, e. g. at a duration and rate which is discriminable and functional in his or her social regulation.

Wolff (1967) has demonstrated high-frequency rhythms of ¾-second and ¼-second cycles in neonatal sucking. He posits that these neonatal microrhythms will be entrained onto external pacemakers, but he states that it is difficult to conceive of external "clocks" for entrainment that would have the appropriate frequencies for these infant microrhythms. We propose that the mother is precisely such an external pacemaker, and provides the infant with the exactly appropriate range of high-frequency rhythms with which to entrain his own endogenous microrhythms (Beebe & Gerstman, 1980).

Turning to the possible clinical implications of this study, the only way this mother was able to alter the pervasively aversive tenor of the interaction was to introduce highly regular hand rhythms. During the course of the 2 minutes analyzed, each time she departed from these rhythmic games, the infant's affective engagement dropped out of the positive range. This one case illustrates the possible potency of introducing rhythmic stimulation in changing the affective climate in the dyad.

In addition to introducing rhythmic stimulation per se, if an optimal range of tempo could be demonstrated in mother-infant pairs experiencing difficulty, mothers might be taught to alter the tempo of their movements and speech. The timing of the mother may affect the quality and strength of the bond established. One wonders what the capacity of psychotic mothers, who clinically often appear to possess jerky rhythms (see Beebe & Sloate, 1980), might be to maintain regular and slow rhythms.

Finally, in considering the relevance of rhythm for the interrelation of cognition and affect, repetition and rhythm are chief means by which the infant acquires cognitive expectancies (Lewis & Goldberg, 1969; Stern et al., 1977; Stern & Gibbon, 1978). The very same rhythmic events are here shown to influence the infant's affective level of engagement. That is, within the structure that rhythm provides, aspects of both affect and cognition are simultaneously organized.

DISCUSSION

Participant:	Has it been evaluated as to who the leader was in that interaction?
Beatrice Beebe:	Yes. Very important question and extremely hard to analyze. From the previous data on the baby's "vetoing" of the mother's attempts to engage him, the mother seemed to lead. She seemed to loom into the baby's face, and one fraction of a second after she began her loom into the baby's face, the baby was already turning away. But essentially it was a simultaneous or nearly simultaneous interaction. My original hypothesis with the present study which I failed to demonstrate was that it was the baby who would slightly decrease affect level which would then be the cue for the mother to change her tempo. I still think it's a good hypothesis, but it wasn't quite statistically significant in this data. On the basis of the way I've analyzed the data so far, it is impossible to say that it is the baby who gets the mother to change her tempo or vice versa.
Stanley Feldstein:	I find that, with the stimulus-response model,

you have to make a lot of conditions and add a lot of constraints to get it to fit the data, whereas with a reciprocal model you can deal with the data as it occurs. It's more difficult because at least in psychology we're used to thinking in terms of stimulus-response models and not mutually reciprocal models. But I think that's really where we ought to be going, particularly with this kind of rhythmic analysis.

Beatrice Beebe: As a matter of fact, none of my data fits a stimulus-response model (see Beebe et al., 1979).

Anne
Schutzenberger: I would like to comment about some French research done by Professor Montagner of Pousanson University. He found that, when the mother sits down at the level of the child, the synchronicity is much better. He also found, as you did, that when she has slow movements, the child is more happy and more responding.... Well, he went a little bit further down the road than you did. He made an analysis of the urine ... of the mother and the child and he proved that, during the week when the child is going to nursery school, his urine and his mother's are different, but on the weekend the child has the same urine analysis as the mother. Which means that the child is matching the mother's rhythm in all the biological functions. He just has a book out on that.

Participant: I noticed that toward the very end of the sequence the child got saturated, and I'm wondering whether that saturation effect may occur gradually as they go along.

Beatrice Beebe:	Actually 2/3-second cycles and 1/4-second cycles roughly alternate throughout the data. However, the period the mother pauses the most occurs in the second minute. This baby has already been videotaped for 20 minutes. He's had it, and the only way the mother's able to get him back was through this rather controlled hand rhythmic stimulation, so the issue of the baby's fatigue is very relevant.
Participant:	It occurs to me that the dance therapist might be doing the same things movement-wise. You could be talking about the same process in dance therapy with chronic schizophrenics, and using verbal analogies, there may be parallels in psychotherapy sessions with non-schizophrenic patients.
Beatrice Beebe:	Well, I am not a dance therapist. I do psychotherapy with borderline schizophrenic adults. I have found that the process of learning to code these films has sharpened my acuity for noticing postural orientations, facial exchanges, and tempo changes in my patients. I seem to have sharpened my perception so that I can tell when a patient isn't telling me a thought by various nonverbal behaviors flickering across the face or the body. To speak more directly to your point, I do think that this is the primal communication paradigm. I think it must apply to patient-therapist paradigms, to paradigms between lovers, etc. Perhaps the exact functional relations are somewhat different, but many of the parameters are very similar.
Participant:	For some social phenomena, there are long time lags before a response. I know this occurs with adult humans. The impression I got from your data, however, was that there was very

little of that, that the behavior looked either simultaneous or immediately responsive rather than having any appreciable delay.

Beatrice Beebe: First of all, I'm only looking at the microlevel, and, as many people have pointed out, rhythmicities occur on a continuum from micro to macro. . . . At the microlevel one tends to see either absolutely co-occurring behavior or movements occurring within an average of ½-second onset to onset latency. If I take all the mother-to-infant and infant-to-mother sequences, i. e., just one-step sequences, and make a distribution, all fall within 1 second (Beebe et al., 1979). Now, the exception to that is inhibition of responsivity, because, of course, those are periods when the infant essentially opts out for stretches of time from the interaction. There are periods, even at the microlevel, where you can see lapses in this very quick type of interlocking, mutual . . . one can't even call it responsivity. We don't know what to call it. I think Condon is the one who's tried to best conceptualize it as co-occurring systems. Furthermore, I would add the caveat that these amazingly temporally meshed sequences probably occur for only stretches, and then the system goes out of "synch" or the mother and infant stop interacting in such a finely tuned way, and the mother has to answer seven telephone calls and attend to three other children, and so on. I don't think either one of them could continue for very long in this temporally tuned, intermeshed way.

Participant: Is the mother saying anything during that sequence, and do you want or need to account for that?

Beatrice Beebe: Very important question. I am now beginning to consider the vocal behavior. I could not deal with all the variables at once. So this is a purely kinesic analysis. I have begun to put the sound back in, and I'll tell you that's very tricky—to synchronize the kinesics of the film with some kind of vocal transcript done separately because you have to syncrhonize them. I understand that the Bell and Howell editor is good for this. I can only give you my impression, which is exactly as we have heard from Dr. Oliva; namely that the major vocal events occur as packages with the kinesic events. I think that Condon and Stern have been saying this all along, although the actual demonstration of it in very, very careful measurement is hard to come by.

REFERENCES

Ambrose, A. *Stimulation in early infancy.* New York: Academic Press, 1969.

Ashton, R. Aspects of timing in child development. *Child Development,* 1976, *47* (3), 622–626.

Beebe, B. *Ontogeny of positive affect in the third and fourth months of the life of one infant.* Doctoral dissertation, Columbia University, University Microfilms, 1973.

Beebe, B. Micro-timing in mother-infant communication. In M. R. Key (Ed.). *Nonverbal communication today: Current research. In preparation.*

Beebe, B. & Gerstman, L. The "packaging" of maternal stimulation in relation to infant facial-visual engagement. *Merrill-Palmer Quarterly,* 1980, *26* (4), 321–339.

Beebe, B. & Sloate, P. Assessment and treatment of difficulties in mother-infant attunement in the first three years of life. *Psychoanalytic Inquiry,* in press.

Beebe, B. & Stern, D. Engagement-disengagement and early object experiences. In N. Freedman & S. Grand (Eds.), *Communicative structures and psychic structures.* New York: Plenum Press, 1977.

Beebe, B., Stern, D. & Jaffe, J. The kinesic rhythm of mother-infant interactions. In A. W. Siegman & S. Feldstein (Eds.), *Of speech and time: Temporal patterns in interpersonal contexts.* Hillsdale, N. J.: Lawrence Erlbaum Assocs., 1979.

Brazelton, T. B., Koslowski, B., & Main, M. Origins of reciprocity: The early mother-infant interaction. In M. Lewis & L. Rosenblum (Eds.), *The effect of the infant on its caregiver.* New York: Wiley, 1974.

Birdwhistell, R. *Kinesics and context.* Philadelphia: Univ. of Penn. Press, 1970.

Brannigan, C. & Humphries, P. Human nonverbal behavior, a means of communication. In H. B. Blurton-Jones (Ed.), *Ethological studies of child behavior.* London: Cambridge Univ. Press, 1972.

Church, J. *Language and the discovery of reality.* New York: Vintage Books, 1961.

Kimberly, R. P. Rhythmic patterns in human interaction. *Nature*, 1970, *228*, October 3, 88–90.

Lashley, K. S. The problem of serial order in behavior. In L. A. Jeffress (Ed.), *Cerebral mechanisms in behavior.* New York: John Wiley & Sons, 1951.

Lewis, M. & Goldberg, S. Perceptual-cognitive development in infancy: A generalized expectancy model as a function of the mother-infant interaction. *Merrill-Palmer Quarterly*, 1969, *15*, 81–100.

Nie, N., Hull, C., Jenkins, J., Steinbrenner, K., Bent, D. *Statistical package for the social sciences.* 2nd Ed. New York: McGraw-Hill, 1975.

Oster, H. Facial expression and affect development. In M. Lewis & L. Rosenblum, *The development of affect.* New York: Plenum Press, 1978.

Salk, L. Mother's heartbeat as an imprinting stimulus. *Trans-actions of the New York Academy of Sciences*, 1962, *24*, 753.

Sander, L., Stechler, G., Julia, H., & Burns, P. Primary prevention and some aspects of temporal organization in the early infant-caretaker interaction. In E. Rexford, L. Sander, & T. Shapiro (Eds.), *Infant psychiatry.* New Haven, Yale University Press, 1977.

Schilder, P. *Contributions to neuropsychiatry.* New York: International Univ. Press, 1964.

Sollgerber, A. *Behavioral rhythm research.* New York: Elsevier, 1963.

Stern, D. A micro-analysis of mother-infant interaction. *J. Amer. Acad. Child Psychiatry*, 1971, *10*, 501–17.

Stern, D. Mother and infant at play. In M. Lewis & L. Rosenblum (Eds.), *The effect of the infant on its caregiver.* New York: John Wiley, 1974.

Stern, D. *The first relationship.* Cambridge: Harvard Univ. Press, 1977.

Stern, D., Beebe, B., Jaffe, J., Bennett, S. The infant's stimulus world during social interaction: A study of caregiver behaviors with particular reference to repetition and timing. In H. R. Schaffer (Ed.), *Studies in mother-infant interaction*. New York: Academic Press, 1977.

Stern, D. & Gibbon, J. Temporal expectancies of social behaviors in mother-infant play. In E. Thoman (Ed.), *Origins of the infant's social responsiveness*. New York: Lawrence Erlbaum Assocs., 1978.

Thomas, A., Chess, S., Birch, H., Hertzig, M. & Korn, S. *Behavioral individuality in early childhood*. New York: New York Univ. Press, 1963.

Tronick, E., Als, H., & Brazelton, T. B. Monadic phases: A structural description analys of infant-mother face to face interaction. *Merrill-Palmer Quarterly*, 1979.

Werner, H. *Comparative Psychology of mental development*. New York: International Univ. Press, 1948.

Wolff, P. The role of biological rhythms in early psychological development. *Bulletin Menninger Clinic*, 1967, *311*, 197–217.

Chapter 4

SOME INTERACTIVE FUNCTIONS OF RHYTHM CHANGES BETWEEN MOTHER AND INFANT[1]

Daniel Stern

I would like to change the title of my presentation to something like *The Importance of Irregularities of Rhythm*. At this conference we have discussed regularities of tempo or rhythm a great deal as important structural units of interaction. Perhaps it is the state of the art, but we seem to overstress the regularities and get exclusively involved in issues of whether a behavior is co-contemporaneous, synchronous, or whatnot. These issues are important to investigate, but I would like to discuss the irregularities, the transition points, the places where the system is apparently breaking down or at least changing. To be more accurate, I will discuss *lawful* irregularities or changes in rhythm. It is impossible to conceive of interaction systems of the sort we are discussing which do not have both regularities and irregularities.

[1] We wish to acknowledge the support of the Jane Hilder Harris Foundation in conducting these researches. Editor's Note: This chapter was edited from a transcript of the lecture, and the informal tone has been preserved.

I am focusing on lawful irregularities of rhythm because I think much important interaction occurs during them. I believe that they are functional units that have a great deal to do with cognition and affect. Let me give some examples.

The first one is the "I'm Going to Get You Game" between a mother and a baby. The "I'm Going to Get You Game" is irregular in the sense that the beat progressively elongates. It consists of saying:

"I'm gonna getcha . . . I'm gonna getcha . . . . . I'm gonna getcha . . . . .Gotcha!"

Let's pretend I have held the pitch and volume constant and only varied the timing. If this pattern were strictly metric, each "I'm gonna getcha" would fall at the same interval as the one before, but it doesn't. The mother stretches the waiting interval each time before repeating "I'm gonna getcha." At each repeat the baby may figure, "Well on the basis of what happened the last time, the next one ought to fall about here." And it doesn't. The mother violates the expectation by progressively stretching the interval while the baby's excitement mounts, and then, wham, gives a "gotcha," the timing of which constitutes the largest violation, and the baby goes into peals of delight.

The actual amount of stimulation that the baby receives in this repetitive run becomes less and less because the mother progressively slows the tempo. One cannot say then that the baby's affect has been generated because there is more stimulation. If anything, the reverse is true; there is less stimulus density. What has happened is that the mother has stretched some expectation which is a cognitive operation on the baby's part. Accordingly, while there is progressively less physical stimulus density, there is progressively more cognitive stimulus density which operates during the silences. (This is in no way different from the appropriate timing in telling the punch line of a joke.) So, here is a lawful temporal irregularity serving a very important functional purpose, generating a moment of affectively positive excitement.

To cite another example, there are definite soothing rhythms, as Beatrice Beebe has discussed (see Chapter 5), which have a certain tempo and regularity. However, a slow, steady tempo is not always the essential element in trying to soothe an upset baby. When the baby starts to get upset, and goes "a a a a a aaaaa" into a fuss cry, the mother often automatically speeds up and tops the baby's rhythm and brings him down. She becomes a pacesetter for the baby, but to do so she must just exceed his or her rate. She will go, for example:

"Hey hey hey hey . come . . come on . . . come on . . . .
yeah . . . . . way to go . . . . . . atta girl . . . . come on
sweetie pie . . . . here we go."

This is not a regular, steady tempo. It has a rapid initial phase with a gradual deceleration. The entire sequence is a functional unit to bring the baby down. (One can also do the reverse, an acceleration, to excite someone.) Now, that doesn't mean that certain tempos are not soothing. We are really talking about different parts of the interaction, and I am purposely focusing on the use of a constantly changing tempo to first initiate soothing. The "soothing," steady tempos which Dr. Beebe is addressing appear in periods where the baby's quiet state is being maintained, not initiated. However, there would be nothing to maintain if initiation were not successful and the initiation was accomplished with a lawful irregularity of tempo.

Before proceeding with other examples of the interactional functions of irregular tempos, it has probably already become apparent that we need to examine how we, and especially infants, appreciate tempo and how infants might create temporal expectancies. An understanding of deviations from absolutely regular tempos depends upon this. Probably most of you know that, when the musical performances of extremely fine musicians such as a Horowitz are examined quantitatively, they are often found to be off the metronome beat within the piece. The musician usually catches up at the end of a measure or every other measure. If they were right on the beat, then the reviewers and the listeners would say that it was a technically good performance, but it was unemotional and uninteresting. There is something about the deviation from the beat, the irregularity or variation from the expected regularity that is "expressive" of feelings and thoughts. This is perhaps most dramatic in jazz, where such deviations are a conventionalized feature of the style, and much of the excitement can be generated by fluctuations of falling behind and then getting ahead of the beat and then slipping back into it.

Another very different phenomenon exemplifies our need to understand in an interactive setting the creation and evaluation of temporal expectancies. I examined on film the time it took Muhammed Ali and Carl Miltenburger to throw a left jab in the World Heavyweight Title Fight in 1966. This was interesting because both men can throw a left jab in well under reaction time, so theoretically, if it is a stimulus-response world, each man would get hit and be knocked out in the first round. Neither could dodge in time. If, on the other hand, they were really sharing the same program the way we imagine mothers and babies and a lot of other people do, if, in fact, they were in perfect synchrony, a punch would never land, the dodge would begin with the onset of the punch. Mind you, these men are highly trained. Each is watching the other do a very small repertoire of behaviors that are quite predictable. They've been through it many times. Clearly, both systems (stimulus-response and perfect synchrony) are not the essential part of the match. The only thing that's interesting in a boxing match is when there is a mess up. When the stimulus-response system fails and when the synchronous, co-occurrent system fails—that's the only time there can be any action. Stated differently, only when one fighter fails to anticipate his opponent's next move and its exact timing will he get hit.

Another example comes from Adam Kendon's study of greeting behavior (Kendon & Ferber, 1973). The question arises as to what is the effective stimulus for one to know what's going on. As Kendon beautifully demonstrated, when people greet one another, they do a variety of things: the head and eyebrows go up, there is some form of palm display on the approach, etc. Actually I hadn't seen Adam for quite a while before today, and we've known each other enough so that, when I saw him, I said, "Hi" in roughly the way he would predict. And he did to me. The important thing, though, from the point of view of this argument is that the duration of my eyebrow raise had to be appropriate to our relationship, the amount of time since we've seen each other, etc. If it wasn't, if it was too short, then he would have said to himself, "What is going on here, what's wrong," and so would I if he'd done that to me. In that situation, the effective functional stimulus event is the discrepancy between the expected and the actual duration of what happened, i. e., an evaluation of a deviation from an internally represented standard or regularity.

Given the above, if we are going to talk about tempos, we have to know something about temporal expectancy. (I will not talk about temporal conditioning, although it is a related field.) There are several ways we know that humans as well as animals might keep track of time or create temporal expectancies. The first is called absolute timing. This is one mechanism whereby we create an expectancy of when the next event in a series of events with a regular tempo is going to occur. Absolute timing is an extraordinary process. Using this process, the estimating error of when the next beat will fall is the same, i. e., is absolute irrespective of the duration of the event to be measured. If, for example, I count seconds, "1, 2, 3 . . .," absolute timing predicts that at each attempt to estimate, I am going to be off by, for example, 100 milliseconds when I call each second. If I then try to call off 10-second intervals, I'll still be off by only 100 milliseconds. This is counterintuitive. If I try to estimate an interval of 10 seconds in my mind, it would seem that I should be off much more than I was when I was estimating a 1-second interval. And that is true, except in estimates below roughly ½ a second. It appears that for durations under ½ a second, human beings using the process of absolute timing can measure either 100, 200, or 500 milliseconds, etc., and their estimate will be in error by the same 15 milliseconds whether the task is to estimate

100 or 500 milliseconds. This is one of the reasons that we have such exquisite timing in music. All musical beats with the exception of largo and the slower regions of andante fall into this realm. (Presto is around 200 milliseconds.) Therefore, when we're in the musical range, we are mainly dealing with our ability to perform absolute timing, which means we can be very, very accurate.

As soon as we get beyond 550 milliseconds, it appears that the absolute timing process is no longer operable; one of two other processes takes over, Poisson timing or scalar timing. I shall discuss mainly scalar timing which seems to apply to what mothers do with infants and probably to how babies appreciate the timing of mothers' behavior. It is called scalar timing because the error in estimation is scaled to the duration of the interval being estimated. I'm going to estimate, for example, the interval from one second to the next. I will be off on the average of 1/10 of a second. I will have a 10 percent error. If I'm going to estimate an interval of 10 seconds, I'll still be off 10 percent, but that means I'll have a 1-second error on the average. If I'm going to estimate 100 seconds, I'll be off by 10 percent, so I'll have a 10-second error. The error is proportional to the duration of the interval.

We were curious about the tempo of movements and vocalizations the mother presented the baby with to see what kind of timing mechanism she might be using and what kind of timing mechanism the baby might have to have in order to be able to form an expectancy of when her next behavior was going to happen. If such mechanisms did not exist, there could not be rhythm sharing of the kind we're talking about. To do this, John Gibbon of Columbia University and I counted the onset-to-onset time of maternal vocalizations to babies.[2] We used the same

---

[2] Counting onset-to-onset times in vocalizations can be severely criticized by anybody who's dealt with languages by saying, "Well, the real action is where the stresses are." But because mothers' vocalizations to infants are so short, they usually only have one stress and sometimes two. It really doesn't matter. In fact, we went back and did the analyses by stress and obtained the same results.

data base Beatrice Beebe reported on in this volume. We had six primiparous mothers talking to their six children at two, four, and six months, and recorded about 1,500 utterances. We found the mothers talked as if they were using a scalar timing mechanism rather than a Poisson mechanism or other possible models. This may be ubiquitous and so not an extraordinary finding, but it does help us understand some of the constraints on the baby's ability to create temporal expectancies.

Let me say a little bit more about what scalar timing really means for the baby. With an infant you have to present something fairly regular in order for them to understand that it belongs to the same class of events temporally. Therefore, speech units ought to be fairly regular to a baby, regular in the sense of having a reasonably tight beat. On the other hand, if anything is exactly predictably the same to the baby, the baby will habituate quickly. Therefore, the ideal rhythm of maternal speech should be regular but with a certain limited amount of variability. That will allow the baby to keep attending to it without habituating and to form expectancies of when the next thing will occur. At the same time the baby can exercise what is probably its strongest cognitive tendency, and that is to make hypotheses and test them with regard to whether he or she is right or wrong, predicting whether something will occur when it's supposed to. If the mother violates what is considered a lawful expectancy which the scalar timing rule will tell, then the baby will say essentially, "Oh, that's part of a different event or a different class of phenomena." It doesn't belong to the same unit. So, I think these timing mechanisms are a very important part of how the baby goes about being able to parse the world of behavior he or she is exposed to.

I might add that with some of the same data that Dr. Beebe talked about, we looked at the kinesic or body movement tempos much as she has discussed, and it seems that the mother was doing essentially the same kind of scalar timing kinesically that she was vocally.

To make the same point in another realm, I think everyone here will accept that the intonational shape or pitch contour of a maternal utterance can be considered itself a vocal signal which carries information about the mother's intent. In other words, the very pitch contour of what she says can be considered a speech act. Another way of putting this is that it's the shape of the envelope, not what's in it, that has the semantic force regardless of the syntactic form. This is, of course, not a new idea. It has simply never been applied to mothers and infants in this age range (birth to six). You'll see in a minute why I am taking a sidetrack into this area and its relation to my central theme about irregularities of rhythm.

The mother's speech contours are extremely important because we know from experimental laboratory studies that babies are capable of discriminating various pitch contours and even melodic patterns by the time they're six months of age, so there's every reason to expect that they would do this with the human voice.

What we did was to pass samples of the mother's speech to her baby through a voice spectrograph and looked at what intonation contours the mothers produced when the baby was in various interactive states. We have identified a number of these contours. The first is like so,

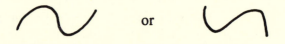

or

a sinusoidal shape. When mothers talk to babies, as you know, they exaggerate the pitch contouring enormously. In these patterns there is a minimum criterion of a pitch excursion of a musical third, and in many of them octave shifts occur. Sinusoidal patterns might typically occur as follows:

"You haven't   been   here   in a long   time."

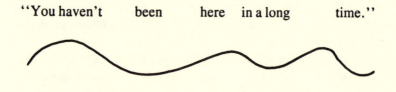

''The puppet's   got your   hand.''

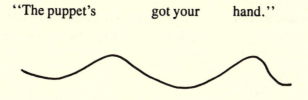

The second pattern, a U-shape, seems to function similarly.

''There   he   is.''

Originally, we just had a Bell shape which typically might be something like,

''Come on.''

''Right.''

We found that we had to distinguish what we called a Bell-Right which looks like two right thirds of a bell because it goes up a little and then way down:

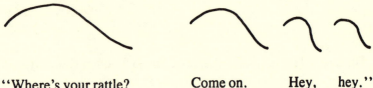

"Where's your rattle?   Come on.   Hey,   hey."

Then we distinguished several kinds of "rises." Yes-no questions, as you all know, have a rising intonation pattern:

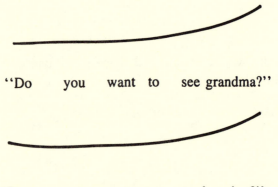

"Do   you   want   to   see grandma?"

"Do   you want   to   go shopping?"

In addition, there are sharper rises which usually go with reiterative questions such as:

"Do   you   want   to see grandma,   huh?"

where you get a marked pitch rise of about six, seven, or eight.

We determined the pitch contour for every utterance and correlated these with all the interactive situations. We also analyzed the grammatical form as to whether it was a command, a question, affirmative, declarative, etc. for all utterances. In addition, we obtained some interactive ratings from the video-tapes as to what the baby was doing at the time that the mother performed the utterance.

We found that there were several form-function correlations during the first months that were of much interest to us. One was when the baby was not looking at mother and expressing neutral affect. In this case, the mother would use

the Sharp Rise (╱).

These seemed to serve the elocutionary function of a request for visual attention. The request for attention could be mild, like a cajole, to very strong, as in a demand.[3] A good example of this pattern would be where the mother would say:

"What's the matter? Huh? Whatcha looking at?

[3] When several sharp rising speech contours are strung together, the speech sounds something like:

I have wanted to go to the police labs to do some analysis of what sirens are most effective because this seems to be fairly effective in getting the baby's attention back. I'm entirely speculating here; I don't expect anyone to take it any further than that.

"Huh?   Come on.   Hey."

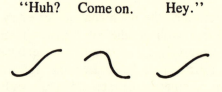

When the baby is looking at the mother and affect is neutral or slightly positive, the Bell-Right shape speech contours are frequent. The intent or semantic force of this shape seems to be something like a request for increased level of engagement. The kind of sentences occurring in the Bell-Right contour can be varied. Commands, affirmatives, declaratives—

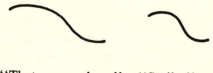

"That   a   boy."   "Smile."

and all have the quality of let's go with some more. The final two forms that were notable occur when the baby is showing a fair degree of positive affect as measured by a smile. At these times, we found the sinusoidal shape and the Bell shape statistically most frequently used. (All of these correlations are statistically significant I should say here.) The mother and infant seem really locked in together so she says something like:

"You're the   cutest little boy in the   whole   world."

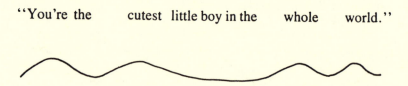

It isn't a question of the length of the utterance because right after she said this the mother may say "whole world" right over again with the sinusoidal inflection. I do not really have a good, concise definition of what the intent or force of this contour is. It seems to be something like, "Continue at this high level of positive engagement, we're having so much fun together," and that is certainly the context in which it most occurs.

These are some relative regularities of speech contour, but I want to get back to where I started and continue the case for a role for irregularity. The question arises here, how does the mother, so to speak, analogue qualify features of her intent. Dr. Oliva talked about this in his presentation. Suppose, in fact, the mother's intent is a request for attention, such as occurs with the rise contour. One way to analogue qualify the message in the sense of intensifying its urgency would be to progressively shorten the rise time of the pitch excursion. For example, she might say:

"Come on, come on,   come on,   come on—   hey."
[A series of rise contours increasing in tempo.]

The real semantic force of the event would now be contained in this sequence of five units. The sequence becomes the functional unit, and its lawful deviation from a preceding regularity constitutes the relevant stimulus.

I think that it is in this manner that mothers go about making the analogue qualifications of their intent. Of course, the same thing is done with volume or by increasing the pitch contour. I am not making the case that the temporal variations are the only ones of importance in this. I simply want to urge that we attend to the changes in rhythm and the deviations from regularity of rhythm because these serve some very important functions. Sometimes the most important interpersonal action is right there.

DISCUSSION

Participant:	As you made the sounds of the mother, you also made movement shape changes in your body. Do you also observe those motions simultaneously with the voice?
Daniel Stern:	Anecdotally, yes. It's something that I would like to examine more fully. For instance, mock surprise, or what I guess would be a 90 on Dr. Beebe's mother affect scale, would come at the uprise of a sinusoidal contour. You do see that. There's something very important in this. The baby is getting at least two channels, auditory and visual. Secondly, everything that I've said will apply to tickling behavior or belly-poking behavior.
Participant:	It seems that people talk to their pets in these ways, especially to small dogs.
Daniel Stern:	Yes. And actually it's a very important point because sometimes people say, "People talk to both small animals and old people that way, so what's the big deal." Speaking teleologically, I think that this kind of speech is mainly designed to be an infant-elicited variation of normal speech pattern which does apply to small animals for very cogent biological reasons, as Lorenz has laid out. The young of any species looks different from the old. They have a bigger forehead. The eyes are set lower. The cheeks are bigger. The nose is small. The chin is smaller, etc., and all of these features elicit certain types of parental, social, and antiaggressive behaviors in all social mammals and nonmammals, so that we're talking about a biological phenomenon which is also enormously influenced by training, model-

ing, etc. The use of such speech to animals and the "incompetent" (old, foreigners, etc.) is probably a derivative. It sounds the same superficially, but there are major differences. The pitch contouring is different in some ways. The speaker raises the absolute pitch but doesn't contour as much. The timing is different. The rhythm isn't as strict. I'm glad you brought it up because it allows me to mention the biological roots of these patterns.

Participant: What about fathers . . . ?

Daniel Stern: We're looking at that. People all around the country are. It's very hard to find fathers who care for babies 50 percent of the time so the study can actually complement the mother's speech analysis. So far, the results are essentially this. There are differences in the "average American family" where the father works and comes home and at the end of the day he's up for only a quick interaction, compared to the mother who's dealt with the baby all day long. What we find is that the fathers usually do more high-level, high-intensity, vocal, and kinesic patterns with the baby for shorter durations and have fewer games in the sense that Dr. Beebe has talked about them. I should clarify that the children love it when the father comes. They expect something different. They expect faster and higher-intensity behaviors, and they get a big kick out of it. On the other hand, if you were to come from Mars and look at a mother and a father, you'd say the similarities are so enormous, the difference is miniscule. I have only seen one family where the mother works and the father stays at home taking care of the baby, and there, essentially, there seems to be reversal in how the two of them talk

Participant:

Daniel Stern:

along the parameters of the study, but that's a case of one. We really do not have any idea how much of this is biologically loaded for males and females.

There must be some mothers who do not follow these kinds of patterns. How are they different?

I have only seen two mothers who talked to babies entirely in an "adult" register with "adult" timing, rhythm, etc. Both were teenage mothers who already decided to give the baby up for adoption. I think it is extremely rare to see a complete absence of this sort of behavior in a bonded mother-infant pair. Now, there's enormous range between 0 and doing it 4+. I'm loath to call it a clinical index because speech is not the only modality. There's touching, there's looking, there's proprioceptive experiences. There are all of the other modalities of stimulation. I'm only talking about this one because it is easier to study, which is no small thing, and because it is more amenable to precise quantification, which the others are not. I have seen mothers who I think are rather impoverished as far as their vocal repertoire is concerned, but I think they are terrific mothers in other modalities so I wouldn't care to predict with regard to vocal patterns alone. I think you'd have to see the total behavior.

REFERENCES

Kendon, A. and Ferber, A. A description of some human greetings. In R. P. Michael and J. H. Cook (Eds.), *Comparative ecology of primates*. London: Academic Press, 1973.

Stern, D. Mother and infant at play. In M. Lewis and L. Rosenblaum (Eds.), *The effect of the infant on its caregiver*. New York: John Wiley & Sons, 1974.

Stern, D. *The first relationship: Infant and mother.* Cambridge: Harvard University Press, 1977.

Stern, D. and Gibbon, J. Temporal expectancies of social behaviors in mother infant play. In E. Thoman (Ed.), *Origins of the infant's social responsiveness.* Hillsdale, New Jersey: Lawrence Erlbaum Press, 1979.

Chapter 5

TEMPORAL ASPECTS OF "SELF-STIMULATING" BEHAVIOR IN ABNORMAL SPEAKERS

Judith Duchan

There is a class of movements called "self-stimulatory" or stereotypic behaviors which is frequently reported as a diagnostic sign for pathology such as psychosis (Creak, 1963) and autism (Rutter, 1968). There are several problems with this. The first is that the criteria for classifying behaviors as self-stimulatory are not made explicit. For example, Koegel et al. (1974) include static activities such as staring and locking hands behind head along with repetitive movements such as hand rubbing and finger flicking. Other clinicians and researchers do not include the static movements.

A second problem is that normal people also engage in such behaviors which suggests that it is not simply the existence of such behaviors that makes one appear deviant but perhaps other factors such as morphology, frequency, or when they occur in the interaction.

Finally, classifying this diverse set of behaviors as self-stimulatory presumes, without doing the necessary analysis that they all serve a single function—that of stimulation. It then follows if it is only stimulation that any one of these behaviors should be substitutable for any other.

This study is a structural analysis of repetitive behaviors in three subjects, a normal teenager, an autistic child, and a senile adult. The attempt is to analyze the patterns of their repetitive behaviors and to look at their interactional embeddedness.

All three of my subjects were videotaped as they were engaged in a somewhat formal interview situation. The tapes had time superimposed on them in tenths of a second for indexing purposes. The segments where the subjects exhibited repetitive behaviors were analyzed for the following:

1. the movement or vocal characteristics of the repetitive behavior
2. beat or tempo changes
3. number of repetitions in an unchanging sequence
4. length of time these identical repetitious sequences lasted
5. other behaviors accompanying the repetitions such as gaze and the interactant's verbalizations
6. reaction of the interactant to the repetitive activity

Multilevel transcripts were made of the repetitive sequences. They were similar to Condon's in that the cycles in the repetition were indicated across the page and co-occuring events were marked on separate lines above and below these cycles. For example, my first subject, Brenda, the normal teenager, was chewing gum throughout the tape. Each chew was marked at its most closed point. If the topology of the chew changed, such as when she changed from an open to closed mouth chew, the change was described and indicated on the main line of the transcript. If Brenda was chewing while someone else was talking, their speech was transcribed beneath Brenda's chews with an attempt to indicate which syllable co-occurred with Brenda's clenched teeth positions. My transcripts are more cursory than Condon's in that they are not frame-by-frame analysis, so the interactional synchrony and self-synchrony awaits verification from a more fine-grained analysis.

First, I'll report results for each of the students separately, and then I will compare subjects in light of the three issues being raised.

Brenda, my teenaged normal subject was videotaped with a classmate and a relatively unfamiliar adult. The adult was a student teacher assigned to teach the two eighth graders philosophical concepts such as logical quantifiers. The first two minutes of the half hour tape were transcribed in sequence and in detail.

Brenda was selected as a subject because she moves throughout the tape. She is what some would call nervous or a fidgeter. There were only three places in the tape where she was still. Many of Brenda's movements were not repetitive — that is, a movement of her hand to her chin could be followed by touching her ear, then picking up a pencil. The repetitive movements were defined as voluntary identical movements which occurred in a continuous series (three or more), and were movements which served no other obvious function. This latter criteria would exclude things such as her hair grooming movements or scratching herself.

In the tape studied, Brenda exhibited three types of such repetitive movements — gum chewing, pencil tapping or flipping, and left to right knee rocking. There was some variability within each. The gum chewing varied in morphology between up-down-closed-mouth chews, rotating-closed-mouth chews, narrow-open-mouth chews, and wide-open-mouth chews. Typically there were a series of identical looking chews such as up-down-closed-mouth ones, which were immediately followed by another series of identical chews, such as wide-open-mouth chews. This sequencing of identical repetitions was also true for pencil tapping and flipping sequences.

Pencil tapping behaviors differed with the place of the tap, sometimes on her chin, sometimes on the table, sometimes in the air (which I have been calling pencil flipping) and with the *direction* of the tap; sometimes a new series begins on a different part of the table, but the relationship between the pencil and hand is maintained. Sometimes she rotates the pencil to the opposite side of her hand and taps some more.

The knee rocking varies in the degree of excursion. It is only done by the right knee, and the excursion varies from 1 inch to its full sway of around ½ foot, where it reaches the left lag, touches it, and then swings back in an equidistant excursion beyond midline to the right. These excursion differences in knee rocks are not distinguishable from one another. That is, it appears they increase and decrease gradually rather than occurring in identical and successive sequences. Thus one does not feel that there are small excursions and then separate large ones as was described before for the small and large excursion chews.

Brenda's repetitive movements, even those within the same class, vary considerably in tempo, number of repetitions in a sequence, and the length of time of the sequence. Further, the cycles within identical sequences also vary temporally. They sometimes have an irregularly spaced progression, while at other times they occur at equidistant intervals from one another.

The variabilities in structural patterning suggest that the repetitive activities are not autonomous acts which Brenda initiates to keep herself stimulated, but that they may be tied to other phenomena which are variable in their temporal occurrence. The multilevel transcripts indicate that this is indeed the case.

An analysis of the onset and offset of gum chewing sequences indicates that Brenda's chewing sequences are closely tied to the course of the conversation. There were 22 repetitive sequences of gum chewing in the first two minutes of the tape. Ten of these, and the longest and most irregular sequences, occurred while no one was talking. The remaining 12 were during or immediately following her or someone else's talking. These 12 sequences consisted of two where she finished talking and chewed her gum once or twice and then stopped, six where she chewed on the first morpheme of someone else's short utterance and then just after the utterance was over (as if she stopped to listen more carefully), and four where she chewed throughout the longer utterance of someone else, stopping either at the end or at a major constituent boundary. These last four chews seemed to occur in synchrony with the stronger stresses of the speech of the interlocuter, but this will have to be determined by more careful microanalysis. Incidentally, this did not seem to be the case for the large knee excursions. One gets the impression that the large knee movements assume their own tempo—slower than the verbal beat and out of synchrony with it because of the difficulty of such a large extremity to keep up with the rapid pace.

There were three occasions where chewing continued but changed in morphology, from open to closed chewing, for example. These all occurred when no one was talking and when Brenda was being asked to answer a question verbally or by writing it on paper. The chewing occurred before she wrote or answered, that is, as she was formulating her answer, and the changes in chewing occurred with an overall change in posture or gaze direction. On these three occasions the chewing stopped when she began writing.

Finally, on no occasion were any of Brenda's repetitive activities seen to interfere with the ongoing interaction. Nor did she at any time appear to be attending to anything other than the ongoing activity. The interlocutors would just as likely begin talking during Brenda's chewing and tapping as they would during her few quiescent periods.

My second subject is Robbie, an eight-year-old autistic child. I am drawing from two tapes of Robbie, the first is of an interaction between Robbie and his mother in which his mother is conducting a daily lesson to teach Robbie what she calls "concepts for daily living." The second tape is of Robbie and his classroom teacher in which she is teaching him object names and functions. They were filmed one week apart. The tapes differ considerably in the amount of repetitive behaviors which Robbie displays—the mother tape has fewer than the teacher tape. While the repetitive sequences vary in frequency between the tapes, they do not vary in morphology.

On both tapes Robbie has the following repetitive behaviors.

There are vocal noises, chin and head hits, and head and body rocks. In the mother tape, Robbie's thumbs are wrapped with a bandaid to prevent his thumb sucking, so there is no thumb sucking on that tape while there is a bit on the teacher tape.

Robbie's vocal noises have an identifiable canonical form which allows one to classify them into three kinds. The first is a "henshui"—a stereotypic form which is two or three syllables in length. The first syllable is usually a very high-pitched consonant and vowel—the consonant is an /h/, the vowel is nasalized. The second syllable is said on a much lower pitch and shorter, and begins with a fricative or affricate followed by a vowel, usually a /u/. The last syllable, if present, is either a vowel or bilabial consonant and vowel. It is also short in duration and low in pitch. Robbie's other noises were an oioioi, said with a glottal fry, and a buccal fry. The noises all involve extremes in articulatory positioning, i. e., front to back vowels, glottal to alveolar movement. The "fry" aspect suggests his focus on kinesthetic as well as, or instead of, auditory features for those sounds.

Robbie's hits are most often chin and head hits with the palm or heel of either hand. Sometimes there are quick sequences made with alternating hands on alternate sides of his head. Head and body rocks are much more jerky than those described for Brenda. That is, at the ends of the excursions there were clear and abrupt changes in direction.

Robbie's repetitive sequences were often combinations of several types of behaviors rapidly following one another such as hits, noises, then rocks. They were sometimes irregular in temporal organization; that is, they were not equidistant, had an unequal number of identical segments per sequence, and were unequal in the amount of time given to each identical sequence. Those sequences which were more regular were where Robbie or the adult was talking. In these cases, he hit himself or jerked on the strongly stressed syllable of the utterances. Sometimes every syllable was stressed as when he said "This is a puh" and hit his leg with his left hand on each word. There were three exceptions to his movement and talk synchrony. In each instance,

Robbie was being corrected by his teacher for a wrong answer and appeared agitated. Incidentally, we found this same infrequent departure from self-synchronous behavior in a normal one and one-half-year-old child we studied and it too coincided with her strong emotional state (Duchan, Oliva, Lindner, 1979).

In Robbie's interaction with his mother, his repetitive behaviors were infrequent, consuming about 10 seconds of a 2-minute sequence. They occurred between activities or when his mother was looking away from Rob. In contrast, his repetitive behaviors were more frequent with his teacher with the longest sequences following the teacher's nonacceptance of Robbie's attempts to perform for her. In both interactions, the adults sometimes continued to talk to Robbie during his repetitive sequences. At other times they waited until the behaviors subsided or told him to put his hands down. The most consistent occasions for which the adults did not pursue the interaction, and instead did things like snap their fingers in front of Robbie's eyes or call him, were those where Robbie was staring out away from the ongoing event in an unfocused way. This is the state which his mother and teacher call "out of it."

My third subject is H, a senile man. The tape is of a clinical interview in which he is being asked to identify objects or pictures by name or function, or he is questioned about his family and his daily experiences. He may ignore the question, say "Yeah" or "I don't know," or repeat the question back perhaps changing it into a statement, but not answering it. An example would be: "Are you looking for something else?" "I'm looking for that something else."

Throughout the 10-minute tape H exhibits three kinds of repetitive activity — thumb stroking, during which he moves one thumb on the other; palm rubbing, when he clasps the fingers of both hands together and rubs the touching palms back and forth; and thumb biting, when he puts his thumb in his mouth and bites it repeatedly with his gums. (If it weren't such a distracting term, it would be more accurately called thumb gumming.)

The variability in the activity is minimal. Thumb stroking

can be done by either thumb in either direction (up, down, or both up and down) and can involve the entire thumb or just the distal third, i. e., the part with the nail. Palm rubbing can have minimal or extensive excursion and thumb biting is of either the right or left thumb in either side of the mouth.

As for Brenda and Robbie, H's repetitious activities vary considerably in number of cycles per sequence and length and tempo. They are most often evenly distributed in time, but can be irregular; they sometimes involve several sequences when, for example, thumb stroking is immediately followed by palm rubbing. However, more than for the other two subjects, H seems to prefer different activities at different times. At the beginning of the tape the primary activity is thumb rubbing, during the middle segment, he bites his thumb, and the last third he rubs his palms and periodically stops this to put his thumbs on the edge of the table scrutinizing them as if lining them up with one another.

A multilevel analysis of H's repetitive behaviors indicates they are easily interruptible by clinician's questioning; however, they, like Brenda's chews and Robbie's hits, are capable of continuing through the flow of the conversation—both during his and his clinician's talk. This is even true for thumb biting, believe it or not. In nearly every case where the clinician asks a question, H shows some change in his activity. This is either at the beginning of the question where he stops or changes the direction of the repetitive activity, or at the end where he resumes or again changes its direction. Sometimes his repetitive movements continue throughout a conversational interchange, sometimes not. An example is the palm rub which starts when the clinician asks "Do you have a son" and continues five times through the pause, stops when he answers "Do I have a son" resumes again after the clinician says "or a daughter" and continues through and beyond his answer "or a daughter?" H's repetitive boundaries, like Brenda's and Robbie's seem to coincide with the stressed syllables of both the clinician and his own verbal productions.

There were three types of events which diverted H from his repetitions: turning pictures, lining up objects, and pictures, and direct questioning by the clinician. Except for during these times, his repetitions were accompanied by an unfocussed gaze which changed in direction, but not in degree of focus.

The clinician seemed to ask her questions throughout the interview regardless of H's repetitive behaviors. There were two exceptions and in each case she interrupted the interview to ask him if he wanted to leave. Both times were when H was biting his thumb, and both times his head was lowered and in violation of what Kendon suggests I call the face-address system. On those thumb biting occasions where H and the clinician had mutual gaze exchanges, the clinician continued her interviewing.

Returning to the initial questions, we can now bring the findings to bear on each. First, do the repetitous behaviors identified in my three subjects qualify as self stimulatory in function? The findings suggest that they are much more than simply self stimulating. That is, they are often also in the service of the verbal beat, they are coincidental with the change points in the conversation, they sometimes appeared to tie closely to emotional states such as frustration, or they might be manifestations of changes in thinking as was postulated for Brenda's changes in chewing when she was preparing to write. The evidence for pure and isolated self-stimulatory functioning of the repetitive activities was most strong for Robbie's glottal fry noises which had a strong kinesthetic component. Finally, if their primary function is, indeed, self-stimulatory, one is still left with many questions, such as why they are temporally irregular when there is not a regular verbal beat to control them.

The second problem was to determine the differences, if any, between repetitive activity in normal and abnormal subjects. The picture gleaned from the interlocuter's reactions and the morphological analysis was first that the most interfering activities were those which prevented mutual gaze, as was seen from the interlocutor's reactions to Robbie's "out of it" states, and H's movement out of the face address system. Secondly, repetitive activities which were more noticeable than others were those that were intrusive on the interaction. Robbie's chin hits and jerky movements are examples, especially in contrast with Brenda's more modulated chews and ballistic knee rocks. Finally, there were some repetitive activities such as noises which interfered with the ongoing activities, in this case because the activity involved conversational exchanges. The behaviors interfering most with face-to-face interaction are hypothesized to be those which would be judged to be most deviant. I plan to look into this further by analyzing reactions to different behaviors in detail.

Finally, I asked at the beginning whether the different repetitive behaviors serve the same functions or were substitutable for one another. Evidence for their substitutability is a temporal grouping phenomenon—that is, several repetitive behaviors often occurred together in rapid succession in each of our subjects. Further, evidence is that all the behaviors with the possible exception of Robbie's noises can assimilate to the verbal beats and change-points in conversational turn-taking. These factors might argue that the particular form of repetitive activity is only a surface incidental, and different repetitives can serve the same function. However, the data also indicate that there are differences in the degree to which the repetitive behaviors can be incorporated into ongoing activities because of their incompatibility—pointing to some degree of inherent functional differentiation.

I think it was Colonel Sanders who first coined the term "finger lickin' good." For this paper I have extended Colonel Sanders to question whether finger *flicking* is good, and the answer, like all good answers, needs qualification with questions such as good for whom or what. It's good for the finger flicker in different ways in different contexts, and it's good for the interaction if it is modulated and peripheral, and if it doesn't interfere with ongoing face-to-face exchanges.

DISCUSSION

Participant: I was struck with the fact that each person you described was in a one down position, the subject was either being taught something or interrogated.

Duchan: Yes. I had a feeling that the teenager was very aware of the camera. It might be that you move more these ways when you are in a one down situation and that is another hypothesis about their function. It would argue against the self-stimulatory hypothesis, I would think.

Participant: In all of the tapes the persons doing the repetitive activity are in anxious or stressful situations.

Duchan: Actually in Robbie's case, the situation with his mother and the other with the teacher were very different in terms of the amount of stress. He wasn't as self-stimulatory in the situation where he was under less stress. It has been suggested that I look at him in situations where no one is around. From casual observation I have noticed that when he plays alone, he does different self-stims. For example he will hold up things to lights for many hours. He likes to look at lint against light. He doesn't do that in the strong interactions, so they are different.

Participant: (Felix Barroso from the Clinical Research Unit, Downstate Medical Center)   One alternative explanation for repetitive movements which we have been studying also, such as self touching, is their relation to attentional strategies. For example, if we give children 10-years-of-age a test where they have to ignore the word and name the color which the word is printed in, there is a lot of self-touching which can be viewed as fidgeting, as nervousness, or as related to the fact that there is a camera filming their behavior. When their repetitive behavior is then compared to their performance in the task (and there are a series of very good measures of performance for that task), we find that those who self-touch the most are the ones who perform better in the tasks. We have now repeated these studies on self-touching and their relationship to different attentional strategies. For example I recently conducted a study using dichotic listening tasks where subjects have to follow one message while ignoring another—a task that my subjects refer to as the psychotic listening task—and it is now very clear the subjects who self-touch particularly doing the hand-to-hand or finger-to-hand movements you were describing, have fewer intrusions of the irrelevant messages and are able to repeat more words from the relevant message.

Duchan: If you touch yourself more you'll do better on the tasks!

Participant: I wonder if you have considered the fact that adults who have blindisms show them less when they are under stress than when they are not.

Duchan: It is my observation that when blind children are in interaction, they don't rock and spin and do self-stimulatory actions as much as they do when they are not in any interaction. So that must involve a different dynamic, one that might have to do with the particular kind of repetitive activity.

REFERENCES

Condon, W. & Ogston, W. A segmentation of behavior. *Journal of Psychiatric Research*, 1967, *5*, 221–235.

Creak, E. Childhood psychosis. *British Journal of Psychiatry*, 1963, *109*, 84–89.

Duchan, J., Oliva, J., & Lindner, R. Performative acts defined by synchrony among intonational, verbal, and nonverbal systems in a one and one-half year old child. *Sign Language Studies*, 1979, *22*, 75–88.

Koegel, R., Firestone, P., Kramme, K., & Dunlap, G. Increasing spontaneous play by suppressing self-stimulation in autistic children. *Journal of Applied Behavior Analysis*, 1974, *7*, 521–528.

Rutter, M. Concepts of autism: A review of research. *Journal of Child Psychology and Psychiatry*, 1968, *9*, 1–25.

Chapter 6

DISCUSSION

Paul Byers

It is customary for a discussant to talk about the papers which have been presented. But I want to respond to the kinds of things I have been hearing in the hallway between sessions. I find that there is some uncertainty or even uneasiness about what this conference is all about.

To begin, I hope that we in the science business of human relations and human communication will someday come up with a better format for doing what we're doing than a serial presentation of papers with a few questions at the end of each paper. We could read the papers more quickly, and then we would have more time for your participation, involvement, and discussion. I think we're coming to the end of this rather formal and old-fashioned conference form.

Gregory Bateson once said that the major problems in the world are the result of the difference between the way nature works and the way man thinks (Bateson, 1976). This is reflected in this conference. There are those who think or believe that communicating — even nonverbally — is a matter of exchanging

133

messages and their science is, one way or another, the study of those messages, their creators or originators, and their effects. Many people do very strongly believe that the universe contains *causes* which have *effects*. On the other hand, there are those of us who begin with the premise that one of man's most necessary pursuits is getting it together harmoniously with others of his own and other species and that communication is the means by which this is done. We don't study messages. We study, instead, the organization of the communication *behavior* between or among interactants.

About a generation ago we began to discover that, if we accept our responsibility as explainers of human behavior, we needed to change not our methodologies but our epistemology. First, let me give you my own definition of communication, and then I'll give an example of what I mean by this epistemological shift. Communication, to me, is simply the ways in which people get it together. That, after all, is most of what we do, one way or another.

I'm an anthropologist, and sometimes I recognize that the earth is a ball out in space with a thin layer of life forms on it. Now, considering the limitations of a ball in space, these life forms either get it together—achieve a living harmony—or the life forms won't survive. We have survived so there are necessarily processes by which this is achieved. And I regard our responsibility as one of trying to explain this all the way from brain structure to social structure. Those of us devoted to the "how nature works" question have begun to discover that in the temporal dimensions, which we are calling rhythms in this conference, there are some fairly uniform principles that seem to apply all the way from brain structure to social structure.

As an example of these uniform principles, Dan Stern talked about the unpredictability of varying a rhythm with a child and getting a kind of higher affect response from the child. On other levels of organization the same thing happened when rhythms were varied. If you are late for an appointment, if you die young, if you don't get to dinner or a date on time, if you interrupt someone's speech—all these variations between the temporal expectations of one person and the behavior of another will produce higher affect, higher energy. In Dan Stern's case the higher affect was called positive, but in other instances the higher affect is negative, and we talk about anger, annoyance, being impolite, etc. That is, the same basic thing happens at the micro- or macrolevel regardless of the content.

The reason we had this conference on rhythms, then, comes from our observation that rhythm—the temporal characteristics of interpersonal behavior—is a dimension of all relationships and that the principles that apply at one level of organization will in some sense apply to any other level. And we can then leave out the content of the exchange, and adjectives we have used to describe the content, or any kind of evaluation. The interpretation of our observations shifts from references to theory (or "why" explanations) to extrapolations to other levels of behavior. We are becoming more genuinely objective.

At the end of his life, Karl Lashley, the brain scientist, said that, if his research proved anything, it seemed to prove that memory didn't exist. In other words, Lashley and others had been looking at memory the wrong way. They were looking at content. Now Lashley's student, Karl Pribram, offers another view (Pribram, 1979). All the information that reaches the surface of our bodies, our perceptual facilities, reaches us as vibration. The only raw, raw, raw data (below sound, sight, heat, motion, etc.) is vibration in the form of wave-front intersections at the sensing organ. This is the only primary reality, and it is transmitted along neural fibers as intermittencies of nerve firing—that is, pulsing in one form or another. All a nerve fiber can do is fire or not fire. At a macrolevel we are calling these intermittencies rhythms or talking about temporal dimensions. It is the programmed brain which translates these vibrational patterns into objective reality so that we can say "That's a tree, that's an exit sign, those people are sitting in chairs." Another order of reality is the social consensus which says, "We are going to call that a man, that a woman, that a chair."

And, if we look behind this, by examining the temporal characteristics above the level of vibration or frequency and into the realm of everyday interpersonal behavior, we begin to see that we have the possibility of understanding not only communication between two or more people but how natural systems work. This doesn't include the content of the behavior, and it doesn't include your feelings, but we're beginning to discover that your feelings are a function—a response or outflow—of temporal relationships. We feel good or bad about the harmony or the mismatch in temporal relationships.

What we're saying in this rhythms business is that there are two people—two or more—out there who have to get it together somehow. If you look at one person at a time, you will never find out much because what we must study is relationships. You have to look between people to understand the process by which two people become, in interaction, one unit. There are rules of organization which apply to interaction which simply do not apply to a single person. We do not talk *to* another person, we participate in a conversation with him. We cannot understand human communication, or tennis, or ping-pong, or chess, or lovemaking by looking separately at the participants. What we think is good about any of those enterprises is our internal response to the temporal relationship as it manifests in sound, touch, and movement with others.

Somewhere in this process there is a wire in the brain which runs off to a component called awareness—which often leads us to suppose that we're consciously doing it. One of the things that we've begun to discover is that the show is very much more determined than we liked to think—and at the same time that the human game is even more interesting because we can both participate in it and we can watch it.

So what we have had today in the presentations under the name of *Interaction Rhythms* are bits and pieces of this attempt to understand what these temporal relations are. If Chapple had gone a bit farther in his presentation, he would have pointed out that we can put electrophysiological measuring instruments on people and discover that, when they get it together, which is observable through out instrumentation as getting into the same rhythm, they feel good and that, when they're out of step, late for the party, out of rhythm, they feel uncomfortable.

Now we don't have full empirical proof of this, but it is pretty clearly beginning to take shape as the way nature works. Whether we're talking about mother and infant and how the conjoint behaviors become organized, whether we're talking about vast groups of people or indeed the whole species, or even animals, the same processes are at work. Your animals tell something about where you're at, and you tell something about where they're at simply by looking at the temporal dimensions of their behavior. And this must require no *thinking* in the usual sense of the word, since we know that animals do not have *our* capacity to think.

All this is to say, again, that human life, animal life, and surely plants have underlying, built-in biological processes for getting it together so there can be a society, can be a couple, can be a human in the context of other humans.

All this may be confusing in academic discussion of research because we're still collecting pieces of the puzzle, and the conservative scientist is hesitant to put them into a grand design too quickly. But I am less conservative, and I hope that this vision of the larger nature-picture will give you some reference points for making sense out of this conference as a whole and of the individual presentations.

I believe that this kind of research—Dan Stern's work is an excellent example—is the most exciting human science thrust that has come along for a long time. We're gradually throwing our preconceptions out the window and saying that we must now look at what happens and how it's organized without diverting ourselves by such red herring questions as "Why?". In fact, we are coming to recognize that the chief effect that our thinking has had on our communication—our getting it together—has been to muck it up. Animals survive. They form groups and societies. And they relate to their natural environment without speech or human-type thinking.

Speech and all that implies enables us to construct an elaborate civilization and hold meetings for intellectual exchange, which is great. But, when Ray Birdwhistell went off to college, his father said to him, "Now you be very careful of paper and pencil. Paper will just lie there and let you put any damned thing on it." (Birdwhistell, 1964)

Science has, in the past, believed in assorted realities. We studied them. But now I remind you that there is no need to make a reality out of rhythm. This is simply a place to stand to observe the way nature works. Its value lies not in any reality but in our opportunity, through the use of temporal relationships, to discover pattern—pattern which emerges in mother-baby behavior and pattern which emerges at all levels of organization of the whole cosmic show. We must, now, free ourselves from the limiting view that humans are essentially individuals who do things to each other. You may choose to see human interaction as stimuli-responses, causes and effects, and all that. You may point out that someone can hit you on the head and that it will raise a bump and hurt. But I will point out that it took two participating (willingly or unwillingly) interactants to achieve the bump and the hurt. If you are attached to the cause-effect view, you blame someone and ask "Why?" which directs you away from the interaction and changes the subject. Even if you protest that you want to avoid future bumps, I will suggest that you will have greater success if you understand the relation of the behaviors in given contexts—if you understand how the phenomena is organized and works—than if you pursue a single cause and simply label the bumpers.

When we get into looking at those communication processes by means of which people get it together and if we have no preconceptions to confuse us, we can begin to look at stuff we can't see—ESP, psychic phenomena, psychic healing, or good vibes. But, if we have preconceptions, we can become confused by them. Rhine at Duke University spent much of his life trying to find out if ESP existed as a human communication phenomenon or process. But in the end it seems to me that he wasn't studying ESP. He was studying his own preconception of how ESP worked. And it was essentially wrong. He studied crosses and plus signs and circles and whether they could be replicated from sender to receiver. He studied content. Now that we are looking at ESP as a possible human process without a priori assumptions, it is becoming much more amenable to scientific understanding.

If you want to know *why* things happen, you will have a rough time at this conference because the content is sometimes trivial, and there is no uniformity in the subject matter. Rhythms are not subject matter. They are process, and they are relationships. The concept of rhythms is a conceptual tool. When we use this tool and assorted technology to examine it, we can arrive at another level of process description. I have come to the view that human communication is a process by which states (physiological states, emotional states, states of consciousness) come to be shared so that humans can cooperate in a society, in a classroom, in bed, or wherever. Since a rhythm (and we have not defined rhythm any more than we have defined consciousness, or life, or death) is a reflex of a state, we can study where individuals are "at" by looking at how their states are reflected in their rhythms as they relate to others. It's an open-ended way to look at anything, and in the case of communication it puts each person in the context of other persons and it allows our aggregates—our groups, our society, our species—to be seen as integral wholes. This is unifying and certainly more satisfying and economic than studying endless fragments or pieces—or individuals.

The word synchrony has been kicked around a lot at this conference, but it has one meaning that may be unfamiliar. Eliot Chapple, who is most associated with the word synchrony, never used the word to refer to simultaneous events. Condon does, of course. That's the dictionary meaning. But beginning with Chapple, it has referred more to reciprocal relationships. My mother once said to me, "I met a very nice woman yesterday.

I don't know how to describe her except that talking to her is like playing a nice tennis game. Back and forth conversation.'' That's synchrony—fitting two interactants together into a harmonious, pleasing whole. Another way of putting this: when two people get it together ''synchronously,'' there is a characteristic higher energy flow. Dan Stern talks about generating positive affect. My mother talked about feeling good. But energy flow is value free. Indian war dances were synchronizing procedures for generating energy to fight battles. A mob may become synchronized and invest high shared energy in lynching someone. A peace march can synchronize the participants who direct the energy into love. In any event the characteristic of synchrony is heightened energy flow. But at this conference you need to be aware that the word is used in two ways.

Although our research is all nibbling away at the same thing—understanding man's behavior—there are epistemological differences between us. Some look through the laundry list of emotions and what elicits them. I can't handle that one myself. I prefer to see that, when emotions are shared, the communication worked. That is, I prefer to see the broader function of human communication as bringing two or more people into a kind of unity which implies shared emotions. There are those of use who look at individual interactants and those who look only at relationships. There are those who believe in reality and those who find it a useless concept. There are those who want to find out what they hypothesized and those who are willing to be quite surprised at what they may find. And there are those who want to find out about particular aspects of the human and those of us who believe that the same principles of organization (i. e., humanness) are going to apply all the way from brain structure to social structure.

Another way of putting all this: Some look in detail at the human individual *differences*. Others look at the underlying *unity* and the processes by which it is occasionally achieved. But unity is required for survival.

DISCUSSION

Virginia Reed: I think we are still running amok because we are using Western man's perceptions of time. These are underlying the instruments we are using now to measure this interaction behavior. We leave out other perspectives. Some people do not measure it these ways. I'd like to suggest two sources in this connection: Fritjof Capra's *The Tao of Physics* (Bantam Books, New York, 1975) and Rudolf Laban's *Choreutics* (MacDonald and Evans, London, 1966).

Paul Byers: Yes. As Karl Pribram has pointed out, the primary reality out there has no time and no space. The clue for this came from the hologram which is an information storage and retrieval system that has no space dimensions as amplitude. The brain is imposing that structure, but we all have them, and that may be the structure through which we organize our relationships.

Daniel Stern: I would like to take exception to what was just said by Paul and Virginia. I think that to the extent that we're going to be scientists (which you don't have to be), one must consider time a reality. It is the same in the East as it is in the West. There would be no way to conceptualize what I have talked about or the beauties of Eastern music, if you didn't have some temporal reality both in your head and out there by which to appreciate them.

I think that the stuff of this conference is so important that we really hurt what we're doing by moving away from the main traditions of Western science to talk about it. I feel that we shouldn't be limited by them in getting new ideas and being creative, but I think we really hurt ourselves if we toss them to the winds. I strongly disagree with what's been said.

Paul Byers: I believe that one of the interesting new directions in research is to put those two things together without doing violence to either of them, and that's happening. One of the things I look forward to in the future of the world is greater diversity of almost everything—life style, possible roles, and so forth, and it may be that we can have a variety of sciences so long as we understand what logics we are using in each and we don't ask who's right. There may be levels of science so that what Dan was disagreeing with me about was that he wants to look at the show in terms of one science and level, and I'm interested in another one. I don't know that they contradict.

Participant: I want to address a different dimension of time, namely, what temporal patterns are continuous through development. In other words, an infant may respond to certain ½- or 1-second rhythms that a mother shows. But those patterns change. Mothers' speech to young children changes as the child grows. Yet there are certain continuities that may persist. For example, at times when we are very aroused, we will do things that may be considered infantile, and they have time dimensions. Developmental phases and continuities in these rhythmic patterns should be a focus of our interest.

Stanley
Feldstein:[1]   In answer to Paul's earlier question of why we have to define rhythm, I think it is fair to say that it's important to define what we're trying to talk about. Definition is one of the major parts of a scientific enterprise, and presumably that's what we're trying to do. We're trying to scientifically assess the components of rhythm at different levels of the hierarchy.

Daniel Stern: I agree with that. I'm not sure we're ready to do a great job of integrating at a lot of levels, although certainly what Alan Lomax did is extraordinary. I think that so much more work has to be done within each level.

Martha Davis: I think that, although it's ambitious and a bit premature, to look at the relationship between the levels and how diverse studies of interaction relate, there is much that can be discussed. Duration of the behavioral "bits" is clearly a useful device for this. But we won't be able to understand these integrations until we attend to more aspects of the behavior than coordination of body parts, changes in spatial direction, and a few more attended to in these studies. I think that, as the analyses become more "macro," more aspects of movement—complex spatial patterns, variations in intensity, group formations other than distance and orientation, etc. — must be included. And I'm sure the same point can be made for paralinguistic phenomena.

[1] This remaining discussion actually occurred the next day at the final panel discussion. It is placed here because of its relevance to Paul Byers' presentation and because his comments are a focal point of it. [Ed.]

Participant:	Perhaps we can resolve the problem of defining rhythm by viewing it in terms of systems theory. To be specific, it is known that one system may behave differently when viewed within a larger system. That doesn't mean it's a different phenomenon. We're just looking from a different point of view, so phenomenon A when put in a context of another system will look as if it behaves differently.
Paul Byers:	My answer to that is that the state of the art is such that we don't know enough yet, and that's one of the reasons we find this kind of lack of agreement.
Alan Lomax:	Well, that was what I was trying to do in my talk, and I thought that's what Chapple did in his talk very successfully. He talked about a series of hierarchies of biological rhythms, and he showed how these related to musical systems and psychological interaction. Coming from the other end, I thought I had met Chapple right in the middle and working with these very big-sized pieces showed how systems of rhythms can define all the cultures that we have the histories of. It seems to me, Paul, that we don't have to be so modest. We have people here who are talking about the rhythms of speech lengths that are defining the differences between personalities and personal qualities and then on the other hand we have a system that defines most of the cultures. Why can't we go ahead and be a little bold? We're dealing with systems really fitting together.
Paul Byers:	I use the concept of rhythm, you use it, almost everybody here has talked of rhythms or temporal dimensions of behavior, but we aren't yet to the point where we know we're talking

about the same thing in the same way. I believe most of us would like to work toward the idea of systems. I think of it in those terms. Alan does, and yet Alan and I can't quite connect, though we believe basically in the same thing.

REFERENCES

Bateson, P. P. G. Unpublished presentation at Lindisfarn, Long Island, 1976.
Birdwhistell, R. L. Personal communication, 1964.
Byers, P. Biological rhythms as information channels in communication behavior. In P. P. G. Bateson and P. H. Klopfer (Eds.), *Perspectives in ethology*, Vol. 2. New York: Plenum Press, 1976.
Pribram, K. *Languages of the brain*. Belmont, California: Brooks-Cole, 1979.

Part II

Each of the chapters in this section deals with paralanguage, the speech "qualifiers" of stress, intonation, fluency, pitch, duration, and so on. Alan Lomax, Madeleine Mathiot and Elizabeth Carlock, and Joseph Oliva discuss the relationships between paralanguage and musical rhythm, each in quite different ways. Extending the work of linguists such as Trager and Smith, they offer refinements of terminology, methodological advances, and new perspectives on the function of paralinguistic patterns. Alan Lomax and Madeleine Mathiot and Elizabeth Carlock present examples of cultural variation in paralanguage and systematic methods for analyzing speech dialect.

In addition to paralinguistic analyses, Alan Lomax discusses cross-cultural comparisons of dance and song in an extraordinary study of expressive behavior around the world. The variety of details of interaction and expressive behavior that he and his colleagues attend to is more extensive than any other in this volume.

Chapter 7

THE CROSS-CULTURAL VARIATION OF RHYTHMIC STYLE

Alan Lomax

Today, rhythmicity occupies the cultural foreground, as Americans, black and white, co-acculturate to the loud and rather monotonous rhythms of disco dancing. The two groups have exchanged dance music for generations, but now, for the first time, they are dancing together on a grand national scale. "Disco" provides a half-way house between the once very different rhythmic cultures of the two groups, so that blacks and whites can dance in the same room to the same music. Whites are learning more Africanisms—torso articulation, ground hugging step, elastic arm style. Since the music, at the moment, is made primarily by white groups, blacks are learning a Europeanized version of their own dance style.

Here rhythm is playing its old role in linking people, by providing a common framework of identification. Rhythm is, after all, a prime mover in social relations. Rhythmic patterns facilitate the co-activity of groups and aid their members in coordinating energies and resources in work, nurturance, defense, social discourse, rites of passage, interchange of information, and, above all, expressive acts. The important role of rhythm in group behavior suggests that we can view the rhythmic aspects of communication as essentially social in nature — a system that binds individuals together into effective groups and links groups into communities and polities. Each such "rhythmic style," passed on generationally, shapes many aspects of each cultural tradition, as these pages will demonstrate.

The term "rhythmic" has been applied by analogy to any simply cyclical or regularly patterned phenomena, but the core concept of rhythm is musical — that is, clear patterns of strong and weak beats organized into definable meters (Lomax, 1978, p. 49). Although rhythmic behavior has been observed in many animal groups, none of them, so far as I know, matches human rhythmic systems in precision, flexibility, number of levels, or elaboration. Among humans, our cross-cultural evidence shows that each main branch of culture employs a different strategy of rhythm and rhythmic coordination, and each of these styles represents a cultural adaptation to an ecological setting. Each model is a cultural invention, culturally transmitted. Each has a clear-cut usefulness in a special social context and is suitable to a particular set of productive relations. In practice these rhythmic models can be best observed at the level of everyday — in long (10 second to 10 minute) stretches of human behavior. This is the level of the overt and the explicit, the level of action and interaction which all humans can and do observe, talk about, adjust, regulate, and criticize. I believe it is the level that basically shapes or at least employs and organizes the units and periodic patterns observed at more microlevels, thus giving rise to the forms which shape human intercommunication (Lomax, 1978).

The cross-cultural study of these paracommunicational phenomena opens up a useful strategy to humanistic study. It is based in the work of the Buffalo linguistic school which was the first to define the paralinguistic level in communication, and to provide a reliable method for describing its components and their effect upon meaning and the expression of personal feeling

(Trager and Smith, 1951). They observed that there were set-qualities and cross-referencing patterns running through whole stretches of conversation, which identified the speakers in terms of age, sex, status, and other cultural modalities and thus acted to maintain the continuity of communication and interaction (Trager, 1958). Both Trager and Birdwhistell (1970), because of the importance of the briefer, more transient paralinguistic data to immediate linguistic concerns, did not extensively investigate the role of the continuous, large-sized, paralinguistic markers as culture indicators. It occurred to me that expressive communication, especially the nonverbal arts of music and dance, largely consist of the manipulation of these large-style nonverbal continua, and that much could be learned about art, about culture, and about the nonverbal by a comparative study of these "bit bits" of paracommunication.

Three holistic, multiscalar rating systems were developed to describe three communicational systems—singing, dancing, and speaking (Lomax, 1975; Lomax et al., 1977; Lomax, 1978, Chap. 10). Because "the pieces" defined by these analytic systems are relatively big and easy to observe, our judges, using preestablished criteria, could rate large bodies of filmed and taped data with high interrater consensus (Lomax, 1976; Ebel, 1951; Markel, 1965; and Lomax, 1978).[1] What was found will throw light upon the social basis of rhythm. Though it paints with a broad brush, the cross-cultural approach helps to remove cultural bias from the study of panhuman phenomena. For example, since the whole species handles rhythm in the very specialized way we have indicated, it is important to become aware of the important cultural variations in rhythmic styles early on, so that the cultural components of particular cases may be accounted for. Often a phenomenon that might otherwise appear to be idiosyncratic or situational will turn out to be the

[1] The average interrater consensus for subjects exposed to the Cantometrics training tapes was about 86 percent. Reliability scores for the individual parameters, calculated by Ebel's Inter-rater Reliability Coefficient, are presented on page 270 of the Cantometrics handbook (Lomax, 1976).

outgrowth of a widespread rhythmic style or the product of its encounter with another style.

Comparative study also leads us to the discovery of the consonance between the different rhythmic systems in cultural traditions. For example, we find that the rhythmic organizations of music and dance vary together cross-culturally; not only that, but the rhythmic style of everyday behavior and conversation, can be seen to vary in analogous ways, thus exposing to view some fundamental characteristics of human communication.

The strategy in the present inquiry is first to examine music and dance, the systems where rhythm is most overt, then to look for analogies and parallel rhythmic phenomena in conversational speech. Employing the cross-cultural, comparative method, we have analyzed the way rhythmic systems work in a sampling of the whole cultural range. These discovered variations have been correlated to cross-cultural data on social structure and culture history. A general framework of explanatory hypotheses has emerged sufficient to explain many of the shifts in the rhythmic arts as reflections of changes in familiar and potent components of social structure.[2]

(1) Level of subsistence productivity is directly related to the amount of new information carried on the rhythmic stream; conversely, the level of repetitiousness in the communication drops as the productive level rises.

(2) The size and potency of the society and its political system are related to the degree of regimentation of performing groups, especially to patterns of dominance by a leading performer.

(3) The importance of women in the main productive system is related to the level of cohesiveness in the rhythmic style.

[2] For a summary of song style/social structure correlations see Lomax, *Cantometrics*, 1976, p. 23 and Appendix 3 for the statistical data. See also: Lomax, 1978.

(4)   The level of discipline in the child-rearing system is related to the regularity of rhythmic patterns.

(5)   Culture provides the continua through which the patterns of rhythmicity are diffused in time and space.

RHYTHMIC STYLE IN MUSICAL SYSTEMS

A sample of 4,000 taped song performances from 400 odd cultures, representing most of the world's cultural traditions, were profiled on 37 scales. Of these measures, phrase length and metrical type are most pertinent to rhythmic style. In most song styles we discovered that phrase length conformed to a model so orderly that the patterns could be timed to a second, and that we could accurately rate phrase length by ear or stop-watch on a 5-point scale, from very short (1–2 seconds) to very long (14+ seconds).[3] Most zones of culture turned out to have characteristic phrase lengths: for example, Black Africa—short; Europe—medium; and Far East—long. These models of how culture handles segmentation of communication are clearly learned early in life, for when our data on phrase length was tested for its cross-cultural social correlations, the strongest associations discovered were with child-rearing (Lomax, 1976, p. 269). The child-rearing data was derived from the Barry, Child, and Bacon studies (1959).

The correlations indicate that short phrases are commonest in cultures where children are not treated indulgently, mid-length phrases where child-rearing focused on obedience, and long phrases where children are treated indulgently or given in to. Phrase symmetry, that is, sung phrases held to one standard length all the way through a performance, is also correlated to emphasis on obedience in child-rearing. Thus, the standard western European song form with its four to eight symmetrically

---

[3] Lomax, A. *Cantometrics*, 1976, pp. 148–150 of handbook and Appendix 3, and training tape V.A2. Phrase Length.

arranged, medium length phrases may symbolize the relatively severe rearing system typical of the western European family traditions, at home or overseas. In general, a relatively brief and orderly approach to handling melodic segments seems to be indicated and reinforced by emphasis on discipline in child-rearing. On the contrary, longer phonations indicate and reinforce systems where children are indulged, for instance, allowed to talk on and on without check.

In describing meter in song performance we noted whether the arrangement of weak and strong beats was *regular* and, thus, easy to count, or *irregular*, and, thus, hard to locate and count. The Cantometric training tape for rhythm makes even an un-trained listener relatively secure in these judgments.[4] Cross-culturally, the only correlation of *regular meter* is with a low level of indulgence for infants, whereas *irregular meters* are associated with a high level of indulgence in the treatment of infants and of children. Thus, here again a regimented approach to timing accents is associated with discipline, and a free and easy timing style both indicates and reinforces a more relaxed approach to child development.

A separate study has shown that the metrical patterns in song and dance seem to vary together. Therefore, we may conclude that the most distinctive structural elements of rhythmicity are implanted by culture early in life, and this makes sense, since they affect the way that every child must shape his or her behavior if he or she is to mesh in with the rhythms of the adults in the environment. In fact, Condon's microanalysis of babies in their cribs shows them shifting their body rhythms to match those of the speaker present (1974).

The Yale child-rearing study clearly indicates the nature of the cultural bias that affects the rhythmic structures employed in expressive systems. It demonstrates that rearing for obedience is

[4]Lomax, A. *Cantometrics*, 1976, p. 45 ff. and training tape V.A1. Overall Vocal Rhythm.

emphasized in full agriculture (where tasks are cyclic and monotonous) and training for assertiveness is emphasized in predatory societies (where more exploratory, independent individuals are socially useful). Thus it appears that the segmental and metrical aspects of rhythmic style may prove to be dependent upon the needs of the subsistence system (Barry, Child, and Bacon, 1959).

A number of other aspects of rhythmicity are even more directly linked to productive relations. The prime discovery of our research, which I sometimes think of as the first law of communication, is that, culture by culture, the level of iteration in communication is inversely related to the level of its subsistence productivity. In other words, the level of repetitiousness decreases and the level of new information increases along a 5-point scale of productivity from Gathering and Hunting to Irrigation Agriculture. In dance this means spatially repetitious, as opposed to complex and varied movement. In song it means: (1) the degree to which repeats fill out the song text, (2) the importance of brief one-phrase melodies, and (3) the presence of one-beat rhythms in the orchestra (Lomax, 1978, Chap. 6).

We turn now to the social aspects of rhythmic style in song, that is, to the ways in which groups synchronize their performances. Vocal coordination is correlated to social structure in several ways. First, the level of rhythmic coordination — singers staying together in tight rhythmic synchrony measure-by-measure — seems to be a good index of the social solidarity of the human community. Very "networky" societies, like American Indian hunter-gatherers and Anglo-Americans, express and maintain their individualism by singing and often dancing in a rhythmically ragged fashion. On the other hand, very *solidary* people, like East Europeans and West Africans, tend to sing and dance in good rhythmic ensemble (Lomax, 1978, Chap. 7).

Cohesiveness/Solidarity

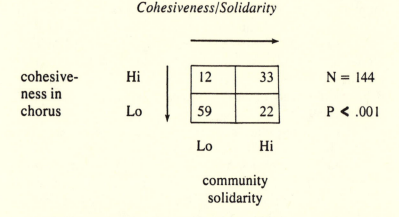

community
solidarity

Vocal blending (Lomax, 1978, p. 163)—matching voice qualities so that the choral effect is unified—is strongly correlated to social complementarity for women: that is, well-blended, harmonized singing characterizes the music of societies where food production and other public activities are shared by males and females, so that the sexes work and associate together day by day. The clear, noise-free singing voice, so essential to a tonally unified chorus, is also characteristic of societies where females tend to have an egalitarian relation to men, thus reducing the tensions felt in everyday relationships and making smooth-flowing rhythmic coordination far easier to achieve.

If the level of vocal rhythmic coordination is symbolic of face-to-face relationships, orchestral organization[5] is a reflection of the superstructure. Socially acephalous or egalitarian organization prevails where there is weak or no government. Clearly ordered orchestration, where leading voices sound prominently, are favored by state-organized societies. In other words, the kind of rhythmic organization of the orchestra seems to reflect the power of the state. *Rhythmic unison*, where all members conform to the same meter—is characteristic of weak states—autonomous tribes; *polyrhythmic structures*, where

[5] Lomax, A. *Cantometrics*, 1976, p. 23, training tape II.B2. The Rhythmic Coordination of the Orchestra.

there are several equal, different, and at times conflicting meters, are characteristic of weak states such as those typical in Black Africa. In *counterpoint*, the most highly regimented scheme, a series of leaders and subordinate parts all work within the same rhythmic framework. Its rhythmic regularity, its regimentation of serial dominance can be viewed as indicators of the societal discipline that comes with state power (Lomax, 1978, pp. 140–141).

Each culture has its favorite ways of ordering the social organization of its singing groups. The cantometric measure of this behavior emphasizes the degree of prominence of the leading voice, and the main *types* of choral organization can be ranged along a scale from group dominance to leader dominance. This scale matches and correlates to Murdock's scale of state organization (Lomax, 1978, pp. 159–160). Thus, we have acephalous groups with stateless cultures versus clear song leaders with sizeable states. Very similar models of ordering and rhythmicizing interaction occur in dance and conversational style, so that this series of examples will be matched later in the other modalities.

Stage 1. *Interlock* is an orderly meshing of several brief, simultaneous, and equal parts. This most egalitarian of patterns is the choral style of the Pigmy and Bushmen gatherers in Africa—the modern culture closest, so far as we know, to man's first life style. *Interlock*, the mode of most unconstrained human gatherings, such as the cocktail party, is commonest in acephalous bands where there is no political authority.

Stage 2. In *Social Unison*, the members of the vocal group sing the same melody to the same rhythm. Though unison is found widely in culture, it is most characteristic of single-unit tribal societies, where no course of action can proceed unless all the members of the group agree to it, and where thus achieved conformity is maximal. Such tribal political systems are typical of the hunter and stone-age gardener cultures of the Circum-Pacific, and *Social Unison* is their characteristic mode of organizing voices into a choir.

Stage 3. In *Overlap* two parts alternate, but not in total

independence, since one overlaps to some extent with the other. This organizational mode might be taken to symbolize a society in which a leading group or leader is clearly established, but still continuously supported by the mass for *overlapping* choral style is most frequent in confederacies of tribes with chiefs or kingly figures who rule in the presence of their councils and subjects.

Stage 4.   *Alternation*, in which two or more parts alternate independently, without overlap, is typical in large states, where political control resides in a ruling group clearly separate from the mass. The slight, but perceptible pause between each alternation can be taken as a sign of the respect relation between the several parties.

Stage 5.   The *Soloist*, performing a complex poem, perhaps in totally free rhythm, represents the favored performance style in large states and can be taken as symbolic of the dominance and the isolation of the ruling figures who control large polities.

In sum, then, one can account for the main aspects of the rhythmic style of a musical tradition as responses to prime features of its social organization, to wit: (1) its child-rearing system; (2) its productive system; (3) its social solidarity; (4) the position of women; and (5) the centralization of political power. One must conclude, therefore, that rhythmic styles function to symbolize and reinforce cultural systems. Elsewhere we have shown that the song performance styles, when subjected to factor analysis, arrange themselves in a regional evolutionary taxonomy which corresponds to the main stages in the evolution of productive systems (Lomax, 1972). Table 7.1 outlines the way that rhythmic systems have shifted across time along with the socioeconomic development of culture. It presents profiles of rhythmic styles for five of the main cultural taxa, arranged in order of increasing productivity, so that one can see the stepwise development in certain of the indicators—in repeats and in vocal organization. Moreover, each of the taxa has a distinctive rhythmic style, suitable to its social system and to its ecological situation. As the following sections on rhythmicity in dance and conversation indicate, these shifts in style are matched in other modes of communication. Thus the organization of rhythm emerges as a basic structural feature of cultural systems, which evolves as they evolve.

RHYTHMIC STYLE IN MOVEMENT SYSTEMS

I have treated the cross-cultural findings about music at some length, because this is the expressive mode which we have most thoroughly researched, and which, therefore, can provide us with reliable guidelines for examining other systems. Moreover, statistical work has shown that there are many correlations between the structural features of the three systems examined — music, dance, and conversation. Table 7.2 pinpoints some of these intercorrelated, matching features. The equal signs indicate that a dance or speech factor that is directly analogous to the one listed in the column for music. The nonequivalent features can usually be shown to have functions similar to their musical parallels. Here is strong evidence that a common rhythmic style infuses these subsystems of culture. Since we have already determined the adaptive function of the musical features of rhythmic style, we are in a position to consider how the matching aspects of dance and speech may have functioned in cultural development.[6]

First let us take a quick look at the rhythmic system in dance. Staying upright on two legs against the pull of gravity is an everlasting human struggle, and dance dramatizes our conquest of this problem. Once the human biped starts to locomote, he needs to move his lower limbs in some steady rhythm or he may stumble and fall. In fact, meter, as Paulay, Bartenieff, and I

[6] Lomax, A. *Folk song style and culture, op. cit.*, Chap. 11. A sample of approximately 500 dances has since been rated on more than 100 predetermined scales. The consensus between two newly trained judges on the 65 best-tested of these measures averaged 82 percent (Ebel's Inter-Rater Reliability Coefficient).

Table 7.1 Regional Types of Rhythmic Style

	African Gatherers	Circum-Pacific Hunters, Incipient Producers	Black Africa Extensive Agriculturalists	Europe Plow Agriculturalists	Old High Culture Irrigation and Plow Agriculturalists
1) Phrase length	Short	Moderate	Short	Moderate	Long
2) Vocal rhythm	Regular	Irregular	Regular	Regular	Free
3) Vocal Coordination	Much	Little	Much	Much, little	Little
4) Repeats	Much	Much	Half	Little	Little
5) Vocal organization	Interlocked	Unison, solo + repeats	Overlap	Alternation, solo + wordy	Alternation, solo + wordy
6) Orchestral rhythmic organization	Polyrhythm	Unison	Polyrhythm	Counterpoint + accompanying	Counterpoint + accompanying

Table 7.2   Intersystem Links

Music	Dance	Speech
Phrase length	=	=
Meter	=	Patterning
Repeats, 1 beat, unison	=	=
Variation	=	=
Blend	Torso	Empathy
Rhythmic unity	=	Sharing the air
Complex orchestra	Regimentation	Dominance
Interlock	Turn-taking	Interlock
Unison	=	Space, pausing
Overlap	=	=
Alternation	Leader/group	Continuous and alternation
Solo	=	=

observed it in the filmed data, is the product of different patterns of coordinating the right and left sides. You can walk in a 1-1-1-1 meter—or in a 1-2-1-2 meter, or even in a 1-2-3-1-2-3. The upper body can simply go along with the legs or it can move to an independent meter or in an accompanying pattern. However, since the upper body is not subject to the constraints of constantly maintaining balance, it is more likely to move in free manipulatory patterns. Free meters may be common in the Orient because rice cultivation, silk weaving, and many other crafts of the region depend upon complex hand movements.

The combinations of the rhythmic patterns in the upper and lower body give rise to more complex meters. For example, Africans produce polyrhythms by moving arms and legs to different meters. One favorite Oriental rhythmic style consists of a steady four in the legs (and the percussion section) while the arms follow a free metered melody of a lead instrument. These remarks merely open up a complex subject and suggest how much light might be shed on musical rhythm by a study of its corporeal basis.

It appears that the same metrical scheme generally enlivens both the song and the dance of a given cultural tradition, probably for the very good reason that so much music is made for dancing. Thus we may assume, although we have not tested this data statistically, that child-rearing is the crucial societal factor in shaping dance, as well as song rhythm, especially since correlational studies show that most of the main factors of song style find their analogues in dance style, and have similar cultural attachments. For example, the level of productivity is reflected in the complexity of the dancer's approach to space. The level of political centralization is symbolized in the degree of regimentation in choreography. The input of women in public affairs seems to affect the level of eroticism displayed in dance movement. In sum, the presence of a particular rhythmic style in the dance of a cultural tradition probably can be explained by reference to the factors that govern musical style.

Stage 1. *African Gatherers.* Turn-taking, which, like vocal interlocking, involves all group members equally in the performance, is the most distinctive feature of this style. Very often even the children participate in this highly redundant, highly rhythmic play. In Bushman examples there are three levels of action—a vocal orchestra of females, clapping in complex polyrhythm; a male feed-line moving with very short, repetitious steps, pulling off into pairs of dancers who mime animal play in brilliant and complex polyrhythms (Marshall, 1966). Palms, buttocks, and bellies are presented in the most openly erotic of all dance styles, in this most complementary of traditions. By dancing and singing all together, these homeless nomads recreate for themselves polyleveled and joy-filled shelters of rhythms in which their people have dwelt from time immemorial.

Stage 2. *Circum-Pacific Hunters and Incipients.* The stone and bone and wooden implements of the primitive hunter tend to restrict his movement to the repetitious, linear, in-and-out movements that conserve the fragile points and edges of his tools. He is a footman, jog-trotting endlessly across vast distances. He is an aggressive individualist, but on the hunt or the fishing grounds he works as a team member, subordinating his independence to a mutually agreed-on strategy. All this can be seen in the main dance styles of Circum-Pacific hunters and planters, who walk, trot, or pace round the dance floor with repetitive, alternating steps, the central body held, the arm movements push-pull and linear, the coordination unison but rough. One-beat rhythms and unison group singing add to the powerfully unifying effect of this powerful, redundant, highly rhythmic style of a male group moving into action.

Stage 3. *Black Africa.* The durability of metal tools permitted larger, multidimensional, more forceful trajectories that influenced the emergence of complex rhythmic patterns. In complementary Black African gardening cultures, a flowing, feminized movement style and a multileveled, overlapping system of intercommunication gave rise to polyparted activities on the part of gang-laborers, drummers, and dancers, each one adding his rhythmic bit to the stimulating, hot pattern. This system turned the routine tasks of field and water transport into pleasurable group experiences. Dancers learned to co-accelerate, to pick up each other's rhythms in collective, improvised rhythmic games that trained both males and females for the strenuous sex life of this expanding, polygamous tradition. The overlapping, interdependent roles of males and females also symbolize the tradition of embedded leadership of the African confederacies.

Patterns of rhythmic organization arise from the need of a society for a certain kind and order of coordination in male/

female relationships, in team work, and in political controls. The Black African system, in which women are so important, focused on personal expressivity and thus on a multileveled handling of parts, but this model loses its authority with the onset of male-dominated pastoralism and plow agriculture and a return is made to the unison model. Moreover, since these societies are larger and more hierarchical, more complex and regimented choreographies emerge.

Regimentation of collective action may be broken down in a number of components. Groups can move in many directions, one direction, or in a pattern of directions. Spacing can be handled loosely, strictly, or shifted in a patterned way. Formations may be loosely or strictly ordered, or they may shift from one form to another. Body parts may move independently, be held, move in unison, or in complex and contrastive ways. Dancers may move raggedly or tightly to the beat, in unison, serially, or in multiparted patterns. Each society adopts its needed mix of these components—direction, spacing formation, limb synchrony, and timing. Where the group is weakly bonded and fissive, as among South American jungle nomads or in a New York disco, dancing may be delightful chaos—a haystack of individualization aiming for simple unison. In another phase of culture, dependent on bureaucracy, audiences are enthralled by totally regimented and choreographed performances.

Stage 4. *Western Europe.* A plowman with his ox could easily cultivate more acres than a corvee of hoemen. This shift in agricultural technique encouraged an individualism of Western Europe which is symbolized in the popularity of solo male stepping, clogging or jigging which show off the leg skills of the plowman. This preference for solo virtuosity shapes much of Europe's dance tradition, both fine art and folk, but in its other distinctive style, Western European villagers developed many forms of regimented choreographies which enacted patterns of courtship, kinship, and social organization. In the often intricate and interwoven maneuvers of these choral dances, made possible by precise footwork, Europeans demonstrate how a well-organized society can define and take possession of terrain. Yet rhythmic patterns remain simple and unison coordination is basic.

The need of king and court for controlled order transformed these rustic country dances into the elaborate spectacles of processional, quadrille, ballet, and exhibition drill, that subject the participants to rigid schemes of rhythmicity, in which formations mesh together like the cog wheels of a Swiss clock, and bodies are precisely synchronized within one rhythmic framework. The ballet, like the symphony, with several components interlocking smoothly under the direction of a conductor or a choreographer, presents an idealized image of the disciplined operation of a large modern nation or corporation under a strong president. With such order as a backdrop, leading dancers depict the triumphs, struggles, and sorrows of the individual in displays of extravagant virtuosity. Sometimes body parts or segments of the company move in an accompanying or contrapuntal rhythmic relation to each other, but all this takes place within one unitary rhythmic framework and the underlying rhythmic style is regimented unison conforming to a simple regular meter.

Stage 5. *The Orient.* Here is a vaster subject, but even so, our survey reveals outstanding characteristics. First, the social substance of dance style is similar to Europe in the prominence of solo virtuosos and of well-drilled companies performing long and intricate choreographic works. The rhythmic baseline, however, is profoundly different from Europe, especially in the Far East. On the one hand, the naturally nonregular rhythmic pattern of arm movement is of paramount importance, coloring much dance movement with its ornamented, flowing, free rhythms. On the other, interaction between dancers is often responsorial in character, like a stylized duel, in which one gives way to a coiling thrust, at the same time beginning to initiate a counter-thrust. Thus a series of long-sustained, free-rhythmed phrases follow one on another, linked in a leader-follower relation, which well-symbolizes the interaction of emperor and vizier, courtesan and client. This style of coordination depends on quick displacement, such that one actor after another can occupy or impact the same spot, and thus a large group of individual workers, serially coordinated, can quickly carry out huge tasks, such as dike building. Translated into dance, the free, conversational rhythms of this style allow the dancer to mime the subtleties of any human interaction. Transformed into ballet, as in the traditional Peking Opera, the segments of a company pour over and under and past each other in incredibly rapid three-dimensional movements that can compress a huge battle into a brilliant drama only minutes in length.

Beyond these few paragraphs lie whole worlds of varied dances, but it is clearly indicated that rhythmic patterning examined cross-culturally, links dance, music, and cultural style.

RHYTHMIC STYLE IN CONVERSATION

The third section of this cross-cultural look at rhythmicity deals with a study of conversational dialogues in which 50 scaled measures were applied to a sample of speech recordings from 100+ of the world's language families. The approach here is similar to that of George Trager's paralinguistics, but the observations pertain to long stretches of recorded dialogue. Two raters, working separately, pooled their judgments on each point. Interrater consensus between the raters, Carol Kulig and Dorothy Deng, was 82 percent (Ebel's interrater reliability co-efficient). The orderliness of this system was tested in an R factor analysis, where its 50 parameters are clustered into 10 homogeneous factors and four uniques. The measures deal with such matters as iteration, periodicity, voice gliding, the social relations of the speakers, tension, and noise (Lomax, 1978). Correlational studies strongly indicate that some of these para-linguistic features—which clearly pervade whole conversational styles—are reliable measures of socioeconomic development, others of male/female balance in culture, yet others, as we shall see, arise from the styles of social interaction that are typical of different regional cultural traditions. Even in the results of this first small, but still representative, sample of world speaking styles, it is possible to see that crucial variation in the mannerisms of conversation are clearly connected to variations found in other cultural realms (Lomax, 1975).

In contrast to song and dance, of course, speech is far less redundant; its rhythmicities are far more elusive. Indeed, I was impressed as I listened to all the papers, by how much more difficult it is to locate stable, repeated pattern in everyday interaction than in expressive behavior. Probably the reason is that too much rhythmicity interferes with the transmission of information at the verbal level and, aside from such activities as collective lifting or pulling or paddling, probably does not allow the individual the free play he needs to deal with the particular segment of the real world his mind, his body, or his work tool encounters. So in everyday action the rhythmic precision seen in music and dance sinks below the easily visible surface to the temporal levels where Birdwhistell located them (1970). The strict, almost ballet-like rhythmic patterns that Birdwhistell found and Condon later mapped at a 48th of a second form the constant undercurrent of everyday speech (Condon, 1967). It seems likely that transmission of information and successful coordination at the level of everyday life would be impossible without this "dance" of microgestures which seems to link all communicating humans below the level of conscious perception.

However, if such a high degree of overt and strict rhythmicity was present in everyday speech, it would distract the listener from the new information that words and sentences convey and would sink the individual speaker in the group, as all redundant expressive behavior tends to do. This is what our cross-cultural study of speaking style seems to have discovered. We found the most rhythmicity in the dialogues of the simplest cultures, that is, those with the fewest stable social bonds and the weakest superstructures. Where group ties are fragile and there is little continuity of social authority to bind the group together across time, there is *the most need for the constant renewal of social bonds through rhythmic interaction*. This may explain why the most alienated sectors of our fragmenting urban society are now literally drowning themselves in the rhythms of disco.

In simple economies most knowledge is in common. Therefore, high rhythmicity in speech does not interfere with transmission of information. Among the African gatherers, the conversational space is fiercely and eagerly and equally shared. As economies evolve and such egalitarian rhythmicity is gradually reduced, several compensatory strategies appear that serve to link speakers. Then, as the word and the expert become the thing, the earlier, highly rhythmic patterns diminish even further. As rhythmicity diminishes, group interaction occupies less time, and the role of the individual specialist, dominating the airtime, transmitting information and orders, grows more important.

The first aspect of spoken rhythmicity to be considered is repetition. As in the case of song, we found significantly more repetition of passages of text in the conversation of simple socioeconomies than in those of complex economies (Lomax et al., 1977, p. 25). This kind of culture is without metallurgy. One-beat rhythm is its musical signature. Push-pull movement and high iteration in speech and song are all highly correlated.

Another factor affecting the rhythmicity of speaking is the degree of variation in tempo, in vocal stance, and in timing. Just as the level of variation in movement turned out to be a highly consensable and sensitive indicator of the level of complexity in culture, so, too, in speech *variation* proved to be associated with complexity. A patterned approach to speaking where tempo is steadily maintained, where vocal stance varies little, and speech bursts are similar in length is found low on the scale of economic productivity, while varied styles are found at higher levels (Lomax et al., 1977, p. 26). In larger, more socially competitive societies, a changeful approach to tempo, role, and timing probably helps to focus attention and keeps the speaker on the air. A varied approach to tempo is also commonest where speech bursts are longer. Moreover, long, varied speech bursts seem to be more frequent in large settlements, whereas shorter, more patterned speech bursts are found in cultures where settlements are small, and where brief, repetitive melodies are also characteristically present. It appears, then, that conversational style tends to become steadily less rhythmic and more varied, as societies grow larger and more complex.

The analogies between the social organization of conversation and of the rhythmic arts are less direct, since little or no everyday conversation is chorally organized. However, a number of interesting findings emerge. The study of how conversational space is shared between two speakers shows that dominance by one speaker for long stretches is most frequent just where solo singing is most common, that is, among the hunters, the pastoralists, and the complex agriculturalists of the Northern Hemisphere, principally in aboriginal North America and Eurasia. At the other end of the scale, rapid switching between speakers seems to be most frequent in the simplest cultures, such as the African gatherers.

A number of other parlametric measures describe the social texture of conversation in terms of frequency of pausing, frequency and kind of interjection, how the speakers space themselves and take their turns, and how tense and noisy the vocalizing is. Having made these ratings, judges found themselves in high agreement about whether the interchange had a supportive or a competitive tone.

The conjunction of the several measures allows us to portray the changes of rhythmic style in conversation across the four regional traditions that in this essay represent the evolution of human culture. As rhythmicity (or redundancy) diminishes and the input of the individual and of information rises, alternative attention- and group-maintaining strategies are employed, and a series of rhythmic interactive styles emerge, each one suitable to a particular human context.

In the recordings we have from the nomadic, band-organized African gatherers, where women provide the bulk of the food consumed, speakers converse with a kind of desperate excitement, filling conversational space with rapid streams of loud, brief, immediately echoed speech bursts. This passionately maintained conversation provides bonding important to these fissive societies, whose members may come or go as they please, unrestrained by authority or local ties. In this style, rhythmicity, redundancy, patterning of delivery, and equal access are all maximal. No one can stay on the air alone for more than a fraction of a second before others echo, comment, support, or deride this contribution. The result is that, when one person recounts some incident to another, the narrative is co-spoken, and conversational space is so closely shared that often the observer cannot distinguish the teller from the listener. This interlocked style is also found in the singing and dancing of the Bushmen and Pigmies, whose culture and way of life represent one of the earliest human adaptations. Their interlocking conversational style, like those of many human crowds, resembles the phonation of certain animal groups and may well be a vestige of one of the earliest ways of languaging. Indeed, it may be through interlocking that language, with its system of socially based references, could have initially developed. Interlock allows co-conversation without interference, and thus it may have offered a highly efficient way for primitive egalitarian communities to speedily reach linguistic agreement on naming or defining a phenomenon.

There is a complete change of rhythmic style with the hunters and planters of the Circum-Pacific. Often the tempo is slow, the mood grave; there are many pauses, which the listener fills with supportive interjections. These pauses vary in length, creating an irregular rhythm and leaving plenty of time for hearers to absorb the information and respond if they wish. Repeats, echoing, short speech bursts, and patterned delivery compose a highly rhythmic mode, suitable in an economy where most possessions are shared. This redundancy, combined with the characteristic slow tempo and frequent pausing, creates a style well-suited to the needs of hunters.

Gathering demands encyclopedic knowledge of the environment, but the act itself is simple. Hunters, however, are technicians and strategists, often operating in situations of physical danger, and their success depends on the fruition of well-laid and skillfully managed step-wise procedures. Reaching agreement on such a plan and carrying it out demands sober exposition and silent absorption by both the leader and his followers. Levi-Strauss depicts this system in operation among the Nambikwara (1944). First the chief listens to his people for a time, as one after another, they bring him information. Then he sums up what he has heard and presents a plan to the whole group. This is an admirable way of reaching the total consensus necessary in a politically weak society, and thus we find variations on the pause-filled, expository model all round the Circum-Pacific, where unison rhythmic organization achieves the same effect in dance and song.

The prime Black African ecological model is of populous, clan-organized villages, organized into political confederacies or kingdoms and supported by a hoe agriculture whose many routine tasks are performed by groups working in rhythm. Women play an important complementary role in the economy. Powerful and often ruthless leaders must constantly enlist the support of their counsels and their subjects, indeed individual success in the society depends upon charm and eloquence. In conversation, repeats and echoing are at a mid-level that approximates the position of this tradition on the productive scale. The cohesiveness essential to group effort, which is dramatically reflected in choral dance and song, appears in a rather feminized and empathetic conversational style, in which drawl, softened attacks, descending cadences, laughter, high pitch, and all sorts of supportive responses and interjections create a warm and intimate social web. These and many other devices, including use of high speed and energy, help speakers to gain and hold the floor in the normally crowded conversational scenes. Here two or more speakers quite normally overlap with each other, but without interfering with information transmission, because of the almost dance-like rhythms of speech. Even when a chief, a tale-teller—or, in America, a preacher—dominates the scene and holds the floor, vigorous responses from and comments by those listening punctuate his message. This changeful, dramatic, overlapping, highly rhythmic style survived the Atlantic crossing and thrives in all the black communities of the New World.

The drawl, the vocal playfulness of Black Africa, colors the dialects of whites in the Deep South, but otherwise rhythmicity has been largely displaced, as everywhere in the complex cultures of Eurasia. In much of Eurasia the individual plowman and owner replaced the singing work-gang and the communal ownership of earlier agriculture. In northwestern Europe, particularly, the conference of equal specialists is a key communication model. One expert after another speaks at length without interruption, encouraged by quiet nodding or almost inaudible interjections. The ancient redundancy of the primitive world is held to a minimum and the appealing and sociable ploys of the gardeners have been reduced as information delivery and dominance become paramount concerns. Conversation style, enlivened principally by variations in timing and vocal stance, often becomes a series of monologues, as it tends to do everywhere in this region of powerful political leaders and individual enterprises, of solo virtuosos and sports champions, of solitary heroes and monotheism. This basic model is handled in a great variety of ways in different cultural settings. For example, the chorally oriented, complementary, and groupy societies of central and eastern Europe employ more empathetic and supportive devices. In northwestern Europe the relative infrequency of high pitch, alteration of voice quality, of emotional ejaculations, of fast tempo, and of overlap lend a more sober tone to most conversation. There are many other regional variations in speaking style, of course, which can not be presented in this brief survey. The observer also encounters individual and situational deviations away from these broad regional styles, but to date our study strongly indicates that these deviations fall within the ranges of the characteristic regional differences discussed.

This essay sketches some of the findings about rhythmicity by the Columbia University Project on Expressive Behavior, with no space to discuss deviations from the main cases discussed. For these and other omissions, I beg the reader's tolerance. This is a first demonstration that rhythmic systems, whatever their mode, are culturally consistent and that these systems have evolved as human socioeconomic systems have evolved. My central thesis is that rhythmicity in communication is largely a function of social and cultural contexts, and that its effects on behavior are best understood if a broad view of these facts is taken into consideration. There are tidal rhythms and biological rhythms; there are subliminal rhythms that knit the species; the animals organize their behavior in loose and engaging rhythmic style. But only human beings have created and adapted a variety of multileveled rhythmic systems in species development. Only human beings control and tune their behaviors in precise multi-modal rhythmic coordination. Only human beings can self-consciously design and elaborate new schemes of rhythmic behavior out of the old. All these rhythmic skills have contributed centrally to the development of human culture.

References

Barry, H., Child, I. L., Bacon, M. K. A cross-cultural survey of some sex differences in socialization. *Journal of Abnormal and Social Psychology*, 1957, *55*, pp. 332–337, 447.

Barry, H., Child, I. L., Bacon, M. K. Relation of child training to subsistence economy. *American Anthropologist*, 1959, *61*, pp. 51–63.

Birdwhistell, R. L. *Kinesics and context*. Philadelphia: University of Pennsylvania Press, 1970.

Condon, W. S. Neonate movement is synchronized with adult speech: interactional participation and language acquisition. *Science*, 1974, *183*, pp. 99–101.

Condon, W. S. and Ogston, W. D. A segmentation of behavior. *Journal of Psychiatric Research*, 1967, *5*, pp. 221–235.

Ebel, R. L. Estimation of the reliability of ratings. *Psychometrika*, 1951, *16*, pp. 407–424.

Levi-Strauss, C. The social and psychological aspects of chieftainship in a primitive tribe, the Nambikwara of N. Y. Matto Grosso. *Trans. N. Y. Academy of Science II*, 1944, *7*, 16–32.

Lomax, A. Culture style factors in face to face interaction. In A. Kendon, R. M. Harris, and M. R. Key (Eds.), *Organization of behavior in face to face interaction*. The Hague: Mouton, Inc., 1975.

Lomax, A. *Cantometrics: An approach to the anthropology of music*. Berkeley: Univ. of California Extension Media Center, 1976.

Lomax, A. *Folk song style and culture*. New Brunswick, N. J.: Transaction Books, 1978.

Lomax, A. The evolutionary taxonomy of culture. *Science*, 1972, *177*, pp. 228–239.

Lomax, A., Berkowitz, N., Deng, D., Kulig, C., and Markel, N. A stylistic analysis of speaking. *Language in Society*, 1977, *6*, pp. 15–36.

Markel, N. N. The reliability of coding paralanguage: pitch, loudness, and tempo. *Journal of Verbal Learning and Verbal Behavior*, 1965, *4*, pp. 306–308.

Marshall, John (producer). *Bitter melons*. Somerville, MA: Documentary Educational Resources, (film) 1966.

Trager, G. L. and Smith, H. L. An outline of English structure. *Studies in Linguistics*, 1951, *3*.

Trager, G. L. Paralanguage: A first approximation. *Studies in Linguistics*, 1958, *13*, pp. 1–12.

Chapter 8

ON OPERATIONALIZING THE NOTION OF RHYTHM IN SOCIAL BEHAVIOR

Madeleine Mathiot and Elizabeth Carlock[1]

Rhythm is considered here as a property of social behavior. The goal is to understand the nature of its behavioral manifestations, rather than its biological foundations. The first part of this paper proposes a stipulative definition of rhythm in social behavior. The second part gives a detailed description of a pilot study conducted on the basis of this definition. The pilot study is an initial step in the operationalization of the notion of rhythm in social behavior.

ANALYTIC DEFINITION OF RHYTHM

A stipulative definition reflects the nature of the phenomenon under consideration by relating it to the broad phenomenon of which it is a type, and by specifying its unique characteristics. In other words, such a definition has a "genus" part and a

---

[1] The first author contributed the theoretical and methodological frame of reference. The second author contributed the application of this frame of reference to the data base.

"differentia specifica" part. Considering the genus part of the definition, rhythm is viewed as sharing a broad characteristic with other forms of temporal patterning, namely, *patterned recurrence*. The broad phenomenon characterized by patterned recurrence is referred to as *periodicity*. (Note that the characterization of periodicity as patterned recurrence implies that this phenomenon is a property of structures postulated as underlying social behavior. It does not itself enter into the constitution of one of these structures.)

We differentiate rhythm from other forms of periodicity, such as cycles, by specifying the structures of which it is a property. In line with the model of social behavior adopted here (see Mathiot, 1978), rhythm is considered a property of the mechanical aspects of this behavior rather than a property of its meaning conveying aspects. In other words, rhythm is a property associated with units pertaining to systems such as the phonological system, the system constituted by spatio-orientational maneuverings (see Kendon, 1977, p. 179) and what Harris (1964) has called the "actonic" components of social activities. It is not a property of sequences of units such as morphemes or lexemes. Patterned recurrences of such units pertain to forms of periodicity other than rhythm.

As specified here, rhythm can be said to be a social phenomenon that is very close to its biological foundations. Thus, Paul Byers (1976) postulates an underlying beat in the nervous system. Lenneberg (1967, pp. 12–13) postulates an intrinsic rhythm in the nervous system acting as a coordinator. Condon and Ogston (1971) sees rhythm in social behavior as determined by the heart beat and so on.

This notion of rhythm in social behavior is in keeping with the notion of rhythm as traditionally applied to music. Thus, musical rhythm can be said to be a property of the ongoing musical flow itself rather than of the recurring melodic units created through this flow. We propose, therefore, that the traditional conception of musical rhythm as interface between *beat* and *tempo* can be applied to rhythm in social behavior. [2] The notion of tempo is understood as standing for any patterned rate of occurrence. It applies, therefore, to any form of periodicity. The notion of beat is based on the perception through the senses of particular forms of patterned prominence. We distinguish two factors in the latter: (1) *points* of perceptual prominence in ongoing behavior; and (2) a *background* against which points of perceptual prominence stand out.

The stipulative definition of rhythm in social behavior proposed here is as follows. It is the patterned rate of occurrence in ongoing behavior of points of perceptual prominence within specified units of the behavioral flow. Viewing rhythm as involving patterned rate of occurrence is the genus part of the definition. Rhythm shares with all forms of periodicity the property of having a patterned rate of occurrence, i. e., tempo. Viewing rhythm as a property of ongoing behavior that involves points of perceptual prominence within specified units of the behavioral flow is the "differentia specifica" of the definition. Rhythm is different from other forms of periodicity because (1) it is immediate, i. e., it is manifested in ongoing behavior, and (2) it is perceptually prominent, i. e., it is perceived through the senses within a background provided by specifiable units.

Within this definition the many researchers who do not distinguish between rhythm and other forms of periodicity can be said to equate rhythm with tempo. In contrast with the normative conception of musical rhythm, no requirement is made in the stipulative definition adopted here for the rate of occurrence of points of perceptual prominence to be absolutely regular. We view differences in the rate of occurrence of these phenomena as one of the factors entering into the characterization of different rhythmic patterns. As a consequence, it is likely that a large variety of rhythmic patterns will be needed to

[2] It would be impossible to do jusice here to the numerous attempts previously made to apply the notions of beat and tempo to rhythm in social behavior. For a recent attempt, see Oliva and Duchan, 1978.

characterize rhythm in social behavior, from very regular or "smooth" ones to very irregular or "erratic" ones.

RHYTHM VERSUS SYNCHRONY

The definition of rhythm adopted here clearly differentiates rhythm from a phenomenon commonly associated with it in the literature, namely, synchrony.

When taken literally, the notion of synchrony refers to the co-occurrence of any two or more phenomena, whether such co-occurrence is patterned or not. As commonly used in the literature, however, the notion of synchrony appears to refer to the systematic co-occurrence of rhythmic patterns. When these co-occurring patterns pertain to differentiated flows in the behavior of a single individual, this patterning has been referred to as "intrasynchrony" or self-synchrony (Condon, *this volume*). When the co-occurring patterns pertain to similar and/or different flows in the behavior of several interacting individuals, this patterning is commonly referred to as "intersynchrony" or "interactional synchrony." Such a conception of synchrony makes it dependent on rhythm, but not vice versa. Note that the lack of synchrony between rhythmic patterns has diagnostic value. For example, Gearing (*personal communication*) proposes to utilize the absence of interactional synchrony to spot "stumbles" which, in turn, are clues for a lack of cultural sharing on the part of the participants. The absence of synchrony can be specified as a lack of co-occurrence between rhythmic patterns, which means that in these cases rhythmic patterns do exist, but they are not synchronized.

The position taken here is that the systematic investigation of any form of patterned synchrony, either intrasynchrony or interactional synchrony, requires the previous identification of the relevant rhythmic patterns which are co-occurring.

OPERATIONALIZING THE NOTION OF RHYTHM:
A STUDY OF BUFFALO ENGLISH

As stated above, the goal of the pilot study was to operationalize the notion of rhythm in social behavior as specified in the stipulative definition. The particular form of social behavior chosen for investigation is the speech flow of native speakers of different ethnic backgrounds from Buffalo, New York. Ethnic forms of Buffalo English are especially well suited to operationalizing the notion of rhythm, since previous sociolinguistic work in the Buffalo community by the second author had suggested that one of the clues utilized by native Buffalonians to spot the ethnic origin of speakers is the rhythm of their speech. This research had also indicated that women's speech is more colored by ethnicity than men's. Consequently, only women were asked to contribute specimens of their speech for the pilot study.

These specimens were obtained by requesting a number of female native speakers of ethnic forms of Buffalo English to talk about impersonal and ethnically nondistinctive topics, such as "catching cold in the winter" or "going to the zoo." The specimens obtained on the basis of this request constitute examples of natural-sounding narrative accounts delivered as monologues. They are not part of a conversational exchange. Two forms of ethnic Buffalo English were retained for the Pilot Study, Buffalo Polish English and Buffalo Italian English. The data base consists of three specimens of Buffalo Polish English and two specimens of Buffalo Italian English.[3] Table 8.1 is a sample of the data base.

The analysis phase consisted of two major tasks. First, to ascertain the patterns of perceptual prominence present in the ongoing flow itself. Second, to ascertain the *rate of occurrence*

---

[3] Full transcripts of the data base may be obtained from the authors.

Table 8.1:   Sample Transcription:
Buffalo Polish-English Specimen 1

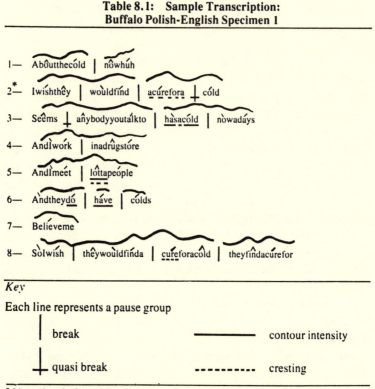

Key

Each line represents a pause group

| break | ———— contour intensity |
| quasi break | - - - - - - - cresting |

* Note that 2, 3, and 8 are very similar rhythmically.

of the points of perceptual prominence of these patterns. The scope of the pilot study is limited to the first major task.

Previous work bearing on this task by eminent researchers such as Pike (1945), Bolinger (1958), Trager and Smith (1951), Crystal (1969), and Brazil (1975) concurs in suggesting that: (1) points of perceptual prominence in the ongoing speech flow itself are constituted by one basic type of vocal elements, namely, prosodic features;[4] (2) the units within which these

4 Note that Crystal (1969, p. 140) considers silence a type of prosodic feature, along with pitch, loudness, and duration. Silence is regarded here as one type of discontinuity entering into the constitution of junctures, i. e., boundaries of speech flow units.

points of perceptual prominence are distributed are constituted by speech flow units resulting from "prosodic analysis," sometimes also called "intonation analysis." Following common practice, prosodic features are defined here as the manifestations of duration, loudness, and pitch.

Prosodic features relate to segmentals, as follows: Being manifestations of properties rather than of entities, prosodic features must have carriers. These carriers are constituted by sequences of segmentals. Segmentals are regarded here as indirectly rather than directly pertinent to the investigation of points of prominence. They are not directly pertinent to such an investigation because they do not themselves enter into the constitution of points of prominence.

The procedure followed in the pilot study is an adaptation of prosodic analysis as developed in a previous study (see Garvin and Mathiot, 1958). This procedure consists of three consecutive steps: (1) ascertaining the speech flow units in the specimens; (2) ascertaining what patterns of prosodic features bearing on perceptual prominence are present in the specimens; and (3) ascertaining the patterns of perceptual prominence in the specimens. All the criteria utilized in the performance of these tasks are based on the perception of the flow by the human ear rather than on an instrumental specification of this flow. This is not to deny the usefulness of an instrumental approach. But we believe that such an approach is appropriate only after the relevant variables have been discovered (which is the goal of the present study). To do this, we first identify relevant phenomena impressionistically, on the basis of overall auditory effect, and then specify by fine-grained auditory analysis the features that are likely to account for the way in which they were perceived.

SPEECH FLOW UNITS

Unlike other attempts to segment the speech flow, we do it on the basis of various types of discontinuities perceived in the flow.[5] These perceptual discontinuities are interpreted as boundary cues and utilized to set the boundaries of speech flow units. The various cues responsible for the perception of discontinuities in the speech flow are viewed as related to different types of junctures. The latter, in turn, serve to classify speech flow units. In short, therefore, speech flow units are first ascertained, then classified, on the basis of the junctures marking their boundaries. Two broad types of junctures are immediately apparent in the specimens, *pauses* and *breaks*.

Pauses are discontinuities in the flow characterized by the presence of an audible silence of varying duration. Breaks are discontinuities characterized as the point at which a new sequence is perceived to be starting.[6] We further distinguished two types of breaks on the basis of the clarity of the perception of these discontinuities, *true break* and *quasi-breaks*. True breaks are perceived as more clear-cut discontinuities than quasi-breaks. Pauses are the boundaries of speech flow units which will be called

[5] The reliance on perceptual discontinuities in the speech flow as the unique means of setting the boundaries of units is what distinguishes the present approach from other attempts at segmenting the speech flow. Halliday (1967) utilizes grammatical criteria to place the boundaries of "tone-groups." Although neither Pike (1948), Trager (1964), Trager and Smith (1951), nor Brazil (1975) state how they segment the speech flow, it is clear that they use basically the same strategy as Crystal (1969). Although Crystal recognizes the need to ascertain units on the basis of their boundaries, "In fact, any process of intonation analysis will take simultaneous account of both boundary cues and internal structures (and ultimately external functions, i. e., distribution of tone-units as wholes), and any comprehensive definition of the tone-unit must also have recourse to a complementarity of cues" (p. 205). In line with the procedure adopted here to segment the speech flow, the internal structure of speech flow units is specified after these units have been determined by setting their boundaries. As a consequence, contours differ greatly with respect to their stress pattern; in the specimens one contour was observed to have two primary stresses, and many contours have no primary stress.

[6] There is a high degree of agreement among both naive and experienced perceivers as to when the break junctures occur. The significance of breaks being perceived as the start of a new sequence rather than as the end of a previous sequence is as yet to be discovered.

lines. Breaks are the boundaries of speech flow units to be called *contours.* A contour bounded on both sides by true breaks is an *independent contour.* A contour bounded on one side by a quasi-break is a *dependent contour* (see Table 8.1). In the specimens no contours bounded on both sides by a quasi-break were encountered. A sequence of one dependent and one independent contour is a *contour cluster.*

PATTERNS OF PROSODIC FEATURES
BEARING ON PERCEPTUAL PROMINENCE

Two factors are considered crucial for the further specification of the prosodic properties of duration, loudness, and pitch as they are manifested within the natural speech flow of different speakers: (1) the *range of variation* of the prosodic features; and (2) the *span* covered by the carriers of these features.

The range of variation exhibited by related prosodic features within the speech flow of the same speaker relates to (1) whether these features are within or beyond the speaker's normal range; and in either case (2) what pertinent contrasts they enter into.

Crystal notes that ''different people strike different norms'' and that ''departures from these norms are not idiosyncratic but are conventional, carrying meaning-contrasts which are shared by speakers of the same speech-community'' (1969, p. 141). It is clear then that the speaker's normal range must be ascertained for the case of each speaker.

Well-documented cases of ''phonemic stress'' and ''phonemic length'' in various languages show that related prosodic features may involve very different types of contrasts. In English phonemic stress is manifested in four degrees of loudness; phonemic length is manifested in two degrees of length. Thus, the pertinent contrasts into which related prosodic features enter must be ascertained separately for each prosodic property.

The crucial distinction pertaining to the span covered by the carriers of related prosodic features of which manifest the same prosodic property seems to be whether this span is of the order of the contour (from smaller than the contour to an entire contour) or whether it encompasses from one to several contours. Related prosodic features whose carriers are of the order of the contour are said to have *"short-span carriers."* Related prosodic features whose carriers encompass from one to several contours are said to have *"long-span carriers."* Loudness is manifested in different degrees, carried both by short-span carriers (e.g., vocalic nuclei within the contour) and by long-span carriers (e.g., several contours within the line). Degrees of loudness manifested in short-span carriers are traditionally regarded as entering into the constitution of *"phonemic stress."* We propose that the different degrees of loudness manifested in long-span carriers be regarded as entering into the constitution of different *"loudness keys."* This interpretation is an extension of Brazil's (1975) notion of key which he proposed for what is regarded here as long-span carriers of pitch. We believe the notion of key applies not just to long-span carriers of pitch but also to those of loudness and of duration.

Related prosodic features with short-span carriers are believed to be directly connected with rhythm. Related prosodic features with long-span carriers are believed to bear on forms of perceptual prominence less directly connected with the ongoing flow itself, and hence less directly connected with rhythm as here defined. Consequently, in the subsequent discussion only features in the short-span carriers encountered in the specimens under study will be taken into account.

Two degrees of phonemic length are contrastive in English, *long* and *not long*. In the specimens, the short-span carriers of relative length are vocalic nuclei within the contour. Variation in the length of vocalic nuclei within the speaker's normal range is traditionally called *"phonemic length."* Only one type of variation in the relative length of vocalic nuclei beyond the speaker's normal range was observed in the specimens to relate to perceptual prominence, *extra length*. This type of variation in relative length is called here *"syllabic extension."*

Loudness refers to a scale of loudness, or intensity, from "soft" or "weak" to "loud" or "strong." In the specimens, the short-span carriers of relative loudness are either vocalic nuclei within the contour, a part of the contour, or the contour as a whole. Degrees of loudness included in phonemic stress in English are viewed here as entering into two contrasts. The first contrast is strong versus not strong. The second contrast is between three degrees of strength. These two contrasts yield four degrees of stress: three strong stresses—*primary, secondary, tertiary*—and one *weak* stress. Only one type of variation in relative loudness beyond the speaker's normal range was observed in the specimens: *extra loudness*, called here *"contour intensity."* The carriers of contour intensity are either a part of the contour or the entire contour (see Table 8.1, lines 5, 6, and 7). Both phonemic stress and contour intensity are regarded as pertinent to the investigation of perceptual prominence in the ongoing speech flow.

We consider pitch here in terms of two interrelated dimensions: change in pitch movement and degree of change.[7] We distinguish between the presence or the absence of change in pitch movement, either an upward movement (*"rise"*) or a downward movement (*"fall"*), versus no pitch movement at all (a *"level"* progression), and we analyze degree of change in pitch movement as "slight" or "sharp" changes in rises or falls.

In the specimens, the short-span carriers of pitch are constituted by parts of the contour or by the entire contour. Variation beyond the speaker's normal range was observed to apply only to degree of change in pitch movement. A single type was encountered in the specimens: *extra sharp pitch rise*. This degree of change in pitch movement is called *"cresting."* Its carriers are a portion of the contour or the entire contour.

[7] Note that the conception of pitch adopted here is different from Crystal's (1969) and from Brazil's (1979). Crystal distinguishes "tone" (defined as direction of pitch movement) from "pitch range." Brazil distinguishes "tone" (defined as pitch level of the tone group as a whole).

Variation within the speaker's normal range was observed to apply both to change in pitch movement and to degree of change in pitch movement, as specified above. We found it valuable to analyze change in pitch movement and degree of change at three parts of the contour: (1) pitch onset; (2) the body of the contour; and (3) the tail of pitch contour. Some of the factors responsible for variation in pitch in these positions are shown in Table 8.2.

Table 8.2   Factors Responsible for Pitch Variation

Contour Pitch Onset	Contour Pitch Tail	Body of Contour	
		Two basic pitch movement configurations:	Pitch
1. level progression: ▬▬▬	1. level progression: ▬▬▬	1. flat: ▬	
2. slight fall followed by onset of rise ✓	2. slight or sharp fall ↘	2. peak(s) and trough(s): ∿ further distinguished in 3 degrees: salient, medium rounded, and flattened	
	3. slight or sharp rise ▬ ▬ ▬		
truncated peak (i.e. no pitch onset or no pitch tail)		elongated, shortened and compact peaks and troughs	Factors
Junctures		Duration	

In the following discussion only the initial results of the analysis of pitch variation are presented. The criteria and procedures used in the analysis are summarized in order not to detract attention from the major points at issue. The initial results are as follows. It appears that both contour-onset and contour-final pitch variation can be assigned to the presence of different types of junctures marking the boundaries of the contour. How many types of junctures should be distinguished remains to be ascertained. Two basic configurations of pitch movements within the contour were observed in the specimens: sequences of peaks and troughs constituted by combinations of rises and falls and instances of level progression. (Note that while the configurations occur over the entire contour the carriers of individual peaks and troughs are portions of the contour.)

An inventory of the manifestations of duration, loudness, and pitch taken into account in the pilot study is shown in Table 8.3.

Note that the three manifestations of these properties that are beyond the speaker's normal range fall at the same extreme end of their respective scale. Thus, contour intensity is extra loudness; cresting is extra sharp pitch rise; syllabic extensions extra syllabic length.

PATTERNS OF PERCEPTUAL PROMINENCE

Patterns of perceptual prominence are ascertained on the basis of how points of prominence stand out within a background of speech flow units. In these specimens we discriminated (1) the different types of points of perceptual prominence; and (2) the distributional patterns into which they entered. In line with the strategy followed in the present approach, points of perceptual prominence in the specimens are first ascertained on the basis of perceptual criteria, i. e., on the basis of the overall perception of the speech flow by the human ear. They are next specified on the basis of the prosodic features entering into their constitution. The latter criteria serve to distinguish two types of points of perceptual prominence observed in the specimens: those constituted by prosodic features within the speaker's normal range (see Table 8.3), and those beyond the speaker's normal range. The first type is called "*beats*." The second type is called "*accents*."

In the specimens, accents are constituted by manifestations

Table 8.3   Analysis of Duration, Loudness, and Pitch in the Pilot Study

Prosodic Properties		Pertinent Contrasts	Short-Span Carriers
Duration	beyond speaker's normal range	'syllable extension' (extra length of vocalic nucleus)	vocalic nuclei within the contour
	within speaker's normal range		
Loudness	beyond speaker's normal range	'contour intensity' (extra loudness)	part of the contour or the entire contour
	within speaker's normal range	primary stress (/) secondary stress (∧) tertiary stress (\ ) vs. weak stress	vocalic nuclei within the contour
Pitch	beyond speaker's normal range	'cresting' (extra-sharp pitch rise)	part of the contour or the entire contour
	within speaker's normal range	2 basic pitch movement configurations (1) peaks and troughs: (2) flats: + how many degrees of pitch change	

of the three prosodic properties that are beyond the speaker's normal range, namely, syllable extension, contour intensity, and cresting (see Table 8.3). Beats are constituted by the conjunction of a peak, i. e., a pitch rise followed by a pitch fall, and a strong stress, either a primary stress, a secondary stress, or even a tertiary stress.

Note that the two factors identified as having an impact on pitch, namely, duration and junctures, do not seem to have an impact on the perception of beats. In other words, beats were perceived as equally prominent irrespective of whether the peak is elongated or shortened (the effect on pitch attributed to duration), or the particular types of junctures marking the boundaries of the contours within which beats occur. Note, in addition, that neither the degree of pitch rise of the peak nor the degree of loudness of the stress seems to have an impact on the perception of beats. In other words, beats were perceived as equally prominent irrespective of whether the peak was flattened or well-rounded, and whether the strong stress was a primary stress, a secondary stress, or even a tertiary stress.

DISTRIBUTIONAL PATTERNS OF BEATS

Distributional patterns are ascertained on the basis of the distribution of stated characteristics within pertinent units, i. e., units displaying contrasts between the stated characteristics. Such units are called distributional frames. Examination of the data reveals that the beats are not distributed without interruption. There are long stretches in which beats occur, interrupted by short stretches without beats. The long stretches in which beats occur are said to constitute the "*beat-flow*." The short stretches without beats are said to constitute "*breaks-in-the-beat-flow*."

When the semantic content of the beat-flow and the breaks-in-the-beat-flow is taken into account, it is clear that the breaks-in-the-beat-flow all involve some form of hesitation as opposed to fluent speech. Fluent speech and hesitant speech have long been of interest to psycholinguists who view these phenomena as a reflection of cognitive planning. Brian Butterworth explains the postulated relation between fluent versus hesitant speech and cognitive planning as follows: "The fluent phase executes the plan formulated in the preceding hesitant phase. That is to say, the temporal rhythm of speech reflects an underlying 'cognitive rhythm' " (1976, p. 8).

In view of their respective distribution (hesitations are scattered throughout the entire text, fluent speech occurs in long stretches), we propose that hesitations enter into a form of periodicity other than rhythm while fluent speech is directly related to rhythm. The following discussion, therefore, is limited to an account of beat patterns within stretches of fluent speech.

Beat patterns are constituted by differential numbers of beats per relevant distributional frame. The unit within which to count the number of beats is the contour rather than the contour cluster or the line. This decision is based on the observation that the boundaries of impressionistically ascertained rhythmic sequences coincide with any breaks and are not limited to true breaks as opposed to quasi-breaks or to pauses.

In the specimens, three beat patterns can be specified in terms of number of beats per contour: one-beat contours, two-beat contours, and three-beat contours. The two types of ethnic English investigated in the pilot study, Buffalo Italian English and Buffalo Polish English, differ as to their respective beat patterns. In the speech flow of the speakers of Buffalo Italian English, one-beat contours and two-beat contours are equally frequent. Three-beat contours do not occur in the specimens. In the speech flow of the speakers of Buffalo Polish English, two-beat contours and three-beat contours are equally frequent. One-beat contours also occur, but much less frequently.

DISTRIBUTIONAL PATTERNS OF ACCENTS

As mentioned above, three types of accents occur in the specimens: syllabic extension, contour intensity, and cresting. Contour intensity occurs in all the specimens included in the data base; cresting and syllabic extension do not. Cresting occurs in the speech flow of the three speakers of Buffalo Polish English, but not in the speech flow of either of the speakers of

Buffalo Italian English. Cresting, therefore, appears to be a characteristic of Buffalo Polish English which may account for the stereotypic description of this form of ethnic English as "sing song." Syllabic extension occurs in two out of the three specimens obtained from speakers of Buffalo Polish English and in one out of the two specimens obtained from speakers of Buffalo Italian English. Syllabic extension, therefore, may be a characteristic of individual speakers rather than of linguistic varieties.

A look at the distribution of the three types of accents throughout the entire text reveals that they occur as follows: (1) only in the beat flow; and (2) individually or either in clumps of two (usually contour intensity and cresting) or in sequential clusters (see Table 8.1). Both the presence and the absence of accents in the beat flow relate to emphasis, a phenomenon pertaining to topic presentation.

These considerations, both distributional and semantic, suggest that accents constitute points of perceptual prominence against the background of the beat-flow. Since the beat-flow is constituted by beat patterns, i. e., by patterns of points of perceptual prominence, two orders of points of perceptual prominence must be distinguished: those entering into *basic patterns* and those entering into *secondary patterns*. Beats enter into the constitution of basic patterns of perceptual prominence. Accents enter into the constitution of secondary patterns of perceptual prominence.

We propose that the distributional patterns of accents are constituted by their *differential positions of occurrence* (i. e., either initially, medially, or finally) within relevant distributional frames. We further propose that two distributional frames are relevant: (1) lines and (2) portions of the text or entire texts. Accents, therefore, can be said to enter into two types of distributional patterns: The first type accounts for where accents occur within the line. The second type accounts for the locations in which lines which have accents occur within portions of the text or entire texts.

TYPES OF PERCEPTUAL PROMINENCE

The three prosodic properties of duration, loudness, and pitch have been shown to be manifested in two types of carriers, short-span carriers and long-span carriers. Only the former are regarded as directly pertinent to the specification of perceptual prominence in the ongoing flow itself. A distinction has been made above between fluent speech and hesitant speech, and it has been shown how the specification of perceptual prominence within the ongoing speech flow relates only to fluent speech. Within fluent speech two orders of patterns of perceptual prominence have been distinguished: basic patterns and secondary patterns. Basic patterns are constituted by beat patterns. Secondary patterns are constituted by accent patterns. Basic patterns occur within the contour, the minimal unit of the speech flow. Secondary patterns occur within the line, portions of the text, or the entire text. These are nonminimal units of the speech flow. Both basic and secondary patterns are patterns of perceptual prominence entering into the specification of rhythm in the speech flow.

CONCLUSION

The pilot study proposes a stipulative definition of rhythm in social behavior and a procedure for the operationalization of part of the stipulative definition, namely, of the notion of patterns of perceptual prominence in the ongoing speech flow.

The procedure was applied to a single type of behavioral flow, the speech flow in monologues. It is believed that this procedure could be extended to other types of speech flows, such as dialogues, and to other types of behavioral flows, such as the body movement flow accompanying the speech flow. This procedure is based on the specification of the notion of rhythm in social behavior as follows: (1) Rhythm is a property of systems rather than a system itself; (2) rhythm is a property of the mechanical aspects of systems rather than of their meaning-conveying aspects; and (3) in speech behavior, rhythm is an attribute of both the minimal and the nonminimal units of the speech flow and is manifested in basic and secondary patterns.

REFERENCES

Birdwhistell, R. L. *Kinesics in context.* Philadelphia: University of Pennsylvania Press, 1970.

Bolinger, D. L. A theory of pitch accent in English. *Word,* 1958, *14,* pp. 109–149.

Brazil, D. Discourse intonation. *English language research,* Birmingham University, 1975.

Butterworth, B. *Semantic planning, lexical choice and syntactic organization in spontaneous speech,* unpublished manuscript, 1976.

Byers, P. Biological rhythms as information channels in interpersonal communication behavior. In P. P. G. Bateson and P. H. Klopfer (Eds.), *Perspectives in Ethology,* Vol. 2. New York: Plenum Press, 1976.

Carlock, E. K. Prosodic analysis of two varieties of Buffalo English. In W. Wolck and P. L. Garvin (Eds.), *The Fifth LACUS Forum.* Columbia, South Carolina: The Hornbeam Press, 1979, pp. 377–382.

Condon, W. C. and Ogston, W. D. Speech and body motion synchrony of the speaker-hearer. In D. L. Horton and J. J. Jenkins (Eds.), *The perspective of language.* Columbus, Ohio: Charles E. Merrill Publishing Co., 1971.

Crystal, D. *Prosodic systems and intonation in English.* New York: Columbia University Press, 1969.

Garvin, P. L. and Mathiot, M. Fused units in prosodic analysis. *Word,* 1958, *14,* pp. 178–186.

Halliday, M. A. K. *Intonation and grammar in British English.* The Hague: Mouton, 1967.

Harris, M. *The nature of cultural things.* New York: Random House, 1964.

Kendon, A. *Studies in the Behavior of Social Interaction.* Bloomington, Indiana: Indiana University Press, 1977.

Lenneberg, E. Biological Foundations of Language. New York: John Wiley & Sons, Inc., 1967.

Mathiot, M. Toward a frame of reference for the analysis of face-to-face interaction. *Semiotica,* 1978, *24,* pp. 199–220.

Oliva, J. and Duchan, J. Three levels of temporal structuring in spoken language. In M. Paradis (Ed.), *The Fourth LACUS Forum.* Columbia, South Carolina: Hornbeam Press, 1978, pp. 460–468.

Pike, K. L. *The intonation of American English*. Ann Arbor, Michigan: University of Michigan Press, 1945.

Trager, G. L. Paralanguage: a first approximation. *Studies in Linguistics*, 1958, *13*, pp. 1–12.

Trager, G. L. The intonation system of American English. In Abescrombie et al. (Eds.), *In honor of Daniel Jones*. London: Longmans, 1964, pp. 266–270.

Trager, G. L. and Smith, H. L. *An outline of English structure*, Occasional Papers 3. Washington, D. C.: American Council of Learned Societies, 1951.

Chapter 9

THE STRUCTURE AND SEMIOTIC
FUNCTION OF PARALANGUAGE

Joseph Oliva

Douglas Greenlee in his, *Peirce's Concept of Sign*, raises the question, when is a sign a sign?

> ... The province of signs is as wide as the world itself. Mental images, objects, events more or less protracted, general signs, as well as systems of signs, may all function significatively. But along with the recognition of this fact should go another equally as important, that not all things do function as signs. The distinction between objects GROSSLY available and those available significatively is basic to Peirce's theory of signs. Establishing this distinction is largely the purpose of his careful and much repeated insistence on the regulation of all signs to the category of thirdness now taken hypostatically ...
>
> (Greenlee: 1973, p. 49)

Semiotics as a general theory of meaning is applicable to anything that counts as a sign, whether verbal or nonverbal. This paper is a structural study of all those phenomena in interactive events (language, paralanguage, and gesture) that contribute to meaning. The progression is from the structure of the sign vehicle to sign function within the framework of Peirce's sign theory. From a structural perspective we are concerned with the interrelationships of co-occurring aural and visual events as they unfold in time. The focus is on the constraints inherent in language, gesticulation, and paralanguage which allow or prohibit the simultaneous occurrence of these sign vehicles in terms of rhythmic structuring.

From the standpoint of function, we are concerned with what counts as a sign (has meaning) and also with the possibilities and prohibitions of co-occurring signs. All signs are subsumable under one or another of the divisions of Peirce's now famous triadic relations of *icon*, *index*, and *symbol*. The icon is representative by virtue of a qualitative configuration of its sign vehicle, or a shared similarity common to it and its object. An index represents its object by being in a contiguous or causal relation to it. One of Peirce's examples of the index is the weathercock which is causally connected and therefore an index of the wind. The symbol represents its object by virtue of a rule or convention and does not depend upon a likeness between the sign-vehicle and what it represents. The three divisions of icon, index, and symbol are not mutually exclusive. Sebeok (1975) notes that "it is not signs that are actually being classified, but more precisely, aspects of signs: in other words, a given sign may—and more often than not does—exhibit more than one aspect, so that one must recognize differences in gradation."

Greenlee's original question restated, would be, if a sign is something that stands for, refers to, or represents something else, how are we to resolve gestural activity such as headbobs, hand movements at rising or falling terminal junctures, sustention of body parts over internal junctures of the speech component, etc., to Peirce's sign object relationship? Also, what are the rules or conventions by which we interpret this relationship? For Crystal (1976) and also Trager & Smith (1951) the parameters of pause, tempo, and rhythm fall within the domain of paralanguage. Their definition of paralanguage excludes kinesic and other nonvocal phenomena that are essential to our analysis of the structure of the sign vehicle.

Rhythm in this study implies the regular recurrence of an event in time. The succession of significant units (whether spatial-temporal or visual-temporal) are not random but are perceived as fixed distributions of significant units in a visual or acoustic gestalt. Rhythm in language is manifested on the surface level by the regular recurrence of prominent stress (/ primary or ∧ secondary) and duration within isometric intonation patterns.

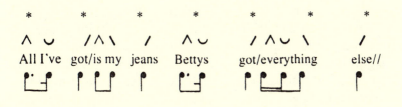

Although it does not appear so in the printed example above, the prominent stresses (characterized by asterisks) are equidistant in time. On the surface level the rhythmic regularity of prominent stresses is obscured by the uneven number of syllables within intonation patterns and the interpolation of weaker syllables (\ tertiary and ∪ weak). The rate of succession of prominent stresses constitutes tempo. Tempo is not to be confused with duration which is a single occurrence on the surface level; tempo has domain and extends over the whole or part of an utterance and the duration of each syllable is marked by musical notation. The native speaker maintains tempo out of awareness and the receiver comes to the interactive event with a set of culturally determined expectancies in terms of regularity of tempo. Any upsetting of rhythmic regularity is perceived as semiotic (afterthought, hesitation, self-interruptions, etc.) or an abnormality. Just as every speaker exhibits voice set as a norm, we can speak of tempo set as characteristic of a particular speaker. Voice set is the range and voice quality we associate with a particular individual, and tempo is the idiosynchratic speed of performance we associate with a particular speaker.

The assignment of the four stresses of English (/ primary, ∧ secondary, \ tertiary, ∪ weak) are also not random but are imposed on the speaker by the lexical and syntactic constraints of the language. The speaker has no freedom of choice about the arrangement of stress distribution.

The fixed distribution of lexical and syntactic stress has yet another constraint and this is the notion of the intonation pattern (Trager and Smith, 1951). The structural function of the intonation pattern as a metrical unit perhaps can be best illustrated by another aural-temporal system, Morse Code. The minimal or significant units of Morse Code are based on the opposition of long and short acoustic units grouped in configurations to represent the alphabet. Because of the reliance on the written system of English, it is a secondary sign system, but the metric patterning operates under the same principle that characterizes the intonation patterns of English. If a subject is presented with a succession of temporally equidistant pulses:

. . . .

either there is no message or he will arbitrarily impose a stronger stress on every other pulse /. /. /. or every fourth, /. . /. . /. fifth, etc. The opposition of long and short still would be unintelligible if transmitted in an uninterrupted sequence (. . . _ _ _ . . . . . _ _ _ _).

We all recognize the possibility of the familiar SOS signal in the initial segment of this transmission. . . _ _ _ . . . , but the message could just as well be . . _ _ _ or . . . _ _ _ and so on through all of the possible permutations in the system. What differentiates signs in this system is the temporal isometricity of corresponding sign units. This means that the sender will use the same amount of time to transmit a configuration of one unit as he would a configuration of three or four units.

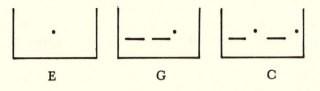

The metric patterning of Morse Code is reflected in the intonation patterns of verbal utterances. The intonation pattern as described by Trager and Smith (1951) extends from nothing to a major juncture or from major juncture to major juncture. Major junctures frame intonation patterns.

All I've got / is my jeans # Bettys got / everything else // consists of: single bar (/) where pitch is level, double cross /#/ where falling pitch occurs and double bar (//) if there is an upward inflection of pitch. Every syllable receives a stress and although the number of stresses within intonation patterns varies, the time expended between major junctures is the same. The perceptual reality of juncture is what makes the unison performance of a text possible by groups of speakers. We have all had the uncomfortable experience of the person reciting out of meter or out of tempo. Chants, prayers, and pledges, of course, are more deliberate than normal discourse, but all depend on the maintenance of tempo and meter.

Rhythm as it is manifested in the speech stream of language is made up of seemingly disparate arrangements of stress patterns but maintains regularity through an underlying succession of prominent stresses; within this variation a temporally uniform pulse is perceived. Units are perceived as different on one level but the same on other levels of analysis. Buhler's principle of abstractive relevance (Garvin 1966) is in operation here. The principle of abstractive relevance stipulates that not everything in a configuration is significant and only those culturally meaningful aspects of the sign are abstracted.

Temporally equidistant succession of prominent beats within a metrical framework performs still another structural function in relation to gesture. There is a maintenance of synchronic co-occurrence of gestural peaks, closure, preparatory gesture, etc., within the metrically rigid recurrence of verbal stresses.

We found support for Kendon's claim that onset of speech utterances and gesticulation are closely connected, with gesture often just preceding speech.

> Phrases of gesticulation tend to appear a little in advance of their associated speech and their preparation begins sometimes well in advance. This suggests that the process of speech utterance begins at one and the same time. The temporal priority of gesture may partly be due to the fact that for a given idea to be expressed in words, it must be strung out in time, whereas the same idea may be expressed in gesture within a single movement or pose of the hand (Kendon, 1975, p. 362).

We also have observed preparatory gestures of the type Kendon refers to in our analysis, but we do not attribute a priority of gesture to them or agree "that the process of gestural encoding is more readily accomplished than that of verbal encoding and so may be faster for this reason"[1] (Kendon, 1975). Rather, preparatory gestures are viewed as physically necessary movements, timed so that the peak, drop, sustention, etc., that follows will, in the case of English, fall on rigidly prescribed prominent stress points. Preparatory gestures are analogous to the movements made by a conductor in providing cues for an orchestral performance. A downbeat is always preceded by an upward swing of the baton and an upbeat is always preceded by a downward preparatory gesture. Although gesture in normal discourse is not quite as deliberate, body parts must be brought into a preparatory position before direction is possible. Most often preparatory gestures anticipate the two prominent stresses within an intonation pattern. Gesture terminates at these points in time so that preparatory gestures always precede strong stresses. If a

---

[1] Kendon has indicated in personal communication that perhaps "preparatory phase" would be a better term than "preparatory gesture."

hand is not already extended for a drop or if the head is not in an appropriate position for a nod, they are brought into position to coincide with the rhythmic beat provided by the syntactic stress patterning. For example, when our subject says:

yù sɔ̂ fræ̂ŋk // læst θ́ɜrzdɛ̃ //

(You saw Frank // last thursday?)

an upward gesticulation of head and hand begins slightly before / sɔ̂ / is uttered and both head and hand reach the peak of this configuration in synchrony with the occurrence of secondary stress on / sɔ̂ /. The hand is sustained in this position over the remaining part of the utterance and is returned to a resting position which coincides with the primary stress of / θ́ɜrzdɛ̃ /. Preparatory gesture is necessary because without it, a sudden upward elevation of the hand on / sɔ̂ / or sudden drop of the hand on / fræ̂ŋk / without preparation would not be what we would expect in terms of gesture in this utterance. To violate the synchrony of gesture and prominent beats is physically very difficult.

Thus far we have considered only those aspects of interaction that are system-derived. The notion of system-derived and field-derived is also taken from Buhler, as interpreted by Garvin (1966, p. 213). In Buhler's formulation system-derived aspects of a sign are the characteristics that it has by virtue of being part of a system while field-derived characteristics arise from a social context or situation. In the interaction of the speech sign with the surrounding field, the system-derived characteristics of the speech sign are modified.

In this study, paralanguage and gesture are viewed not as accompaniments to language, or parallel structures or systems, but as integral and inseparable components of an interactive event. They are seen not as a separate system but as a level or plane of diacritics that modify a verbal gestalt and are field-derived. In this sense, the sign is altered by upsetting equilibrium in terms of those elements in the initial acoustic image that are subject to modification. These mutable elements (and those that are immutable) are present or potentially present in the speech event from the beginning so that we are not imposing another parallel system but either consciously or out of awareness are altering a gestalt.

The difference between paralinguistic or field-derived units and system-derived units is that communication takes place analogically rather than digitally. This is also true of gesture when in accompaniment with spoken language. The system-derived units of language (segmental and suprasegmental pho-nemes of pitch, stress, and juncture) are digital as opposed to the continuous gradation (loud-soft, fast-slow, overhigh-overlow, etc.) of paralinguistic features and the nondiscrete configura-tions of gesture.

The loose patterning that results from gesture and paralan-guage is not random but is the variation that the speaker is free to impose on the system. These alterations of the sign are culturally derived (we can point out different ethnic typologies) and give the illusion of system because in altering the sign they become sign vehicles. Language, paralanguage, and gesture display interdependent relationships, and all three simultaneously con-stitute the sign so that it is possible to look upon this phenomena as several functions being carried by the specific communicative behavior within a given context.

The gesticulatory and paralinguistic units have no "se-mantic" value in and of themselves, nor can they be assigned a conventional value such as Ekman and Friesen's (1969) category of emblem where we have a "direct verbal translation or dictionary definition" of nonverbal phenomena. The linguistic sign is symbolic and depends on convention, or a rule of interpretation. The sign function of nonverbal behavior under consideration here is not symbolic or interpreted by convention; nor is it iconic because there is no similarity between the sign vehicle and what it represents. These particular gesticulatory movements and paralanguage are indexical in that they point to or draw attention to a change or deformation of the sign vehicle itself. This deformation is significative as a potential sign and belongs to the subclassification of "symptom."

In my observation an important qualification of Peirce's division of signs (icon, index, and symbol) should be made. The division is valid because we do not observe simultaneous symbolic systems, e. g., we cannot understand two independent streams of speech at once or two simultaneous deaf signs. We also cannot process two iconic signs at once or two indexical signs such as pointing in two different directions. The co-occurrence of the same species of sign vehicle is possible only when each is in a different mode (e. g., visual versus aural) or when the content is the same but the expression is different or when one sign is empty of symbolic or referential meaning as in the aspects of paralanguage and gesture discovered here.

REFERENCES

Crystal, D. Paralinguistic behavior as continuity between animal and human communication. In W. McCormack & S. Wurm (Eds.), *Language and man: anthropological issues*. The Hague: Mouton, 1976, pp. 13–28.

Ekman, P. & Freisen, W. The repertoire of nonverbal behavior: categories, usage, and coding. *Semiotica*, 1969, pp. 49–98.

Garvin, P. L. Karl Buhler's contribution to the theory of linguistics. *Journal of General Psychology*, 1966, *75*, pp. 212–215.

Greenlee, D. *Peirce's concept of sign*. The Hague: Mouton, 1973.

Kendon, A. Gesticulation, speech, and gesture theory of language origins. *Sign Language Studies*, 1975, *9*, pp. 349–373.

Peirce, C. S. *Collected papers of Charles Sanders Peirce* (8 volumes). Cambridge, Mass.: Harvard University Press, 1931–35.

Sebeok, T. A. Six species of signs: some propositions and strictures. *Semiotica*, 1975, *13*, pp. 233–260.

Trager, G. & Smith, H. *An outline of English structure*. SIL Occasional Papers 3.

Trager, G. Paralanguage: a first approximation. *Language in culture and society*. New York: Harper and Row, 1964, pp. 274–288.

Part III

Impression formation or person perception has been an important subject in social psychology for many years. Traditionally, physical appearance, social role and class, and personality characteristics have been examined in relation to person perception. These chapters represent a new direction in this research, namely, the role of the temporal aspects of speech in impression formation. Stanley Feldstein and Aron W. Siegman have done extensive experimental research on the rhythms of dialogue, particulary in dyadic conversations and psychotherapy. In this section they and their colleague at the University of Baltimore, Cynthia L. Crown, offer a special perspective not directly dealt with by the other authors—the impact of interaction rhythms on social perception.

Chapter 10

IMPRESSION FORMATION IN DYADS:
The Temporal Dimension

Stanley Feldstein

Impression formation is a process that has been tagged by a host of different labels, such as *person perception, interpersonal perception, social perception,* and even *social cognition.* Although each label may have connotations not shared by the others, it is unlikely that those connotations represent critical differences. Tagiuri (1969) argues, with some justification, that the labels use the term *perception* inappropriately. Perhaps, then, the phrase *impression formation* is better for being somewhat less assuming than the other labels. Tagiuri (1969) also defines person perception as those " . . . processes by which man comes to know and to think about other persons, their characteristics, qualities, and inner states" (p. 395). I confess that the definition seems to me philosophically somewhat presumptuous, and I prefer to think that impression formation, or any of the other labels, refers to a process that enables, or is used by, individuals to develop conjectures or hypotheses about other persons, or, if you will, fictions that represent those persons. Thus, it is one of the most important processes in which we engage! It functions as a mediating variable in almost all interpersonal transactions. It influences, if not dictates, the kinds of behavior in which we engage (often determining, for example, whether the behavior is appropriate). And ultimately, it affects how we ourselves are perceived by others.

The efforts my associate, Ms. Cynthia Crown, and I have made to examine certain of the behaviors involved in impression formation were initiated a relatively short time ago and have been concerned with the formation of first impressions. In this chapter, I shall begin by briefly discussing the various types of behaviors that seem likely to influence the formation of interpersonal impressions. Then I shall review, in somewhat more detail, the role of the voice in impression formation. Lastly, I shall talk about the behavior that is of particular interest to Ms. Crown and me, namely, the temporal patterning of dialogues. In the next chapter, Ms. Crown will present the results of our research efforts.

CATEGORIES OF BEHAVIOR

Given that we see a person who we do not know well, or know at all, upon what do we base our impressions of him or her? The answer has at least three parts. One part has to do with the characteristics of the person to whom we are attending, the so-called "target person;" another part has to do with our own characteristics; and the third part with the social and role contexts in which the target person and we find ourselves. In any case, an intuitive answer regarding the characteristics of the other person is that almost any observable characteristic may serve as an interpersonal cue. Clearly, gender and age are such cues. Apart from them, however, it seems possible to delineate roughly about four broad categories of behavior, so to speak, that probably contribute to the formation of impressions. The four are *body movements, postures and clothing, facial features and expressions, visual behavior*, and *vocal behavior*.

The order in which they are mentioned is fortuitous; it is unlikely that the relative importance of their separate contributions can, at present, be meaningfully assessed. In part, each contribution must certainly depend upon not only the number of cues involved in the category but also the salience of each cue, which is a weight that surely depends not only upon the situation but upon the observer.

Body

Consider the impression conveyed by an individual who slouches while standing, or by a person who sits stiffly upright, or the quite different characteristics attributed to the person who lopes along like Groucho Marx and the person who strides forward with head high and spine straight. Speed of walking may itself provoke different attributions. Hayward and Neetz (1978), for example, found that fast walkers are "perceived as more aggressive, selfish, less considerate, and less friendly" than are slow walkers. The attributions elicited by all of these differences are a function partly of the differences, partly of cultural expectations, and partly of the general history and idiosyncratic interpersonal history of the observer.

I might note, incidentally, that inasmuch as I often walk quickly, I know that the characterization of fast and slow walkers obtained by Hayward and Neetz is not accurate in every instance. But accuracy of interpersonal perception is another issue, and one that is of questionable relevance to the search for the cues involved in the formation of, at least, first impressions.[1]

It used to be the case that different social situations and circumstances demanded different modes of attire. That these demands were common knowledge permitted variations in the

---

[1] It seems to me that the role of accuracy in interpersonal perception has not been assessed adequately, although thoughtful discussions have been published (e. g., Cline, 1964; Cook, 1971; Hastorf, Schneider, & Polefka, 1970; Schneider, 1976; Tagiuri, 1969) about the difficulties of investigating the issue and its implications for social and clinical psychology.

extent to which they were met to seem informative with regard to social class and personal characteristics (Douty, 1963; Hamid, 1968). The less formal and possibly less compelling demands of today, however, may make judgments about social class more difficult but judgments about personal characteristics somewhat easier. (Perhaps the most dramatic illustration of the effects of clothes upon interpersonal perception is their absence in situations in which they are expected to be present.)

Face

Facial features and their movements act as cues not only for the perception of emotion (Darwin, 1872; Ekman, 1978; Izard, 1971) but also for the perception of psychological character and stability, and a host of clichés such as "strong face," "weak chin," and "guilty expression" call attention to their use. An example of an old horror-movie cliché that has been raised to the status of comedy is the uncontrollable facial twitch, which presumably reflects a psychological disturbance or the approach of a psychotic episode. (Some of you may recall the deterioration of Inspector Clouseau of Pink Panther fame!)

Eyes

The role of visual, and especially gazing behavior in impression formation is being given increasing attention. A person whose eyes dart rapidly back and forth is usually thought to be frightened, whereas a person with an unmoving, wide-eyed stare is likely to be considered at least strange and possibly terror-stricken. Is the man who "looks you straight in the eye" honest and forthright or merely rude? What about a woman who looks you straight in the eye? Impressions are affected by whether an individual tends to look at his or her conversational partner or to avert his or her gaze (Berscheid & Walster, 1973; Exline & Fehr, 1978; Hillabrant, 1974; Kleinke, 1972; Kleinke, Staneski, & Berger, 1975; Scherwitz, & Helmrich, 1973). There is evidence that the direction in which gaze is averted influences interpersonal impressions (Massillon, & Hillabrant, 1978). Even pupillary size has been shown to affect such impressions (Hess & Petrovich, 1978).

In short, all of these behaviors play some role in the formation of interpersonal impressions, particularly when they provide the only empirical information an observer has upon which to base his impressions of the individual he observes. In the event, however, that verbal interaction occurs, then all of the cues provided by the voice become available to the observer. But what are those cues provided by the voice that influence the forming of impressions?[2]

Voice

There have been many studies, some dating back to at least the early 1930s (e. g., Allport, & Cantril, 1934), that have been concerned with relationships between the voice and various types of interpersonal attributes. Relatively few of the studies, however, were interested in the issue of how such attribution is affected by specific aspects of the voice. Among these specific aspects are *pitch, loudness, voice quality, intonation,* and, *accent,* as well as those parameters that index the timing of the speech sounds and silences. These appear to be the cues provided by the voice, and there are many colloquial expressions that attest to their role in impression formation. "Loud mouth," for example, suggests a person who is arrogant, vain, and "pushy" in interactions with others, but refers behaviorally to vocal intensity and quality. "Smooth talker" and "fast talker"

[2] Clearly, *what* is said (the semantic content of the interaction) may influence the formation of impressions. It seems to me, however, that certainly in a first encounter (although also in later encounters, to some extent) the ways in which something is said exerts more influence than the semantic meaning. It seems likely that when the words themselves affect impression formation, it is because they are unusual, shocking, or put together in unexpected ways.

both imply, in varying degrees, persuasiveness that is not entirely trustworthy, but they refer behaviorally to speech fluency and speech rate, respectively.

Although some systematic investigations of specific vocal cues began appearing in the literature several decades ago, most have appeared only recently. Extensive reviews of the earlier and later studies have been published by Sanford (1942), Kramer (1963), Siegman (1978), and Scherer (1979). However, it may be worth highlighting the findings briefly.

Pitch, loudness, and voice quality are the perceptual counterparts of three electroacoustically measurable parameters called *frequency, intensity*, and *timbre*, respectively. The three acoustic parameters essentially characterize the distribution and level of vocal energy. The fundamental frequency of a voice corresponds to the rate at which the vocal chords vibrate and together with the other voice frequencies partly determines what is perceived as the pitch of the voice. The intensity of a voice, or its amplitude, or energy level, is perceived as loudness although, as with frequency and pitch, the relations between the acoustic and perceived descriptions of the voice are not perfect. The perceptual counterpart of timbre, which is also called *voice quality* and concerns the energy composition of the voice spectrum, is even more difficult to specify. Adjectives such as harsh, breathy, guttural, and resonant are a few of the many that have been used to describe the subjective perception of timbre, or voice quality.

All three of the parameters appear to play some role in the identification of gender by means of the voice, although frequency seems to be the most important (Siegman, 1978). There is also evidence that frequency is associated with the attribution of certain personality traits and the most interesting studies concerned with this relationship have been conducted by Scherer and Brown and their associates. In general, Scherer (1979) has found that different characteristics are attributed to speakers with higher fundamental frequencies than to speakers with lower fundamental frequencies, and that the characteristics associated with the fundamental frequencies of German speakers are different from those attributed to American speakers. However, he has also found that the characteristics attributed to speakers with higher fundamental frequencies seem to indicate in some cases psychological stability, perseverance, and self-restraint whereas in other cases they indicate emotional lability and tension. To account for the difference, Scherer suggests that an increase in fundamental frequency may be a function of either increased muscle tone or increased psychological arousal, and that the two sources have distinguishable acoustic consequences and thus elicit different attributions. Using computer-manipulated changes in the variance of fundamental frequencies, Brown, Strong, and Rencher (1973; 1975) found that decreases and increases in the variability of male speaker's fundamental frequencies are associated with similar changes in ratings of the speakers' benevolence, although decreases in variance are also associated with decreases in ratings of competence.

A number of studies (Markel, Phillis, Vargas, & Howard, 1972; Scherer, 1978; Trimboli, 1973) seem to have clearly related vocal intensity and its subjective counterpart, loudness, to the expression and perception of extraversion and introversion. Another very recent investigation by Page and Balloun (1978) found that increasing the intensity or, to use their term, the ''volume'' of a voice resulted in ratings of increased aggressiveness but decreased self-assurance.

Timbre, or voice quality, has received perhaps the least systematic attention, probably because it is the most difficult to rate subjectively or even to describe objectively. There are some suggestive findings (Mallory & Miller, 1958; Moore, 1939) that harsh and resonant voices are associated with dominance and extraversion whereas breathy voices are associated with introversion and anxiety.

Apart from its apparently minimal role in gender identification, relatively little attention has been given to the function of intonation in person perception (Uldall, 1960). On the other hand, the influence of accent in impression formation has been examined quite extensively of late. For example, in Britain, the Standard English accent is related to highly favorable traits indicating competence whereas regional accents are rated more favorably in terms of traits having to do with personal integrity and social attractiveness (Cheyne, 1970; Giles, 1970, 1971; Giles & Powesland, 1975; Strongman & Woosley, 1967). In the United States and Canada, accents associated with low-status ethnic groups tend to be assigned unfavorable personality traits (Anisfeld, Bogo, & Lambert, 1962; Anisfeld & Lambert, 1964; Lambert, 1967; Lambert, Anisfeld, & Yeni-Komshian, 1965).

TEMPORAL PATTERNING

Although it is not usually distinguished as such, note that each category of behavior involves a temporal dimension. Moreover, the dimension seems to play some role in impression formation, whether it concerns speed of walking or rate of facial twitch or the duration of a glance. It was, indeed, Chapple (1940) who first suggested the related notion that the timing of body and muscle movements (in conjunction with speech) in interactions may provide culture-free indices of personality. Ms. Crown and I are interested in the timing not of body or facial or visual behavior but of speech alone, and especially speech within the context of two-person interactions. It seems to us that the timing of the speech sounds and silences in monologues and dialogues offers still another set of parameters that can influence the impressions of those who listen to the monologues or participate in the dialogues. Aronovitch (1976) found that faster speech rates were associated with ratings of extraversion, confidence, boldness, and dominance for both men and women. Apple, Streeter, and Krauss (cited by Scherer, 1979) report that speakers with slower rates were viewed as less persuasive, more passive, and weaker than those with faster rates. In an experiment by Brown, Strong, and Rencher (1973), in which speech rates were altered by a rate changer, the slower rates were related to judgments of less competence and the faster rates to judgments of less benevolence. A further report by Brown and his associates (Brown, Strong, & Rencher, 1975) described the relationship between benevolence and speech rate as curvilinear in that the slowest and fastest rates were judged to reflect the least benevolence.

The results of an experiment by Addington (1968) showed that when speakers increased their tempo, they were perceived to be extraverted. Ramsay (1968) failed to find such a relationship. He had not, however, manipulated tempo experimentally. Ramsey did find that extraverts used shorter pauses than introverts and Siegman and Pope (1965), using the same extraversion scale (Eysenck, 1967), found that the speech of their extraverts contained fewer long pauses than did that of their introverts. Siegman and Pope also discovered that their extraverts used shorter latencies. Scherer (1979), too, found a negative correlation between extraversion and *number* of silent hesitation pauses but no relation between extraversion and the *duration* of the pause. However, the results of a recent thesis by Sloan (1978) demonstrated that her extraverts did use a faster tempo and shorter pauses than her introverts. A particularly interesting feature of her experiment was that it attempted to distinguish between actual extraversion and the vocal stereotype of extraversion by having each of the introverted and extraverted subjects talk as if she were an introvert *and* an extravert. The results indicated that when they role-played extraverts, all the subjects used shorter pauses and faster tempos than when they role-played introverts. Of possibly greater interest is that even when they role-played extraverts and introverts, the extraverts used shorter pauses and faster tempos than did the introverts!

More recently, Ms. Crown and I (Feldstein, & Crown, 1978) examined the conversational exchanges of extraverts and introverts. We did something, however, that other investigators appear to have either not done or not reported. We used race and gender as independent variables and our results were surprising and puzzling. Our estimates of speech rate and pausing varied with extraversion in the expected directions, but they only distinguished black extraverts from black introverts! Thus, with regard to the white subjects, our results appear to be at variance with those of many previous studies.

One characteristic of dialogue that does not exist in monologue is the *speaking turn*, and a beginning has been made in exploring the relation of turn-taking to personality characteristics. Scherer (1979) reports that frequency of turns was related, in his study, to peer ratings of dominance for both his American and German speakers. Turn length was positively related to peer ratings of conscientiousness and emotional stability but only for his American speakers. Gallois and Markel (1975) explored the speaking turn as an index of "social personality" but never clarified what that meant. In a study some of my colleagues and I reported (Feldstein, Alberti, & BenDebba, 1979), we found that the duration of the speakers' turns seemed to be related not to their own personality characteristics but to those of their conversational partners.

Some Methodological Issues

For the most part, those studies that have been concerned with the relationship between how people talk and the characteristics that others attribute to them have tended to use two methodological strategies to obtain the attributes. The majority of studies have used spoken or constructed monologues for their stimulus speech samples. These were rated by groups of independent judges. Others have used, for their stimuli, speech samples excerpted from the interactions of two or more persons, or the interactions themselves (Sadd, Welkowitz, & Feldstein, 1978). In neither case, however, were the stimuli rated by those who participated in the interactions. Instead, the attributes were again provided by groups of judges who listened to the stimuli. (Some of the studies that Siegman, 1979, has done are exceptions to this observation.)

Yet it is within the context of conversational interactions

that interpersonal impressions are most frequently formed! Might we not, then, use conversations as the stimuli and the conversationalists as the judges? In other words, why not ask those who participate in conversations for their impressions of each other and correlate those impressions with the vocal parameters derived from the conversations? The most cogent objection to such a strategy is that in a face-to-face interaction the participants' impressions of each other may be, and probably are, influenced by all of the behaviors I have been discussing. Given the richness of the context, how are the results obtained to be interpreted? As always, there are at least two possibilities. The first is that no evidence is uncovered of a relationship between the temporal parameters of the conversations and the impressions of the participants. Such a result, while unsatisfying, presents no special interpretive problem. The other possibility is that some significant correlations are obtained among the temporal parameters and the participants' impressions. This outcome raises the old issue of causality.

The question is whether the impressions were elicited by the temporal patterning of the conversations or by other nonverbal cues highly correlated with the temporal patterning. This cannot be answered adequately within such a naturalistic study, although some useful information might be obtained by analyzing and correlating all of the possible nonverbal and vocal cues in the situation with one another and with the impressions. A limited attempt to implement this approach was recently made by Shrout (1978) in a study of impression formation and nonverbal behavior. Hayes and Bouma (1977), however, address themselves directly to the question after stating it in the form of an "alternative hypothesis": "... when talk levels are reported in the literature to be correlated with some social attribute (e. g., 'task leadership') that relationship is artifactual because those impressions are 'really' produced by some other information with which talk is highly correlated—such as what the speaker had to say or how he said it" (p. 115). The credibility of this hypothesis is considerably reduced by the results of a delightful set of experiments conducted by Hayes and his associates (Hayes, Meltzer, & Bouma, 1968; Hayes & Meltzer, 1972). The experiments used flashing lights to characterize the sound and silence patterns of actual conversations. That is, one light was used for each speaker, and it remained on while the speaker was talking and off while he was silent. The results indicated that an impressive array of traits were attributed to the speakers solely on the bases of the patterns of the flashing lights (i. e., the speakers' vocal activity patterns). These results are obviously exceedingly pertinent to my own concerns about the relation between temporal speech patterns and impression formation. Again, however, the impressions of the speakers were obtained from observers who did not participate in the conversations. Still, the best answer to the question, even when the impressions are those of persons who participate in the conversations, can only come from an experiment that controlled all but the temporal cues.

There are, on the other hand, some good and rather obvious reasons for beginning with naturalistic conversations to explore the influence of conversational rhythms on impression formation. First, it is initially simpler to ask subjects to engage in conversations and then provide their impressions of each other than to design the technologically difficult and expensive experiment that would be needed to establish causality. More importantly, the difficulty and expense of such an experiment could only be justified by the appropriate results of a naturalistic study. But these, after all, are the considerations usually used in planning research.

Another issue concerns the ways in which the participants' impressions of each other are characterized. Participants can simply be asked to describe each other in terms (words) of their own choosing. Or they can be provided with a set of terms, such as an adjective checklist, from which they are free to select the ones they believe are appropriate. Or they may be given a set of bipolar adjectival scales and asked to rate each other on all of the scales. Our concern, in other words, is with the choice of an adequate dependent variable. The three approaches mentioned above have different problems of reliability and generalizability and even questions about their validity may be raised. Employing bipolar adjective scales is probably the most useful experimental strategy, but do people think about or perceive others in such terms? Still another approach is to have each of the participants complete a personality questionnaire as he thinks his conversational partner would do it. Such an approach, however, is fraught with other problems. As the next chapter reveals, Ms. Crown and I decided to use adjective scales in our initial studies. It may well be, however, that a variety of approaches ought to be explored with at least one goal being to test the possibility of obtaining convergent validity.

Still other issues that have important methodological implications for the design and analysis of studies of impression formation in dyads have to do with the likely occurrence of mutual accomodation within the dyads (e. g., Dabbs, 1969; Feldstein & Welkowitz, 1978; Giles & Powesland, 1975; Natale, 1975) and the effect of the participants' own motivations and personality upon their perceptions of each other (Assor, Aronoff, & Messé, 1978; Kaplan, 1976; Messé, Stollak, Larson, & Michaels, 1979). These issues are quite complex and any reasonably useful discussion of them beyond noting their existence would carry us well beyond my intended scope of the chapter. Suffice it to say that the occurrence of interpersonal accomodation and the operation of the perceivers' motivations upon their interpersonal perceptions renders the investigation of impression formation in dyads high-risk research; the high risk is that the results of such investigations may often be worthless!

CONCLUDING REMARKS

The primary aims of this chapter are to provide a discussion of some of the background issues and problems that seem to be related to the study of impression formation and a rather brief review of the various types of behavior that might be expected to play a role in the forming of impressions (plus some of the pertinent literature). A number of points made during the discussion and review seem to me worth repeating. One is that the temporal dimension of behavior appears to provide potent cues for the formation of impressions. Another is that the exploration of impression formation ought to utilize the context in which impressions are most often formed, that is, the context of dyadic interactions. Within such a context, it may well be that the temporal patterning of verbal exchanges proves to be quite influential in the forming of at least first impressions.

Finally, a point very much worth re-emphasizing is that of the extraordinary importance of impression formation as a process that is involved in the shaping of almost every facet of our lives. Schneider (1976) asserts that Solomon Asch single-handedly initiated the formal study of impression formation *per se* in psychology. Yet questions about how we perceive others, how we arrive at such perceptions, and whether such perceptions have any "validity," surely form part of the very justification of psychology as a discipline and field of inquiry, and are part of the much broader concern with how we come to "know" the world about us.

ACKNOWLEDGMENT

The chapter was prepared while the author was a Visiting Professor (during the academic year of 1978–1979) with the Department of Research Psychology and the Psychotherapy Research Section of the Clarke Institute of Psychiatry (Department of Psychiatry of the University of Toronto, Canada). He is indebted to the Clarke Institute for its generous support and facilities.

REFERENCES

Addington, D. W. The relationship of selected vocal characteristics to personality perception. *Speech Monographs*, 1968, *35*, 492–503.

Allport, G., & Cantril, H. Judging personality from the voice. *Journal of Social Psychology*, 1934, *5*, 37–55.

Anisfeld, M., Bogo, N., & Lambert, W. E. Evaluational reactions to accented English speech. *Journal of Abnormal and Social Psychology*, 1962, *65*, 221–231.

Anisfeld, M., & Lambert, W. E. Evaluational reactions to bilingual and monolingual children to spoken languages. *Journal of Abnormal and Social Psychology*, 1964, *69*, 89–97.

Aronovitch, C. D. The voice of personality: Stereotyped judgments and their relation to voice quality and sex of speaker. *Journal of Social Psychology*, 1976, *99*, 207–220.

Assor, A., Aronoff, J., & Messé, L. A. *Cue-specific and general effects of psychological motives on impression formation.* Paper presented at the American Psychological Association, Toronto, Canada, August, 1978.

Berscheid, E., & Walster, E. Physical attractiveness. In L. Berkowitz (Ed.), *Advances in experimental social psychology* (Vol. 7). New York: Academic Press, 1973.

Brown, B. L., Strong, W. J., & Rencher, A. C. Perceptions of personality from speech: Effects of manipulations of acoustical parameters. *Journal of the Acoustical Society of America*, 1973, *54*(1), 29–35.

Brown, B. L., Strong, W. J., & Rencher, A. C. Acoustic determinants of perceptions of personality from speech. *International Journal of the Sociology of Language*, 1975, *6*, 11–32.

Chapple, E. D. Personality differences as described by invariant properties of individuals in interaction. *Proceedings of the National Academy of Sciences*, 1940, *26*, 10–16.

Cheyne, W. M. Stereotyped reactions to speakers with Scottish and English regional accents. *British Journal of Social and Clinical Psychology*, 1970, *9*, 77–79.

Cline, V. B. Interpersonal perception. In B. A. Maher (Ed.), *Progress in experimental personality research* (Vol. 1). New York: Academic Press, 1964, 221–284.

Cook, T. D. *Interpersonal perception.* New York: Penguin Press, 1971.

Dabbs, J. M. Similarity of gestures and interpersonal influence. *Proceedings of the 77th annual convention of the American Psychological Association*, 1969, *4*, 337–338.

Darwin, C. R. *The expression of the emotions in man and animals.* London: John Murray, 1872. (Reference from the University of Chicago Press editions, Chicago, 1965.)

Douty, H. I. Influence of clothing on perception of persons. *Journal of Home Economics*, 1963, *55*, 197–202.

Ekman, P. Facial expression. In A. W. Siegman, & S. Feldstein (Eds.), *Nonverbal behavior and communication.* Hillsdale, New Jersey: Lawrence Erlbaum Associates, 1978, 97–116.

Exline, R. V., & Fehr, B. J. Applications of semiosis to the study of visual interaction. In A. W. Siegman, & S. Feldstein (Eds.), *Nonverbal behavior and communication*. Hillsdale, New Jersey: Lawrence Erlbaum Associates, 1978, 117–158.

Eysenok, H. J. *The biological basis of personality*. Springfield, Illinois: Thomas, 1967.

Feldstein, S., Alberti, L., & BenDebba, M. Self-attributed personality characteristics and the pacing of conversational interaction. In A. W. Siegman, & S. Feldstein (Eds.), *Of speech and time: Temporal speech patterns in interpersonal contexts*. Hillsdale, New Jersey: Lawrence Erlbaum Associates, 1979, 73–87.

Feldstein, S., & Crown, C. L. *Conversational time patterns as a function of introversion and extraversion*. Paper presented at the Eastern Psychological Association, Washington, D. C., March, 1978.

Feldstein, S., & Welkowitz, J. A chronography of conversation: In defense of an objective approach. In A. W. Siegman, & S. Feldstein (Eds.), *Nonverbal behavior and communication*. Hillsdale, New Jersey: Lawrence Erlbaum Associates, 1978, 329–378.

Gallois, C., & Markel, N. N. Turn taking: Social personality and conversational style. *Journal of Personality and Social Psychology*, 1975, *31*, 1134–1140.

Giles, H. Evaluative reactions to accents. *Educational Review*, 1970, *22*, 211–227.

Giles, H. Patterns of evaluation to R. P., South Welsh and Somerset accented speech. *British Journal of Social and Clinical Psychology*, 1971, *10*, 280–281.

Giles, H., & Powesland, P. F. *Speech style and social evaluation*. New York: Academic Press, 1975.

Hamid, P. N. Style of dress as a perceptual cue in impression formation. *Perceptual and Motor Skills*, 1968, *26*, 901–906.

Hastorf, A. H., Schneider, D. J., & Polefka, J. *Person perception*. Massachusetts: Addison-Wesley, 1970.

Hayes, D. P., & Bouma, G. D. Patterns of vocalization and impression formation. *Semiotica*, 1977, *13*(2), 113–129.

Hayes, D. P., & Meltzer, L. Interpersonal judgments based on talkativeness. *Sociometry*, 1972, *35*(4), 538–561.

Hayes, D. P., Meltzer, L., & Bouma, G. D. Activity as a determinant of interpersonal perception. *Proceedings of the American Psychological Association*, 1968, 417–418.

Hayward, S. C., & Neetz, R. A. *Effect of walking speed on interpersonal distance and person perception*. Paper presented at the American Psychological Association, Toronto, Canada, 1978.

Hess, E. H., & Petrovich, S. B. Pupillary behavior in communication. In A. W. Siegman, & S. Feldstein (Eds.), *Nonverbal behavior and communication*. Hillsdale, New Jersey: Lawrence Erlbaum Associates, 1978, 159–182.

Hillabrant, W. The influence of locomotion and gaze direction on perceptions of interactive persons. *Personality and Social Psychology Bulletin*, 1974, *1*, 337–339.

Izard, C. E. *The face of emotion*. New York: Appleton, 1971.

Kaplan, M. F. Measurement and generality of response dispositions in person perception. *Journal of Personality*, 1976, *44*, 179–194.

Kleinke, C. L. Interpersonal attraction as it relates to gaze and distance between people. *Representative Research in Social Psychology*, 1972, *3*, 105–120.

Kleinke, C. L., Staneski, R. A., & Berger, D. L. Evaluation of an interviewer as a function of interviewer gaze, reinforcement of subject gaze and interviewer attractiveness. *Journal of Personality and Social Psychology*, 1975, *31*, 115–122.

Kramer, E. Judgment of personal characteristics and emotions from nonverbal properties of speech. *Psychological Bulletin*, 1963, *60*, 408–420.

Lambert, W. E. A social psychology of bilingualism. *Journal of Social Issues*, 1967, *23*, 99–100.

Lambert, W. E., Anisfeld, M., & Yeni-Komshian, G. Evaluational reactions of Jewish and Arab adolescents to dialect and language variations. *Journal of Personality and Social Psychology*, 1965, *2*, 84–90.

Mallory, E., & Miller, V. A. A possible basis for the association of voice characteristics and personality traits. *Speech Monographs*, 1958, *25*, 255–280.

Markel, N. N., Phillis, J. A., Vargas, R., & Howard, K. Personality traits associated with voice types. *Journal of Psycholinguistic Research*, 1972, *1*, 249–255.

Massillon, A. M., & Hillabrant, W. *Effects of a stimulus person's nonverbal displays on impression formation*. Paper presented at the American Psychological Association, Toronto, Canada, August, 1978.

Messé, L. A., Stollak, G. E., Larson, R. W., & Michaels, G. Y. Interpersonal consequences of person perception processes in two social contexts. *Journal of Personality and Social Psychology*, 1979, *37*, 369–379.

Moore, G. E. Personality traits and voice quality deficiencies. *Journal of Speech Disorders*, 1939, *4*, 33–36.

Natale, M. Convergence of mean vocal intensity in dyadic communication as a function of social desirability. *Journal of Personality and Social Psychology*, 1975, *32*, 790–804.

Page, R. A., & Balloun, J. L. The effect of voice volume on the perception of personality. *Journal of Social Psychology*, 1978, *105*, 65–72.

Ramsay, R. W. Speech patterns and personality. *Language and Speech*, 1968, *11*, 54–63.

Sadd, S., Welkowitz, J., & Feldstein, S. Judgments of characteristics of speakers in a natural stress situation. *Perceptual and Motor Skills*, 1978, *47*, 47–54.

Sanford, F. H. Speech and personality. *Psychological Bulletin*, 1942, *30*, 811–845.

Scherer, K. R. Personality markers in speech. In K. R. Scherer, & H. Giles (Eds.), *Social markers in speech*. London: Cambridge University Press, 1979.

Scherer, K. R. Inference rules in personality attribution from voice quality: The loud voice of extraversion. *European Journal of Social Psychology*, 1978, *8*, 467–487.

Scherwitz, L., & Helmrich, R. Interactive effective eye contact and verbal content on interpersonal attraction in dyads. *Journal of Personality and Social Psychology*, 1973, *27*, 405–408.

Schneider, D. J. *Social psychology*. Massachusetts: Addison-Wesley, 1976.

Shrout, P. E. *Impression formation and nonverbal behaviors: Effects of observer/target sex*. Paper presented at the American Psychological Association, Toronto, Canada, August, 1978.

Siegman, A. W. The telltale voice: Nonverbal messages of verbal communication. In A. W. Siegman, & S. Feldstein (Eds.), *Nonverbal behavior and communication*. Hillsdale, New Jersey: Lawrence Erlbaum Associates, 1978, 183–244.

Siegman, A. W. The voice of attraction: Verbal correlates of interpersonal attraction in the interview. In A. W. Siegman, & S. Feldstein (Eds.), *Of speech and time: Temporal speech patterns in interpersonal contexts*. Hillsdale, New Jersey: Lawrence Erlbaum Associates, 1979, 89–113.

Siegman, A. W., & Pope, B. Personality variables associated with productivity and verbal fluency in the initial interview. *Proceedings of the 73rd annual convention of the American Psychological Association*, 1965, 273–274.

Sloan, B. *Speech tempo in extraversion and introversion*. Paper presented at the Eastern Psychological Association, Washington, D. C., March, 1978.

Strongman, K. T., & Woosley, J. Stereotyped reactions to regional accents. *British Journal of Social and Clinical Psychology*, 1967, *6*, 164–167.

Tagiuri, R. Person perception. In G. Lurdgey, & E. Aronson (Eds.), *The handbook of social psychology* (Vol. 3). Massachusetts: Addison-Wesley, 1969, 395–449.

Trimboli, F. Changes in voice characteristics as a function of trait and state personality variables. *Dissertation abstracts international*, 1973, *33*, 3965.

Uldall, E. Attitudinal meanings conveyed by intonation contours. *Language and Speech*, 1960, *3*, 223–234.

Chapter 11

IMPRESSION FORMATION AND THE CHRONOGRAPHY OF DYADIC INTERACTIONS

Cynthia L. Crown

Mark Twain once said, "It's better to keep your mouth shut and appear stupid than to open it and remove all doubt," thereby calling attention to the importance of speech sounds and silences in impression formation. It only remains to demonstrate the relationship empirically and the present chapter describes some first approaches to that end. It reports two studies, both of which were concerned with the relation between the temporal structure of dyadic conversation and the impressions that the participants formed of each other.

STUDY ONE

The first study[1] Dr. Feldstein and I conducted involved relatively unconstrained conversations. Its purpose was to explore

[1] This report of the first study is based upon a paper Dr. Feldstein and I (1979) presented to the Eastern Psychological Association.

225

the possibility that the attributions made by conversational participants about each other are a function of the time patterns of their verbal interaction. The data of the present study were collected as part of another study (Feldstein, 1977), the results of which indicated that conversational time patterns are influenced by the race and gender of the participants.

Method

The participants of the study were 96 white and 74 black undergraduate university students who were either paid for their participation or used their participation to fulfill one of the requirements of their introductory psychology course. Of the 96 white students, 43 were men and 53 were women; of the 74 black students, 24 were men and 50 were women. The average age of all the students was 19.1 years, with a sigma of 1.9 years. The participants were assembled into dyads such that they formed 10 groups. Each group of dyads represented a different combination of gender and race; the 10 groups exhausted the number of possible combinations.

Each pair of potential participants was shown into the waiting room of the laboratory and asked to consider signing a consent form that described the experiment as an attempt to better understand the verbal ways in which people become acquainted with each other. Those who agreed (and all did) were taken to a very comfortably furnished, sound-damped and -proofed room in the laboratory and asked to engage in a 15-minute conversation, the purpose of which was to enable them to get to know one another.

After the conversation, each person was asked to describe him- or herself and his or her conversational partner in terms of a set of 20 bipolar, 7-point adjective scales (Table 11.1).[2] For the

[2] The set of scales was assembled by Drs. S. Feldstein, C. C. Dahlberg, and J. Jaffe for use in a drug study conducted by them ("Effects of LSD-25 on Psychotherapeutic Communication," NIMH Research Grant No. MH-11670, 1965–1971).

analyses presented here, we asked a group of independent judges to decide which adjective of each pair was negative and which was positive, and we scored the positive pole of each scale 1 and the negative pole, 7. The score used in the statistical analyses was the sum of the 20 scales.

Table 11.1 Bipolar Adjective Scales

DECISIVE	INDECISIVE
UNINTELLIGENT	INTELLIGENT
BORING	INTERESTING
WARM	COLD
DEPENDENT	INDEPENDENT
INCONSIDERATE	CONSIDERATE
RESPONSIVE	UNRESPONSIVE
MEAN	KIND
DEPRESSED	CHEERFUL
RESERVED	OUTGOING
ADJUSTED	MALADJUSTED
CALM	EXCITABLE
ATTRACTIVE	UNATTRACTIVE
NEAT	SLOVENLY
POISED	SELF-CONSCIOUS
SENSITIVE	INSENSITIVE
IMPATIENT	PATIENT
CANDID	SECRETIVE
REJECTING	ACCEPTING
SELFISH	UNSELFISH

The parameters that are used to index conversational time patterns are speaking turns, vocalizations, pauses, switching pauses, and simultaneous speech (Feldstein, BenDebba, & Alberti, 1974; Jaffe & Feldstein, 1970). All are derived automatically from the sound-silence sequences of conversations by a special analogue-to-digital converter system (Cassotta,

Feldstein, & Jaffe, 1964). Of the five parameters, only vocalizations, pauses, and switching pauses were examined in this study. A vocalization is a segment of speech uttered by the participant who has the floor (or speaking turn) that is uninterrupted by any silence discernible to the normally functioning human ear. A pause is an interval of joint silence bounded by the vocalizations of the participant who has the floor, and a switching pause is an interval of joint silence that begins after a vocalization of the speaker who has the floor and is terminated by a vocalization of the other speaker, who thereby obtains the floor. It is credited to the participant who relinquished the floor.

Two values of the three parameters were used in the data analyses: their average durations and proportionality constants. (The proportionality constant of an event usually implies that the durations of the event are exponentially distributed and it is identical to the probability that the event will continue.) Another measure — the proportionality constant ratio (PCR) — was computed by dividing the proportionality constant of pauses into the proportionality constant of vocalizations. Previous research (Feldstein, 1976) found the PCR to be highly correlated with words-per-minute, a measure of speech rate.

Results and Discussion

The data we obtained were subjected to hierarchical multiple regression analyses. For the major aim of the study, seven regression equations were used, one for each of the two values of the three temporal parameters and one for the PCR, and we determined the order in which the independent, or predictor, variables entered the equations (Cohen & Cohen, 1975). There were four sets of independent variables. The first set to enter each equation consisted of the gender and race of the participants. The second set involved the average durations or the proportionality constants of one of the temporal parameters or the PCR. The third set was comprised of the products of race and gender, and of the product of each with the variable in the second set.

The fourth and final set consisted only of the products of race times gender times the values of the temporal variable in set two. Given the order in which the independent variables entered each equation, the product variables carried the effects of whatever interactions may have occurred among the three variables.

The dependent, or criterion, variable in each equation consisted of the perceptions of the participants by their partners, that is, the sums of their partners' ratings of them on the set of 20 adjective scales. However, the participants' ratings of themselves on the 20 scales were used as the dependent variable in the solutions of another seven regression equations otherwise identical to those described above. These seven equations served to explore a minor interest of the study, namely, the possibility that an individual's self-perceptions influence or are influenced by his or her conversational time patterns (Feldstein, Alberti, & BenDebba, 1979).

Only two of the main effects concerned with the partners' impressions of each other are interesting. The first is that women were perceived by their partners in more positive ways than were the men whether their partners were men or women ($F_{1,168} = 4.595, p = .03$).

The second is of borderline significance ($p = .06$) but is worth noting because the study was exploratory. In general, those speakers whose probabilities of continuing to pause were high tended to be viewed more negatively by their partners than were those speakers whose probabilities were low. Of particular interest here is that those speakers whose probabilities of continuing to pause were high also viewed themselves in more negative ways than did those whose probabilities were low ($F_{1,166} = 4.889, p = .03$). The finding with regard to their partners' perceptions, however, is modified by an interaction effect ($F_{1,162} = 4.036, p = .04$) which indicates that the white males and black females in the study were viewed by their partners more negatively when their probabilities of continuing to pause were high than when they were low. On the other hand, white females tended to be seen in more positive ways as their probabilities of continuing to pause increased. The perception of black males, however, was not noticeably affected by their pause probabilities (Fig. 11-1a).

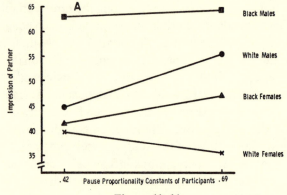

Figure 11–1A

The analysis of the switching-pause probabilities also yielded an interaction effect ($F_{1, 162} = 4.289$, $p = .04$). White men and black women were assigned more negative attributes the more likely it was that their switching pauses would continue (Fig. 11-1b). For the same behavior, however, black men and white women were assigned more positive attributes.

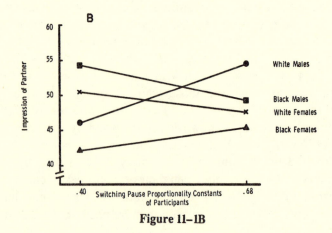

Figure 11–1B

Finally, another interaction effect $(F1,162 = 5.158, p = .02)$ was obtained that involved the PCR, or speech rate. The effect indicates that the faster their rates of speech (that is, the higher their PCRs), the more positive were the characteristics attributed to the white men and black women by their partners. The black men, however, were viewed more negatively when their speech rates were high than when they were low, and the perception of the white women by their partners was not related to their speech rates (Fig. 11-1c).

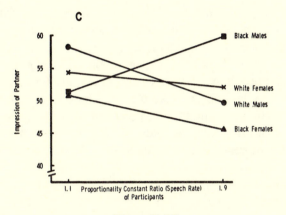

Figure 11–1C

The results suggest that the impressions that the conversationalists formed of each other appear to be related, at least in part, to the silences of their verbal exchanges and to their rates of speech. It may be, however, that the silence and speech-rate variables are mediating relationships between the participants' impressions and other aspects of their conversations to which we were not attending.

Similarities in impressions of the white men and black women as contrasted with a different set of impressions which grouped the black men and white women were not expected. This grouping of white men with black women and black men with white women may reflect subcultural status patterns.

STUDY TWO[3]

Whereas the purpose of the second study was the same as that of the first one, the second study involved interviews rather than unconstrained conversations and the subjects were all female. We could not therefore pursue the examination of the gender and race influences on interpersonal perception indicated in Study One. The purpose of this second project, then, was to examine the relationship between how the interviewers paced their verbal interactions and how they were perceived by the interviewees.

An issue not addressed in the first study is concerned with whether a speaker's own temporal patterns are related to his impressions of his conversational partner. Possibly the ways in which a speaker paces his interaction with another speaker depends upon how he views that person. If, for example, he decides that he does not like the other person, he may not say much at all. Thus, another purpose of this study was to explore the relations between the interviewees' *own* temporal patterns and their impressions of the interviewers.

Method

The interviewees of the study were 63 female university undergraduates who volunteered to participate in order to fulfill one of the requirements in their introductory psychology course. Twelve other female undergraduates who were students in a course concerned with interviewing skills served as observers in the study. The interviewers were five women in their second year of graduate study, who wished to obtain interview experience.

The interviews were only moderately constrained in that the interviewers' verbal responses included not only structured questions but also questions based upon the specific remarks of

[3] Although methodologically similar, the study reported here is not any of those discussed by Dr. Aron Siegman in his chapter.

the interviewees. However, the interviews did involve four conditions created by the behavior of the interviewers: warm, cold, warm followed by cold, and cold followed by warm. In the warm and cold conditions, the interviewers behaved toward the interviewees in a manner that was "warm" or "cold," respectively, during the entire interview whereas in the other two conditions the interviewers were "warm" or "cold" during the first half of the interview and the opposite during the second half of the interview. For the warm condition, the interviewers were instructed to establish eye contact with the interviewees, smile, nod their heads, lean forward, and use the interjection, "mm-hmm," at appropriate times. They were instructed, however, to refrain entirely from initiating such behaviors in the cold condition. Using each other as interviewees, the interviewers practiced the conditions several times before participating in the experiment. In addition, each interviewer conducted two pilot interviews and were evaluated by the experimenter for their proficiency in creating the conditions.

One further manipulation was introduced. Four standard questions were asked in each interview. However, each was followed by two questions, the content of which was determined by the interviewer during the interview (although it was presumably relevant to the content of the preceding standard question). The manipulation involved the content of the standard questions. In half of all the interviews, the questions were of an intimate nature; in the remaining interviews, they were of a nonintimate nature. (The distinction between intimate and nonintimate content was determined by a separate study.) The content and type (intimate or nonintimate) of the questions and the conditions were counterbalanced across the interviewers. A series of 16 practice interviews held prior to the study helped in the anticipation and clarification of most areas of potential misunderstanding. In the rare instance, however, in which an interviewee did not understand a question, it was rephrased.

A measure of impression formation was used that had an already defined factor structure and could, therefore, be interpreted in specific ways. The instrument is one of seven alternative instruments developed by Goldberg and his associates (1977). They attempted to uncover the underlying groupings of words in the English language that refer or seem to refer to personality characteristics. Their assumption is that individual differences that play an important role in interpersonal transactions are bound to become encoded into the language.

The instrument is called the Layman Unconstrained Taxonomy because it was developed by Mark Layman of the Goldberg group (Goldberg, 1978, p. 82), and represents the most ambitious attempt by the group to structure the domain of trait terms. It is unconstrained in the sense that it was not guided by any particular theoretical scheme but is based upon the judgments of Layman and of professional lexicographers. Analysis of the instrument indicated that over half of its variance is accounted for by five factors: dominance, antagonism, conscientiousness, creativity, and emotional stability.

Potential interviewees were shown into the waiting room of the laboratory by the interviewers and asked to complete a consent form that described the experiment as an effort to compare the social histories of students from the university with those of students from several of the local colleges. After agreeing to participate, the interviewees were taken to the same room used in the first study and asked to sit in a comfortable chair across from the interviewer. They were informed that they were not required to answer any of the questions they were to be asked, but that it would be very helpful to the interviewer and the study if they would answer all of the questions as thoroughly as possible. They were also told that the interview would be observed by another student through the vision screen (built into one wall of the room) for the purpose of rating the interviewer on various interviewing skills, but that the content of the interview would be maintained in the strictest confidentiality.

The interviewees were asked to indicate when their answers were completed by simply saying "finished" in order that there be no ambiguity about when they relinquished the floor. As a consequence of this request, one of the temporal parameters used in the first study, switching pauses, was not used in this study. Recall that a switching pause is an interval of silence initiated by the speaker who has the floor and terminated by the other speaker (who thereby obtains the floor). The switching pause is presumed to be a pause of the speaker who initiates it based upon the assumption that, within ordinary conversation, it is not necessarily the case that because the speaker who has the floor has stopped phonating he has relinquished the floor. The assumption fails, however, in an interaction in which the speaker who has the floor declares his intention to relinquish it. In that case, the silence that follows the declaration becomes the time in which the person who did not have the floor can begin to speak, in effect, his reaction time or *latency*. Thus, in the second study, the parameter, latencies, was used instead of switching pauses. Following the interview, the interviewees were asked to complete some forms to obtain demographic information and ratings of the interviewees' impressions of the interviewer. After they completed the three forms, the interviewees were told about the specific ways in which their interviews would be analyzed.

Results

Two manipulation checks were conducted. In order to determine whether the four conditions were successfully induced, the observers of the study monitored the interviews through the vision screen and separately rated the first and second halves of the interviews on a set of adjectival scales.[4] In all cases their ratings appropriately reflected the conditions they observed. In addition, during the debriefing the interviewees were requested to note whether they felt they had been asked intimate or nonintimate questions. In all but two cases, the interviewees' reports were consistent with the type of questions in their interviews.

[4] Although the observers were unaware of the conditions they observed, they were probably aware of important interview variables as a function of their participation in the interviewing course and it is difficult to know how or whether such knowledge affected their assessments.

As in the first study, the present data were analyzed by means of hierarchical multiple regression equations. Again, the order of the independent variables were such that the variables representing the experimental conditions and the type of questions were entered into the equations first along with one of the temporal parameters. (The frequencies as well as the average durations and proportionality constants of the parameters were used in the study.) These were followed by the products of pairs of the three variables and the products of the three variables ordered so as to yield the appropriate interaction effects.

The dependent variable in each equation was one of the five factors of the Layman Taxonomy. Inasmuch as the regression analyses indicated that only three of the factors were significantly related to the temporal patterns of the interviewers and interviewees, I shall confine my comments to those three factors. They are called by Layman, "dominance," "conscientiousness," and "creativity."[5] Inasmuch as these labels seem to imply more than the adjectives of which they are comprised, I shall refer to them as factors A, B, and C, respectively.

[5] Note the adjectives that define the dominance factor: self-assertive, vigorous, bold, cheerful, gregarious, self-assured, persevering, purposeful, pretentious, attractive, passionate, and creative. They seem to suggest an individual who has a firm sense of self and security and is self-confident. If the label, dominance, is meant and taken to imply just these characteristics, then it is adequate. I suspect, however, that it is often thought to include other traits such as demanding, selfish, manipulative, etc., that it is, in other words, often confused with domineering. The factor, conscientiousness, is primarily described by the adjectives: methodical, responsible, exact, rational, realistic, mature, sophisticated, loyal, scholarly, articulate, and intelligent, although intelligent loads somewhat more heavily on another of Layman's five factors. Conscientiousness does seem, therefore, to be a fair label for these traits. The most unfortunate label is that of the factor, creativity. It is defined by the traits: liberal, reflective, perceptive, just, intricate, and—unofficially—intelligent. But creativity means so many different things to different people that to use it as a label for the particular combination of the above traits seems quite arbitrary. The two factors, incidentally, that were found not to be related to any of the temporal variables in the present study were called by Layman, antagonism and emotional stability.

Interviewer Behavior.   The analyses of the influence of the interviewers' temporal speech behavior upon the perceptions of the interviewees yielded two main effects. Interviewers tended to be rated as more liberal, reflective, perceptive, just, and intricate (i. e., they received higher ratings on factor C), $F_{1,54} = 4.16, p < .05$ and $F_{1,54} = 4.16, p < .05$. Although the number of latencies a speaker uses is related to the frequency with which he has the floor or, in other words, the number of turns he takes, the two counts are not identical. It is possible to begin speaking as soon as one is given the floor, in which case no latency occurs. It is also possible to use few or many vocalizations and they may be long or short; their frequency and duration are not necessarily related unless the time available to the speakers is fixed. In any case, it is not clear why those interviewers who began to talk as soon as they obtained the floor should have been thought to be more reflective; intuitively, one might have guessed the opposite to be true.

The other significant findings were that the perceptions of the interviewees were influenced jointly by the behavior of the interviewers and the various conditions of the interviews. I shall describe these findings in terms of the temporal parameter involved.

Vocalizations.   The interviewers' average durations of vocalizations interacted with two conditions of the interviews such that those interviewers who tended to use longer vocalizations were rated as more liberal, reflective, perceptive, just, and intricate when they participated in the cold-to-warm condition (i.e., interviews in which the behavior of the interviewers changed from cold to warm) but as *less* liberal, reflective, etc., when they participated in the warm-to-cold condition ($F_{1,51} = 12.46, p < .01$). However, the factor C ratings do not appear to have distinguished between the two conditions of those interviewers whose vocalizations tended to be generally shorter (Fig. 11-2a).

There was also an interaction of the warm and cold conditions with the proportionality constants of the interviewers'

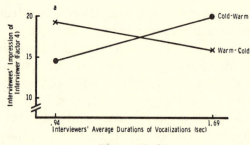

Figure 11–2A

vocalizations such that those interviewers in the warm condition whose probabilities of continuing their vocalizations were high received much higher factor B ratings than those whose probabilities were low ($F_{1,50} = 5.09$, $p < .05$). People with high probabilities of continuing these vocalizations were perceived as being much more methodical, responsible, exact, rational, and mature or, in short, conscientious. However, a relatively minimal difference in factor B ratings was associated with the proportionality constants of the interviewers' vocalizations in the cold condition (Fig. 11-2b).

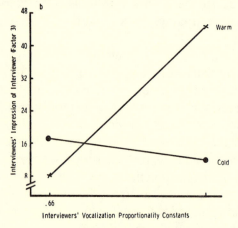

Figure 11–2B

Differences in types of questions asked interacted with the proportionality constants of the interviewers' vocalizations in relation to factor B ($F_{1,52} = 4.80$, $p < .05$). In those interviews in which intimate questions were asked, those interviewers with low probabilities of continuing their vocalizations were seen as more conscientious than were those with high probabilities. In those interviews in which nonintimate questions were asked, however, ratings of conscientiousness do not appear to have been strongly related to the proportionality constants of the interviewers' vocalizations (Fig. 11-2c).

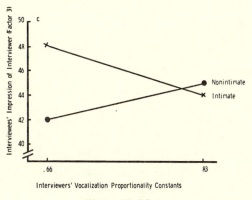

Figure 11–2C

Latencies. The interviewees' perceptions of their interviewers' degrees of conscientiousness were related to the joint effects of question type, the warm-to-cold and cold-to-warm conditions, and the proportionality constants of the interviewers' latencies ($F_{1,47} = 5.63$, $p < .05$). The major contribution came from those interviewers who asked nonintimate questions (Fig. 11-3). Those interviewers who were thought to be more conscientious were either in the cold-to-warm condition and were likely to continue their latencies once they had begun, or in the warm-to-cold condition and were likely to discontinue their latencies shortly after they had begun. None of the other temporal parameters of the interviewers' speech apparently influenced the interviewees' perceptions.

These complex results are difficult to describe but it may help to imagine what interviewers with these patterns are like. Interviewers seen as self-assured, persevering, purposeful, lib-

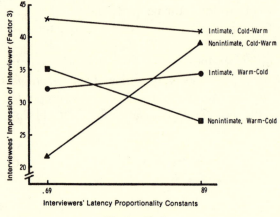

Figure 11-3

eral, and reflective were those who, in the cold interviews, tended to discontinue their vocalizations shortly after having begun them, and to ask nonintimate questions. In the warm interviews, they tended to continue their vocalizations after having begun, whether they asked intimate or nonintimate questions. Interviewers who were seen as more responsible, exact, mature, articulate, and scholarly, asked nonintimate questions either in the cold-to-warm condition and were likely to continue their latencies once they had begun, or in the warm-to-cold condition and were likely to discontinue their latencies shortly after they had begun. Interviewers were also rated as conscientious who behaved warmly and tended to continue talking after having started, and those who tended to discontinue talking when they asked intimate questions.

Interviewee Behavior.   We are concerned here with the relation between the interviewees' perceptions of the interviewers and the interviewees' own temporal behavior in the interviews. Although the analyses were done and the graphs drawn as if the former were being predicted by the latter, they could have done and drawn in the opposite way. Our present state of knowledge is unable to dictate the appropriate direction. Intuitively, it seems to me reasonable to expect that the interviewees' behavior is, at least in part, a function of their perceptions of the interviewers and I shall discuss the results from this perspective.

The analyses of the interviewees' temporal parameters yielded two main effects and a host of interactions. Those interviewees who perceived their interviewers to be less conscientious tended to have longer latencies when they took the floor ($F_{1,54} = 6.09, p < .05$). In addition, those interviewees who rated their interviewers high on factor A (i. e., saw them as more self-assertive, vigorous, bold, gregarious, etc.) were less likely to continue a latency after having begun one ($F_{1,54} = 4.26, p < .05$).

Vocalizations. The proportionality constants of the interviewees' vocalizations interacted with question type ($F_{1,50} = 5.25, p < .05$). Those interviewees who were asked nonintimate questions and were likely to continue their vocalizations after having started, rated their interviewers high on conscientiousness, whereas those who were asked nonintimate questions and were *not* likely to continue phonating gave their interviewers low rating on conscientiousness (Fig. 11-4a).

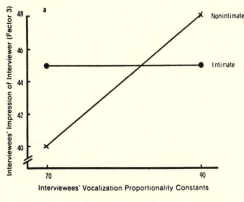

Figure 11–4A

Latencies. The number of latencies engaged in by the interviewees interacted with the warm and cold conditions of the interviews and with the type of question that was asked ($F_{1,47}$

$= 7.43, p < .01$). This interaction suggests that there is not much of a difference between the factor A ratings given by those interviewees with few or many latencies who were asked intimate or nonintimate questions in the warm interviews or intimate questions in the cold interviews. However, those interviewees who initiated many latencies tended, when they were asked nonintimate questions in the cold interviews, to view their interviewers as considerably more self-assertive, vigorous, self-assured, persevering, etc., than did those interviewees who initiated few latencies in the same situation (Fig. 11-4b).

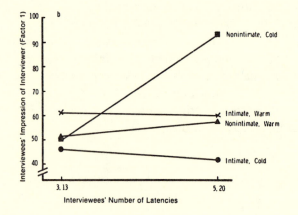

Figure 11–4B

Pauses.   The remaining interaction effects involve the pauses of the interviewees. As can be seen in Fig. 11-5a, the average duration of the interviewees' pauses are related to their perceptions of the interviewers' degrees of conscientiousness, but only for those interviewees who were asked intimate questions in the warm interviews ($F_{1,47} = 4.45, p < .05$). Of them, those interviewees who rated their interviewers high on conscientiousness had much shorter average pause durations than those who gave low ratings to their interviewers on conscientiousness.

In addition, those interviewees with long average pause durations tended to perceive their interviewers to have been

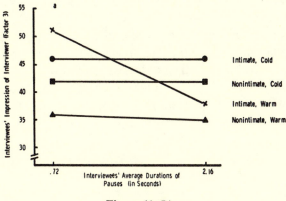

Figure 11–5A

more liberal, reflective, perceptive, etc., if they had been asked nonintimate questions than if they had been asked intimate questions ($F_{1,50} = 9.18$, $p < .01$). Put another way, those interviewees who rated their interviewers high on the characteristics associated with factor C had either been asked nonintimate questions and had long average pause durations, or had been asked intimate questions but had short average pause durations (Fig. 11-5b).

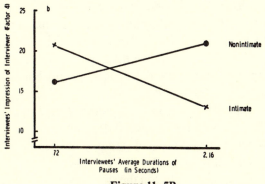

Figure 11–5B

Finally, the interviewees' perceptions of the interviewers as self-assured, bold, persevering, etc. appear to have been jointly affected by the proportionality constants of the interviewees' pauses and by the type of interviews in which they participated ($F_{1,52} = 4.46$, $p < .05$). Specifically, of the interviewees whose pause probabilities were high, those in the warm interviews rated the interviewer much higher on the characteristics of factor A than did those interviewees who were in the cold interviews (Fig. 11-5c). There were, however, no marked differences between the perceptions of the interviewees whose pause probabilities were low.

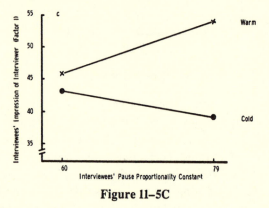

Figure 11–5C

Discussion

The results of this second study lend further support to the notion that the temporal patterning of an individual's participation in a dialogue is partially responsible for the impressions formed about him or her by the other person in the dialogue. Together the studies indicate this process occurs both in unconstrained conversations and in interviews. Considering the findings of the experimental studies conducted by Hayes and his associates (and reported in Hayes and Bouma, 1977), in which they transformed conversational patterns into light patterns to which consistent trait attributions were made, and considering the striking differences between the two studies reported here in terms of type of interaction, type of participants, and type of attribution scales, at least the evidence for the notion is gathering.

On the other hand, the present two studies make it quite

clear that the relation between impression formation and the temporal patterning of interaction is complex. For example, the characteristics attributed to the interviewers depended not simply upon their sound-silence patterns, but also upon the type of questions they asked, upon whether their behavior in interaction was warm or reserved, and even upon the sound-silence patterns of the interviewees. And in the first study, the impressions that the participants formed of each other appear to have been based not only upon their sound-silence but upon their gender and race. Moreover, in the second study, the same temporal behavior elicited different impressions depending on the specific situational, or contextual, cues. An obvious implication of the present findings is that studies investigating the relation between impression formation and sound-silence parameters need to take both contextual and demographic variables into account.

The findings of the second study provide evidence that the interviewees' impressions of the interviewers were related to the temporal patterns of the interviewees' own participation in the interviews. They suggest, in more general terms, that the interpersonal perceptions of a pair of interacting individuals correlate with the speech sounds and silences of both the perceived and the perceiver. Unfortunately, however, the results provide no information about whether the perceiver's speech patterns influence his or her perceptions or vice versa. I mentioned earlier that arguments can be made for either case, although it may be that the influence is mutual. Research is obviously needed to clarify the issue.

Both studies are correlational in approach, and there has been no cross-validation, so caution is needed in interpreting and generalizing the results. For instance, given the importance of gender and race in the relationships depicted by the findings of the first study, it is not clear that the findings of the second study can be generalized to male and/or black interviewers and interviewees. Yet the relationships revealed in the second study are sufficiently strong to deserve further attention; the amounts of variance (of the impression scores) for which the interaction effects reported here account range from 5 to 25 percent. More-over, it is important to remember that these reliable relation-ships are the results not of a group of judges, all of whom are responding to the same configuration of speech and silence patterns, but of a group of individuals, each of whom is respond-ing to a different configuration of speech and silence patterns, one in which he/she has participated.

CONCLUDING COMMENTS

It is interesting to know which of the temporal parameters correlate with which of the factors of the Layman Taxonomy as the present study indicates. It would also be interesting to know the combined contribution of all the parameters that play a role in impression formation either to particular impressions (factors) formed by the perceivers or to the total pattern of impressions they form about their interviewers or conversational partners. Such an analysis is now being conducted.

The results of both studies suggest that further research is warranted, especially experimental investigations that control for various other types of nonverbal behavior that may be con-tributing to interpersonal perception, or investigations in which the temporal parameters are varied in order to assess more carefully and specifically their influence on impression forma-tion. Still another approach would be to experimentally induce the impressions that dyad participants form about each prior to their conversation and then examine the effect of the manipula-tion on the temporal patterns of the participants.

At present, however, the evidence of the studies reported here, and of the relatively few that are beginning to be reported elsewhere (e. g., Brown, 1980; Siegman and Crown, 1981), indicates that the chronography of dyadic verbal interaction does play a notable role in impression formation.

ACKNOWLEDGMENT

The author is deeply indebted to Drs. Stanley Feldstein and Marilyn Wang for their unstinting help in the preparation of the chapter. She is also grateful to the Statistics Center of the University of Maryland Baltimore County and Computer Center of the University of Maryland College Park for the generous amount of computer time they contributed to both studies.

REFERENCES

Brown, B. L. Effects of speech rate on personality attributions and competency evaluations. In W. P. Robinson, H. Giles, & P. M. Smith (Eds.), *Language: Social psychological perspectives.* London: Pergamon, 1980.

Cassotta, L., Feldstein, S., & Jaffe, J. AVTA: A device for automatic vocal transaction analysis. *Journal of the Experimental Analysis of Behavior,* 1964, 7, 99–104.

Cohen, J., & Cohen, P. *Applied multiple regression/correlation analysis for the behavioral sciences.* Hillsdale, New Jersey: Lawrence Erlbaum Associates, 1975.

Feldstein, S. Rate estimates of sound-silence sequences in speech. *Journal of the Acoustical Society of America,* 1976, *60* (Supplement No. 1), S46, (Abstract.)

Feldstein, S. Race and gender effects on conversational time patterns. In P. C. Ellsworth (Chair.), *Demographic and personality influence on nonverbal behavior in conversation.* Symposium presented at the American Psychological Association, San Francisco, August, 1977.

Feldstein, S., Alberti, L., & BenDebba, M. Self-attributed personality characteristics and the pacing of conversational interaction. In A. W. Siegman & S. Feldstein (Eds.), *Of speech and time: Temporal speech patterns in interpersonal contexts.* Hillsdale, New Jersey: Lawrence Erlbaum Associates, 1979, 73–87.

Feldstein, S., BenDebba, M., & Alberti, L. Distributional characteristics of simultaneous speech in conversation. *Journal of the Acoustical Society of America,* 1974, *55,* (Supplement) S42. (Abstract.)

Feldstein, S., & Crown, C. L. *Interpersonal perception in dyads as a function of race, gender, and conversational time patterns.* Paper read at the Eastern Psychological Association, Philadelphia, April, 1979.

Goldberg, L. R. *Language and personality: Developing a taxonomy of trait descriptive terms.* Invited address to Division 5 of the American Psychological Association, San Francisco, August, 1977.

Goldberg, L. R. *Language and personality: Developing a taxonomy of personality-descriptive terms.* (A progress report and research proposal.) Unpublished manuscript, University of Oregon, and Institute for the Measurement of Personality, 1978.

Hayes, D. P., & Bouma, G. D. Patterns of vocalization and impression formation. *Semiotica,* 1977, *13*(2), 113–129.

Jaffe, J., & Feldstein, S. *Rhythms of dialogue.* New York: Academic Press, 1970.

Siegman, A. W. & Crown, C. L. Interpersonal attraction and the temporal patterning of speech in the initial interview: Replication and clarification. In W. P. Robinson, H. Giles, & P. M. Smith (eds). *Language: Social Psychological Perspectives.* London: Pergamon, 1981.

Chapter 12

INTERVIEWER-INTERVIEWEE NONVERBAL COMMUNICATIONS:
An Interactional Approach[1]

Aron W. Siegman
and Mark Reynolds

The studies reported in this paper are part of a larger research program, the major purpose of which is to identify the factors that facilitate communication within the initial interview. To prevent misunderstanding, it should be stated at the outset that we are primarily concerned with the information-gathering interview, the kind which frequently precedes therapeutically oriented interviews.

Early studies in this program focused on the characteristics of the interviewer's messages — such as their ambiguity-specificity level, their length or duration, and their topical focus — and the effects of these variables on interviewees' responses (e. g., Siegman & Pope, 1972). More recent studies have been concerned with the effects of interviewer-interviewee relationship variables on interviewees' verbal and nonverbal behavior. The

[1] An earlier version of this paper was presented at the Conference on Interaction Rhythms, New York City, March 24, 1979, under the title: *The Voice of Attraction: Interpersonal Attraction and the Temporal Patterning of Speech.*

present paper will summarize the results of three recent studies on the effects of interviewer warmth, and one study on the effects of "rapport building" on interviewees' productivity level, self-disclosure,[2] and the temporal patterning of their responses.

These studies were guided by the assumption of reciprocity between the social reinforcement value of the interviewer-interviewee relationship and the flow of communication between the two. It was assumed that interviewees will be more productive and more self-disclosing when interviewed by someone whom they like and feel attracted to than when interviewed by someone whom they feel neutral about, and certainly by someone whom they dislike. Reinforcement-based attraction theory provided the theoretical basis for this assumption. Interviewees should want to prolong exchanges that are pleasant and rewarding and to terminate those that are unpleasant or outright painful—either of which they can achieve by manipulating the duration of their responses or productivity level. Furthermore, it has been suggested that the fear of being rejected is the major reason why people tend to withold information that is of an intimate nature and potentially self-damaging. Such fear should be less of a concern to the interviewee if the interviewer is warm and accepting rather than reserved and neutral. Finally, we

---

[2] Thus far the development of a reliable and valid index of this variable within the context of the interview has been an elusive goal. Originally we classified each clause in an interviewee's response as being affective and evaluational or merely factually descriptive and interpreted the resulting ratio as an index of self-disclosure (Siegman & Pope, 1972). More recently, we have used interviewees' productivity levels in response to highly intimate versus nonintimate questions as an index of self-disclosure. We have also used a questionnaire consisting of items varying in intimacy level and have asked interviewees to indicate which of these items they would rather not discuss during a hypothetical follow-up interview. A high score on this questionnaire indicates low self-disclosure. All of these measures have been found to correlate moderately with each other, but the correlations have not been sufficiently high enough or consistent enough to produce adequate concurrent validity for any one of them.

expected that a warm and friendly interviewer demeanor would elicit interviewee speech which is characterized by the absence of relatively long and/or frequent silent pauses. The theoretical justification for this last hypothesis is much looser than for the hypotheses involving interviewee productivity and self-disclosure. We simply assumed that silent pauses in speech reflect self-monitoring as well as monitoring of one's partner, for which there should be less of a need when talking to someone whom one likes and is attracted to than when talking to someone whom one dislikes.

While obvious applied clinical concerns motivated us to assess the effects of interviewer warmth on interviewee productivity and self-disclosure, our interest in nonverbal behavior, especially in the vocal channel, provided the impetus to look at the temporal patterning of interviewees' speech, especially at their pausing behavior.

There is ample evidence in the nonverbal literature that interpersonal attraction, i. e., the liking of another person, expresses itself in identifiable patterns of gazing and proxemic behavior (Exline & Fehr, 1978; Patterson, 1978). On the assumption that interviewees are more attracted to a warm and friendly interviewer than to a reserved and neutral one—an assumption which has been amply demonstrated in our own and in other laboratories (e. g., Heller, 1968, 1972; Johnson, 1971a, 1971b)—our interviewer warmth studies should provide us with the opportunity to experimentally investigate the relationship between interpersonal attraction and pausing behavior.

In the "rapport building" study, we also looked at how silent pauses, speech rate, and other temporal aspects of the interviewees' speech affect the interviewer's perception of the interviewees' personality, the interviewer's attraction to the interviewee, and the interviewer's sense of satisfaction with the interview. Previous findings indicate that long silent pauses and a slow speech rate are sources of negative personality attributions, whether the attributions were solicited from conversational partners about each other or from "third-party" judges

(Brown, 1980; Crown, *this volume*; Feldstein & Crown, 1979). In the "rapport building" study we wanted to find out whether a relatively slow speech rate and long silent pauses on the part of interviewees tend to elicit similar negative attributions from their interviewers. If we can establish that interviewer warmth, which in our studies was encoded primarily nonverbally, affects interviewees' speech, which in turn affects the interviewer's perception of and nonverbal behavior toward the interviewee, we will have identified the essential features of a truly inter-actional model of interviewer-interviewee nonverbal behavior. But we are running ahead of our data. Let us, therefore, back-track and proceed with the actual studies and their findings.

THE EFFECTS OF INTERVIEWER WARMTH VERSUS INTERVIEWER NEUTRALITY ON INTERVIEWEE VERBAL AND NONVERBAL BEHAVIOR: THREE EXPERIMENTAL INVESTIGATIONS

We have recently concluded three separate experimental studies on the effects of interviewer warmth versus interviewer neutrality on various aspects of interviewees' behavior. In all three studies we used a between-subjects comparison design. Specifically, the interviewer, a male in the first two studies and a female in the third study, behaved in a consistently warm and friendly manner in response to some interviewees, and in a consistently neutral and reserved manner in response to others. In the warm and friendly condition, the interviewer leaned forward, smiled and, nodded on an intermittent but noncontingent forward, smiled and nodded on an intermittent but noncontingent basis.[3] In the neutral and reserved condition, the interviewer from any social reinforcers. Judges who were naive about the warm-neutral manipulation rated the interviewers' warmth and friendliness from behind a one-way screen. These ratings, as

---

[3] "Noncontingent" is used in the sense of not reinforcing a specific category of responses.

well as the postinterview ratings obtained from the interviewees themselves, indicated that the interviewers' behavior was indeed perceived as intended.

In order to control the interviewees' expectations regarding the interviewer's warmth, the interviewees were given a "set," i. e., preinterview instructions, which were designed to lead the interviewees to expect either a warm and friendly interviewer or a neutral and reserved one. In the first study, the interviewer's actual behavior was always consistent with the interviewees' expectations. In the subsequent two studies, this was true only for one-half of the interviewees, with the remaining interviewees coming into the interview with an expectation or set which was contrary to the interviewer's actual behavior. This allowed us to assess not only the effects of the interviewer's behavior, but also of the interviewee's expectations, and the interaction between the two (Table 12.1).

Table 12.1   Design of Third Interviewer Warmth Study

| Group | Interviewer Condition | | N |
	Iee Expectation	Ier Behavior	
W-W	Warm	Warm	14
R-W	Reserved	Warm	14
R-R	Reserved	Reserved	14
W-R	Warm	Reserved	14

The interviewer always followed a prepared script of moderately ambiguous questions, usually with some of the questions focusing on the interviewees' family relations, and others on their school experiences (Table 12.2). The interviewers were somewhat older students, with prior interview experiences. Additionally, they were trained to behave in the appropriate manner in the two contrasting interview conditions. The interviewees were students enrolled in introductory psychology courses.

In all three studies we looked at the effect of interviewer warmth on interviewees' productivity level, usually indexed by the interviewee's total vocalizations, or talking time, per response.[4] In order to prevent the interviewer from subtly influencing the interviewee's productivity levels, the interviewees were instructed to signal when they had finished their response by saying "finished." Thus, the interviewees were in complete control of their response durations. In two of the studies we tried to assess the effect of interviewer warmth on interviewee's self-disclosure, and in all but the first study we monitored the effect of interviewer warmth on the temporal patterning of interviewee's speech.

Table 12.2   Interviewer's Questions in Third Interviewer Warmth Study

1. Tell me what you can about your father.
2. Tell me what you can about your brother, X (or sister Y).
3. Tell me what you can about your high school experiences.
4. Now tell me what you can about your mother.
5. Now tell me what you can about your sister, X (or brother Y).
6. Tell me what you can about your experiences here at the the University of X.

The one finding which emerged consistently from all three studies is that interviewer warmth and friendliness is reciprocated in kind. Interviewer warmth elicited similar behavior on the part of the interviewee, i. e., smiling, head-nodding, etc. Furthermore, on postinterview rating scales the interviewees indicated greater liking and attraction to the warm than the neutral interviewers. The effect of the interviewer warmth manipulation on interviewees' attraction scores was a strong one, with very few reversals, if any, between the W-W (warm set and warm interviewer behavior) and R-R (reserved set and reserved interviewer behavior) conditions. Consequently, it has been suggested (Siegman, 1979, 1980) that our warm-reserve manipulation can also be viewed as a manipulation of the interviewees' attraction to their interviewer—a position which will be adopted in the present paper.

[4] Previous findings (Siegman & Pope, 1972) indicate that this measure correlates .92 and better with the conventional but more laborious procedure of counting the number of words or clauses per response.

The second conclusion which can be stated with a strong degree of confidence is that in same-gender interviewer-interviewee dyads, interviewer warmth per se does not enhance interviewee productivity, nor does interviewer reserve per se inhibit interviewee productivity. In fact, in male interviewer-female interviewee dyads, the subjects responded to the friendly male interviewer with extremely brief responses, although they clearly preferred him to the reserved interviewer.[5]

Perhaps the major challenge of the finding that interviewer reserve has little, if any, adverse effects on interviewee productivity is how to reconcile this finding with the widespread belief among clinicians that interviewer reserve inhibits interviewee productivity. A reconciliation is made possible by evidence obtained in our second and third interviewer warmth studies which indicates that to expect a warm and friendly interviewer and to find him reserved and neutral instead has an inhibiting effect on interviewees' productivity level. Since we have found that interviewees expect their interviewers to be warm and friendly, it may very well be that the inhibiting effect of interviewer reserve and neutrality reported by clinicians reflects not the interviewer's reserve per se, but rather the interviewees' disappointment in having their expectation of a friendly interview disconfirmed.

Interviewer warmth significantly increased interviewees' self-disclosure, when the latter was measured by asking the interviewees after the interview which among a list of items varying in intimacy level they would rather not discuss during a

[5] Heller and his associates (1968, 1972) who also investigated the effect of interviewer warmth on interviewees' productivity levels were similarly unable to confirm the widely accepted assumption of a positive correlation between the two, except in populations that were selected on the basis of special demographic or personality characteristics.

Johnson (1971a, 1971b) studied the effects of warmth within the context of conflict resolution and interpersonal influence. His findings, like ours, indicate that warmth does not have a generalized facilitating or beneficial effect on all behavior. Instead, its effects are specific and depend on the particular variable one is looking at.

subsequent interview.[6] Interviewees in the warm conditions checked off fewer high-intimacy level items than interviewees in the reserved conditions, although there was considerable between-subjects variability on this scale. The results obtained with a more direct assessment of interviewees' self-disclosure were inconclusive.

What about the effects of the interviewer warmth-reserve manipulation on the various temporal measures? There is clear-cut evidence in our second and third interviewer warmth studies that a reserved and neutral interviewer demeanor is associated with an increase in the frequency and the duration of interviewees' within-response pauses, and hence with a decrease in interviewees' speech rate (which is largely a function of within-response pausing).

Since the third interviewer warmth study was specially designed to examine the effects of interviewer warmth on the temporal patterning of interviewees' speech, and included a broad variety of temporal indices, its findings will be presented in somewhat greater detail. In this study, we looked at the following temporal measures: Reaction time or response latency (RT), average pause duration (APD), pause duration ratio (PDR), silence quotient (SQ), pause frequency ratio (PFR), speech rate (SR), and articulation rate (AR).

The RT index refers to the interval between an interviewer's question and the interviewee's response. The APD, the PDR, and the SQ are all measures of within-response silent pauses. The APD is based on silent pauses 300 msec and over. The PDR includes all silent pauses 300 msec and more per response, and the SQ silent pauses 2 seconds and more per response, each divided by the summed duration of vocalizations per response. The PFR refers to the number of pauses 300 msec and over in a response divided by vocalization time. The SR is calculated by dividing the number of words in a response by the duration of that response (in seconds) without removing the silent pauses,

[6]Due to the nature of the scoring procedure, a high score reflects low self-disclosure.

and the AR by dividing the number of words by the summed duration of vocalizations per response, which excludes all silent pauses 300 msec and over. More detailed operational definitions of these measures can be found elsewhere (Siegman, 1978a, 1978b, 1979, 1980).

Interviewer warmth did not account for a significant proportion of the variance in interviewees' RT scores. However, the interaction of interviewer warmth by sequence was significant, reflecting the fact that during the initial part of the interview the interviewee responded with significantly shorter RT's in the warm than in the reserved conditions ($F1,52 = 4.07$, $p < .03$). This difference, however, dissipated as the interview progressed.

Interviewer warmth was a significant source of variance in relation to all three indices designed to measure the duration of within-response pausing, i. e., APD, PDR, and SQ, and in relation to speech rate, which as pointed out earlier, is a function of within-response pausing. Interviewees obtained longer pauses and slower speech rates in the interview conditions in which the interviewer assumed a reserved and neutral manner rather than a warm and friendly one (Table 12.3). The effect was not only clearly significant, but there was little overlap between the conditions. For example, taking the interviewees' mean PDR score in the W-W and the R-R conditions as a cut-off point, only 2 out of the 14 subjects in the W-W condition scored above this point, and only three subjects out of the 14 in the R-R condition scored below it.

What is the meaning of the inverse relationship between interviewer warmth and interviewee silent pausing? Elsewhere (Siegman, 1978a, 1979, 1980), it has been suggested that silent pauses in speech reflect information processing, including the information processing that is related to self-monitoring or to the monitoring of one's partner. If self-monitoring and/or monitoring of the interviewer is the critical intervening variable, one could at least argue that an outright cold and rejecting interviewer is likely to elicit a maximum of such monitoring. Alternatively,

Table 12.3   Mean and SD (Standard Deviation) of Subjects' Temporal Scores in the Third Interviewer Warmth Study[1]

Variable	W-W Condition		R-W Condition		R-R Condition		W-R Condition	
	Mean	SD	Mean	SD	Mean	SD	Mean	SD
Reaction time[2]	.990	.476	.987	.290	1.09	.708	1.147	.535
Silence Quotient	.074	.071	.080	.073	.148	.096	.143	.140
Pause Duration Ratio	.411	.227	.530	.252	.823	.685	.711	.718
Average Pause Duration	.838	.218	.989	.292	1.321	.586	1.188	.781
Pause Frequency Ratio	.154	.047	.169	.042	.197	.059	.178	.048
Speech Rate	2.560	.375	2.420	.417	2.151	.613	2.142	.577
Articulation Rate	1.039	.084	1.082	.188	1.052	.143	.971	.163

[1] Adapted from Siegman, 1979, Table 5.5.

[2] Logarithmic transformations of mean number of words per response.

interviewee uncertainty may be the mediating variable. A reserved and neutral interviewer manner is inherently ambiguous, and therefore is likely to create in the interviewee a state of uncertainty, which in turn is associated with hesitant speech (Siegman & Pope, 1972). According to this explanation an unambiguously cold and rejecting interviewer manner may not be associated with an increase in interviewees' silent pauses. Clearly, we next need to look at the effects of a neutral and reserved interviewer demeanor versus an outright cold and rejecting one on the temporal patterning of interviewees' speech.

As pointed out earlier, this study allowed us to assess not only the effects of interviewer warmth or reserve, but also the effects of expecting such interviewer behaviors. Interviewees' expectations regarding interviewer warmth or reserve had a significant effect on only one temporal variable, i. e., interviewees' articulation rate. The expectation of a reserved and neutral interviewer accelerated interviewees' articulation rate. However, this effect was significant only during the first part of the interview ($F1,52 = 5.85, p < .05$), and dissipated as the interview progressed.

Thus, while a reserved interviewer manner clearly had the effect of decreasing interviewees' speech rate, the mere expectation of a reserved interviewer had the very opposite effect on interviewees' articulation rate, at least during the initial part of the interview. One possible explanation may be that the expectation of a reserved and neutral interviewer tends to increase interviewee's arousal level. There is some evidence (Siegman, 1978b) that anxiety arousal decreases short silent pauses and accelerates articulation rate, but not speech rate. At any rate, the results of this study suggest that speech rate (which is a function of pause duration) and articulation rate are distinct variables. The absence of a significant correlation between these two indices in the W-W and R-R conditions provides additional support for the above distinction.

Let us now summarize the effects of interviewer warmth on interviewees' verbal and nonverbal behavior as they were manifested in the three studies summarized in this paper. (1) There was ample evidence that interviewer warmth and friendliness is reciprocated by interviewee warmth and friendliness. (2) There was no consistent evidence that interviewer warmth per se facilitates productivity (in fact, under certain conditions, i. e., with male interviewers and female interviewees, it may inhibit it. (3) There was some evidence suggesting that interviewer warmth facilitates self-disclosure, but this relationship was associated with a very large variance score. (4) Interviewees spoke with significantly longer within-response pauses when responding to warm and friendly interviewers than when responding to neutral and reserved ones. A discussion of the methodological implications of this latter finding will be postponed until later in this paper. At this point, however, we need to raise a critical question: Considering the findings discussed thus far (and assuming, of course, that they are reliable and that they possess ecological validity), is it possible that the importance generally attributed to interviewer warmth and friendliness has been exaggerated? To answer this question, we need to summarize the results of yet another study.

INTERVIEWEES' NONVERBAL BEHAVIOR AS A FUNCTION OF RAPPORT AND AS A SOURCE OF PERSONALITY ATTRIBUTIONS

One major purpose of this study was to assess the effects of "rapport building" in the interview on the interviewees' productivity and self-disclosure levels. It is widely assumed among clinicians that rapport building, which typically consists of an exchange of relatively innocuous remarks and pleasantries between the interviewer and interviewee in a convivial atmosphere, is an essential prelude to a successful interview, with success defined in terms of productive and self-revealing interviewee responses. We also looked at the effect of rapport on the temporal patterning of interviewee's speech.

Another major objective of this study was to ascertain the

effects of the interviewees' temporal speech patterns (especially the effect of relatively long silent pauses), and of interviewees' productivity levels on the interviewers' perception of the interviewee, their attraction to the interviewee, and their perception of the interview as having been successful or unsuccessful.

Method

Interviewers and Interviewees. The interviewers were three male and three female graduate students in psychology, each of whom interviewed six male and six female undergraduate students who volunteered for an interview study. The interviewers had all taken a course in interviewing techniques and were specially trained for this particular interview.

Due to mechanical problems five interviews could not be analyzed. Altogether, then, there were 67 analyzable cases, with 17 subjects in the male interviewer-male interviewee condition, 17 subjects in the female interviewer-female interviewee condition, 16 subjects in the male interviewer-female interviewee condition, and 17 subjects in the female interviewer-male interviewee condition.

The Interview. The interview (Table 12.4) consisted of nine questions, with the first question always being: Tell me something about your family. The remaining eight questions were divided among four topics (father, mother, self, and sexual experiences), with one personal or intimate question and one impersonal or relatively neutral question in each of the topics. The sequence of the two types of questions, i. e., intimate versus nonintimate, was alternated between subjects. No attempt was made to counterbalance the sequence of the four topics, except that of father and mother. The first question provided the interviewees with a brief adaptation period. Only subjects' responses to the remaining eight questions were analyzed.

The design of the present study included two control conditions: a "no-rapport" condition, and a "confederate-rapport"

Table 12.4   The Interview Schedule in the Rapport Study

Items	Intimacy
1. Tell me as much as you can about your family.	
2. What aspects and personality characteristics of your father do you like best?	Low
3. What aspects and personality characteristics of your father may indicate maladjustment?	High
4. What aspects and personality characteristics of your mother do you like best?	Low
5. What aspects and personality characteristics of your mother may indicate maladjustment?	High
6. What do you feel best about and proudest of in your past?	Low
7. What do you feel the guiltiest about and ashamed of in your past?	High
8. How do you feel about sex education in the schools?	Low
9. How can you tell when you are becoming sexually aroused?	High

condition. In the latter condition, a rapport-building period preceded the interview, but it was conducted by someone other than the interviewer. Rapport building, whether conducted by the interviewer or by a confederate, consisted of brief (about 3 minutes) superficial exchanges between the interviewer and interviewee, such as ''Did you have any difficulty finding this lab?'' Specifically, both the male and the female interviewers who participated in this study were divided into teams, with each team consisting of two interviewers. The two members of each team, who were always of the same gender, served as each other's confederate. The purpose of the confederate-rapport condition was to test the hypothesis that interviewees' attraction to the interviewer is the mediating variable in the alleged facilitating effect of rapport building on interviewees' productivity and self-disclosure scores. If there is any validity to this position, the hypothesized facilitating effect of rapport should obtain only if the interviewers themselves conduct the rapport-building session.

Dependent Variables.   The interviewees' attraction to interviewer scores, their productivity and self-disclosure scores, and their scores on the various temporal indices were the major dependent variables for the part of this study which focused on the effects of rapport building on interviewees' behavior. The temporal variables were: RT, APD, PFR,[7] and the summed duration of vocalizations per response or productivity, all of which have been defined earlier. Additionally, this study included one other temporal index: the proportionality constant ratio, or PCR, which is the ratio of the probability of continuing to talk to the probability of remaining silent. It has been shown that this automatically obtained index is a reliable measure of the more laboriously obtained speech rate (Feldstein, 1976).

In the second part of this study we attempted to ascertain the influence of the interviewees' vocal nonverbal behavior—especially their response latencies and within-response pauses—on the interviewers' attitudes toward the interviewees. In this analysis, the temporal indices together with interviewees' productivity scores constituted the independent variables, and the interviewers' attraction to the interviewees, the number of positive personality traits which they attributed to the interviewees (from a list which contained both positive and negative traits), and their perception of the interview as successful or unsuccessful, constituted the major dependent variables.

Results and Discussion

The effects of the rapport manipulation can be summarized rather succinctly. Interviewee rapport was not a significant source of variance in interviewees' attraction scores. However, the interaction of interviewer gender × interviewee gender × interviewer rapport was marginally significant ($05 > p < .10$), with interviewees showing a tendency of being more attracted to their interviewers in the rapport than in the no-rapport condition, except in male-male dyads (Table 12.5).

[7] In this study we also analyzed the frequency of pauses per response, and controlled for productivity level by using the latter as a covariate. This analysis produced different findings than those which were obtained with the PFR.

Table 12.5 Subjects' Mean Attraction, Productivity, and Self-disclosure Scores in Rapport Study by Interviewer and Interviewee Gender

Gender		Attraction		Prod. non-intimate Qs[1]		Prod. Intimate Qs[1]		Self-disclosure	
Ier	Iee	No rapport	Ier rapport	No rapport	Ier rapport	No rapport	Ier rapport	No rapport	Ier rapport
Male	Male	9.83	9.00	19.7	14.3	12.7	14.9	4.50	5.08
Female	Male	8.33	10.20	17.5	23.1	13.1	18.4	3.21	8.09
Male	Female	8.80	11.20	14.0	17.4	9.6	12.3	10.55	3.25
Female	Female	8.25	9.00	14.1	17.9	5.3	14.8	8.82	2.38

[1] In seconds.

Interviewer rapport was a significant source of variance in interviewees' productivity scores as was the interaction of rapport × intimacy. Interviewees were more productive in the interviewer-rapport condition than in the no-rapport condition, but only in response to intimate questions (Table 12.5). Although interviewer rapport per se had no significant effect on interviewees' self-disclosure scores the interaction of interviewer rapport × interviewee gender was significant. Female interviewees indicated significantly greater readiness to disclose intimate information in the interviewer-rapport condition than in the no-rapport condition. Males, on the other hand, showed a nonsignificant trend in the opposite direction, especially in cross-gender dyads (Table 12.5). We have no obvious explanation why rapport building facilitated self-disclosure in females but not in males. However, the very different effects of interviewer rapport building on interviewees' productivity levels in response to highly intimate questions than on their questionnaire-derived self-disclosure scores, underscores the importance of distinguishing between these two indices of self-disclosure (although we have no basis for assigning greater validity to the one over the other).

From a theoretical point of view it is important to note that attraction was probably not the mediating variable in the facilitating effect of interviewer rapport building on interviewees' productivity level (in response to intimate questions) and on the female interviewees' declared readiness to disclose intimate information. First, the confederate-rapport manipulation had pretty much the same effect on interviewees' productivity level in response to the intimate questions and on their self-disclosure scores than the interviewer-rapport manipulation (Tables 12.6 and 12.7). This makes it unlikely that attraction to the interviewer is responsible for the beneficial effects of interviewer rapport building, at least not as far as interviewee productivity and self-disclosure are concerned. Second, the pattern of interviewees' productivity and scores in the interviewer-rapport and no-rapport conditions does not correspond to their attraction scores in these two conditions (Table 12.5).

Table 12.6   Interviewees' Mean Productivity Scores[1]
as a Function of Rapport and Question Type

Question type	No rapport	Ier rapport	Confederate rapport
Intimate	10.42	15.07	16.25
Nonintimate	16.52	17.98	25.07

[1] Based on logarithmic transformations.

Table 12.7   Interviewees' Mean Self-disclosure Scores
as a Function of Rapport and Interviewee Gender

Iee gender	No rapport	Ier rapport	Confederate rapport
Male	3.85	6.46	3.86
Female	9.68	2.78	9.35

The rapport manipulation, either alone or in interaction with the other independent variables in this study, had no clear-cut significant effect on any of the temporal indices.

INTERVIEWEES' SPEECH STYLE AS THE BASIS FOR THE INTERVIEWER'S ATTRACTIONS

In order to determine the relationship of the interviewees' productivity levels and of their temporal speech patterns to the interviewers' perceptions of the interviewees, a series of regression analyses were performed in which interviewees' productivity levels and their temporal indices served as the independent variables and the interviewers' ratings of the interviewees and of the interview as the dependent variables. Since in this study the interviewees' responses yielded two productivity scores and two sets of temporal indices—one for the intimate interviewer questions and one for the neutral probes—it was possible to determine which of the two accounted for the greatest variability in the interviewer's ratings (Table 12.8).

**Table 12.8 R^2 Values in Regression Analyses of
Interviewer Ratings as a Function of Interviewees' Vocal Behavior**

Interviewees' Vocal Indices	Interviewers' Ratings			
	Attraction	Positive Adjectives	Negative Adjectives	Interview Success
Productivity Neutral	04	00	00	00
APD Neutral	07	01	26	08
RT Neutral	04	00	08	08
PCR Neutral	00	23	01	00
Total Neutral	16	24	34	16
Productivity Intimate	00	01	02	04
APD Intimate	00	01	02	08
RT Intimate	00	01	03	03
PCR Intimate	00	16	13	02
Total Intimate	01	21	20	15

The contribution of the various nonverbal measures derived from the interviewees' responses to the neutral questions accounted for 16 percent of the variance in the interviewers' attraction scores. In other words, variations in interviewees' nonverbal behavior in response to the neutral questions accounted for 16 percent of the variance in the interviewers' attraction ratings. The greatest contribution came from interviewees' APD scores (7 percent): the longer the interviewees' pauses the lower the interviewer's attraction scores. Variations in interviewees' productivity and temporal scores in response to the intimate questions can be attributed to the nature of the material and do interviewer's attraction ratings, presumably because long silent pauses or a slow speech rate in response to highly intimate questions can be attributed to the nature of the matieral and do not reflect negatively on the speaker's personality and/or competence. The contribution of the experimental conditions (including the demographic variables) to the variability in the interviewers' attraction ratings was only 12 percent.

The contribution of the various nonverbal measures derived from the interviewees' responses to the neutral questions accounted for 24 percent of variance in the interviewer's attribution of positive traits to the interviewees. The greatest contribution came from interviewees' PCR scores (23 percent). The faster the interviewees' speech-rate, the more positive the interviewer's perception of the interviewee. Variations in interviewees' productivity and temporal scores in response to the intimate questions accounted for 21 percent of the variance in the interviewers' attribution of positive traits. The contribution of the experimental conditions and of the demographic variables of this study to the variability in the interviewers' positive ratings was only 14 percent.

The contributions of the various nonverbal measures, which were derived from interviewees' responses to the neutral questions, to the interviewers' attribution of negative traits to the interviewees was 34 percent. The greatest contribution came from subjects' APD scores (26 percent), the longer the interviewee's silent pauses, the more negative the interviewer's perception of the interviewee. Variations in interviewees' productivity and temporal scores in response to the intimate questions accounted for only 20 percent of the variance in the interviewers' attribution of negative traits. The contribution of the experimental and background variables to the variability in the interviewers' negative attributions was 15 percent.

Finally, the contributions of the nonverbal measures to the interviewers' perception of the interview as successful was about 15 percent, whether these measures were obtained from the neutral questions or from the intimate questions. Again, the pausing indices (APD and RT0), rather than the interviewees' productivity levels, were the best predictors of the interviewers' ratings. The interviewers perceived the interview as successful when the interviewees gave fluently articulated responses.

Perhaps the most surprising finding of this study is that interviewees' vocal nonverbal behavior, particularly their temporal speech patterns, accounted for so much of the variability in the interviewers' attribution of positive and negative personality traits to the interviewees, more so than the rapport manipulation and interviewee gender. A slow interviewee speech-rate and relatively long interviewee silent pauses detracted from the interviewers' liking of the interviewee, unless the slow speech-rate and the silent pauses could be attributed to the intimate nature of the material.

One important implication of these findings is that the personality attributions made by interviewers on the basis of the interviewees' nonverbal behavior depend on the context in which the latter occur. Long silent pauses that occur within the context of responses to highly intimate questions are much less a source of negative attributions than are silent pauses that occur within the context of responses to relatively neutral questions. Apparently, the interpretation of nonverbal cues on the part of interviewers, and probably on the part of listeners in general, involve subtle and complex discriminations.

Elsewhere (Siegman & Reynolds, 1979), we have argued against a simple-minded apporach which assigns invariant meanings to specific nonverbal behaviors, be they vocal, visual, or from some other nonverbal channel of communication. Evidence was presented that the meaning of nonverbal behaviors is a function of the context in which they occur: the nature of the topic, the relationship, etc. Of course, this is not different from verbal behavior, where meaning is contextually determined. The results of the present study indicate that such distinctions are also taken into account by listeners (at least by interviewers) in the person perception process. At some level, the interviewers responded differentially to pauses in response to intimate questions than to pauses in response to neutral questions. To argue that such distinctions are made does not necessarily imply that decoders are aware of making them, in the sense of being able to verbalize which particular cues they are responding to. As pointed out by Zajonc (1980), affective responses and preferences do not require the mediation of complex cognitive processes.

Viewed together, the two sets of findings, i.e., those obtained in the interviewer warmth experiments and those of the present study, suggest an interactional model for nonverbal behavior in the interview. Interviewees respond fluently, i.e., with a faster speech-rate and fewer silent pauses, to interviewers whom they like and whom they are attracted to than to interviewers whom they dislike. In turn, interviewers attribute more positive and fewer negative traits and are more attracted to interviewees who speak fluently, without long silent pauses, than to nonfluent interviewees. It is suggested that this type of complex feedback system may very well provide the proper model for understanding the role of nonverbal behavior not only in the interview, but in all dyadic communication. Nonverbal, vocal cues are a source of interpersonal perceptions and attributions, which in turn influence nonverbal, vocal behaviors. This mutual influence process may also provide an explanation for the matching of temporal speech patterns that occur among partners in dyadic intersections, be they conversations or interviews (Feldstein & Welkowitz, 1979). Unduly slow speech on the part of one of the partners will elicit a negative evaluation from the versa.

Let us now return to the question posed earlier in this paper: Is there an empirically based rationale for the widespread assumption that it is preferable for an interviewer to be warm and friendly rather than neutral and reserved? Considering the findings of our interviewer warmth studies that a reserved and neutral interviewer demeanor is associated with a slow interviewee speech-rate and with long interviewee within-response silent pauses, and considering the findings of the present study that this speech style detracts from the interviewer's positive evaluation of the interviewee, we can now give an affirmative answer to the above question. It does not seem too far-fetched to suggest that the interviewer's negative impressions about the interviewee are likely to influence the interviewer's subsequent nonverbal behavior, and perhaps even verbal behavior, in a way which is likely to further increase the interviewee's silent pauses. Thus, warm versus neutral interviewer demeanors may very well trigger cycles of benign versus unpleasant interviewer-interviewee interactions. The implications of these speculations for the interview in general, and especially for the personnel-assessment interview, are serious indeed because they suggest that the interviewer's own nonverbal behavior (i.e., a reserved manner) can trigger an interviewee nonverbal response (i.e., long silent pauses) which will result in a negative assessment of the interviewee, without the interviewer necessarily being aware of his or her contribution to the negative evaluation.

SUMMARY AND GENERAL DISCUSSION

In recent years it has been popular to invoke a reinforcement-based attraction paradigm in order to account for a host of social-psychological findings (Byrne, 1971), including phenomena such as congruence in dyadic conversations (Matarazzo & Weins, 1967) and reciprocity of self-disclosure (Jourard & Friedman, 1972).

Taking a similar theoretical posture, we hypothesized that interviewees would be more productive and self-disclosing to warm and friendly interviewers than to reserved and neutral ones. For similar reasons, we hypothesized that interviewers who engage their interviewees in a rapport-building session prior to the actual interview will elicit more productive and self-disclosing interviewee responses than interviewers who dispense with rapport building altogether or who let others do it for them.

We found no support for the widespread assumption that interviewer warmth per se facilitates interviewee productivity or that interviewer reserve per se inhibits interviewee productivity. The general belief to the contrary is probably buttressed by the fallacious reasoning that if something is positively valued its consequences too are positive, and conversely, if something is negatively valued its consequences too are negative. Elsewhere (Siegman, 1980) it has been suggested that this type of reasoning may be responsible for the failure to recognize some of the positive consequences of anxiety arousal on speech.

The results of one study suggest that interviewer warmth

may facilitate interviewee's readiness to disclose intimate information (at least as this variable is indexed by a postinterview self-disclosure questionnaire). However, the significance of this finding is attenuated by the relatively high level of intersubject variability which characterizes this relationship. The results of another study suggest that "rapport building" facilitates interviewee productivity in response to intimate questions, and self-disclosure in female interviewees. It must be noted, however, that interpersonal attraction was probably not the mediating variable in the facilitating effects which did occur.

Two findings, however, were clear and unambiguous and held up under repeated replications. Moreover, the effects were not only statistically significant but of a substantial magnitude. One finding is that interviewer warmth and friendliness is reciprocated in kind. Interviewees respond to warm and friendly interviewers with warmth and friendliness on their part. Furthermore, inteviewees indicate greater attraction and liking of interviewers who behave in a warm and friendly manner than interviewers who behave in a neutral and reserved manner, with little overlap between the two conditions. The other, and less expected, finding is that interviewer warmth or reserve have a significant effect on the interviewees' within—response silent pauses and speech rates. Specifically, a warm and friendly interviewer demeanor was found to be associated with shorter silent pauses and a faster speech rate than a neutral and reserved interviewer demeanor.

The discovery of nonverbal correlates of interpersonal attraction is important in its own right. It is important because the more nonverbal cues are involved in the giving or withholding of affection, the more likely it is that such behavior can be decoded in a reliable and valid manner. Previous research indicates that pupil size, eye contact, and interpersonal distance are all correlates for interpersonal attraction (Exline & Fehr, 1978; Hess & Petrovich, 1978; Patterson, 1978). The results of our interviewer warmth studies suggest that hesitation pauses can now be added to this list. Furthermore, as discussed elsewhere in some detail

(Siegman, 1979, 1980), the availability of indices like average pause duration and speech rate as measures of interpersonal attraction has many advantages. Unlike the paper and pencil measures currently being used by social psychologists (Byrne, 1971), temporal indices like speech rate allow us to monitor changes in interpersonal attraction over time. As pointed out earlier in this paper, interviewees initially demonstrated longer RT's to neutral than to warm interviewers, but this difference dissipated with time. The same was true of interviewees' articulation rates as a function of expecting a warm versus a reserved interviewer. Interviewees expecting a reserved interviewer initially responded with an accelerated articulation rate, but this effect too dissipated as the interview progressed. By way of contrast, other effects may not become apparent until the interview has progressed some. For example, in naturalistic interviews it may take some time before the interviewee decides that the interviewer is either warm or reserved. Temporal indices of interpersonal attraction will allow us to determine at what point this decision has occurred. Most importantly, such indices will allow us to track changes in the interviewee's interpersonal attraction as a function of changes in the interviewer's behavior, and vice versa. [x]

[x] The results of a recently completed study (Siegman & Crown, 1979) indicate that the time variable also moderates the relationship between interviewer warmth and interviewee productivity. In this study, which used female interviewers and interviewees, interviewer reserve initially increased the interviewees' productivity levels. However, this effect dissipated with time, and eventually the interviewees became less productive with the reserved than with the warm interviewers. In this study, the most productive interviews were obtained by interviewers who modulated their behavior, and alternated between a reserved and friendly demeanor. It would apear that initially interviewer reserve has a challenging impact and hence the increase in interviewee productivity. However, this relationship will persist only if the increase in interviewee productivity will have the effect of modifying the interviewer's behavior, i.e., change it from reserved to warm and friendly. If it does not, interviewer reserve will eventually cease to elicit productive interviewee responses.

The relationship between interviewer warmth and the temporal patterning of interviewee's speech takes on special significance in light of the finding that the latter is a major source of personality attributions which interviewers make about their interviewees. Temporal indices such as average pause duration and speech rate contribute significantly to an interviewer's attraction to the interviewee and to the types of personality attributions which interviewers make about their interviewees. Interviewers prefer and assign more positive traits to interviewees whose speech is free from relatively long silent pauses—which contribute to a slow speech rate. However, this depends on the context. Long silent pauses and a slow speech rate that occur when an interviewee is discussing highly intimate material does not detract from the interviewee's attractiveness. Different non-verbal cues contribute to different classes of attributions, and each depends on the context in which they occur.

Let us now return to the relationship between interviewer warmth—reserve and temporal patterning of interviewee's speech. According to our findings a reserved interviewer manner is likely to elicit relatively long silent pauses in the interviewee's responses, which in turn may cause the interviewer to dislike the interviewee. It was suggested that the interviewer's negative feelings toward the interviewee are likely to influence his or her nonverbal, and perhaps even verbal, behavior in a manner which is likely to further increase the interviewee's silent pauses. It is suggested that this kind of complex feedback system may very well provide the proper model for understanding the role of nonverbal behavior in dyadic communication, including the initial interview.

REFERENCES

Brown, B. L. Effects of speech rate on personality attributions and competency evaluations. In H. Giles, W. P. Robinson, & P. M. Smith (Eds.), *Language: Social psychological perspectives*. Oxford: Pergamon Press, 1980.

Byrne, D. *The attraction paradigm*. New York: Academic Press, 1971.

Exline, R. V., & Fehr, B. J. Applications of semiosis to the study of visual interaction. In A. W. Siegman & S. Feldstein (Eds.), *Nonverbal behavior and communication*. Hillsdale, N. J.: Erlbaum Associates, 1978.

Feldstein, S. Rate estimates of sound–silence sequences in speech. *Journal of the Acoustical Society of America*, 1976, *60* (Supplement No. 1), 546. Abstract.

Feldstein, S., & Crown, C. L. *Interpersonal perception in dyads as a function of race, gender, and conversational time patterns*. Paper read at the Eastern Psychological Association, Philadelphia, April, 1979.

Feldstein, S., & Welkowitz, J. A chronography of conversation: In defense of an objective approach. In A. W. Siegman & S. Feldstein (Eds.), *Nonverbal behavior and communication*. Hillsdale, N.J.: Erlbaum Associates, 1978.

Heller, K. Ambiguity in the interview interaction. In J. M. Shlien (Ed.), *Research in psychotherapy*. Vol. III. Washington, D. C.: American Psychological Association, 1968.

Heller, K. Interview structure and interview style in initial interviews. In A. W. Siegman & B. Pope (Eds.), *Studies in dyadic communication*. New York: Pergamon, 1972.

Hess, E. H., & Petrovich, S. B. Pupillary behavior in communication. In A. W. Siegman & S. Feldstein (Eds.), *Nonverbal behavior and communication*. Hillsdale, N.J.: Erlbaum Associates, 1978.

Johnson, D. W. Effects of warmth of interaction, accuracy of understanding and the proposal of compromises on listener's behavior. *Journal of Counseling Psychology*, 1971, *18*, 207–216. a.

Johnson, D. W. Effects of the order of expressing warmth and anger on the actor and the listener. *Journal of Counseling Psychology*, 1971, *18*, 571–578. b.

Jourard, S. M., & Friedman, R. Experimenter subject distance and self-disclosure. *Journal of Personality and Social Psychology*, 1972, *25*, 278–282.

Matarazzo, J. D., & Wiens, A. N. Interviewer influence on duration of interviewee silence. *Journal of Experimental Research on Personality*, 1967, 56–69.

Patterson, M. L. The role of space in social interaction. In A. W. Siegman & S. Feldstein (Eds.), *Nonverbal behavior and communication*. Hillsdale, N.J.: Erlbaum Associates, 1978.

Pope, B., & Siegman, A. W. Relationship and verbal behavior in the initial interview. In A. W. Siegman & B. Pope (Eds.), *Studies in dyadic communication*. New York: Pergamon Press, 1972.

Siegman, A. W. The meaning of silent pauses in the initial interview. *Journal of Mental and Nervous Disease*, 1978, *166*, 642–654. a.

Siegman, A. W. The telltale voice: Nonverbal messages of verbal communication. In A. W. Siegman & S. Feldstein (Eds.), *Nonverbal behavior and communication*. Hillsdale, N. J.: Erlbaum Associates, 1978. b.

Siegman, A. W. Interpersonal attraction and verbal behavior in the initial interview. In R. St. Clair & H. Giles (Eds.), *The social and psychological contexts of language*. Hillsdale, N. J.: Erlbaum Associates, 1980.

Siegman, A. W. The voice of attraction: Vocal correlates of interpersonal attraction in the interview. In A. W. Siegman & S. Feldstein (Eds.), *Of speech and time: Temporal speech patterns in interpersonal contexts*. Hillsdale, N. J.: Erlbaum Associates, 1979.

Siegman, A. W., & Pope, B. The effects of ambiguity and anxiety on interviewee verbal behavior. In A. W. Siegman & B. Pope (Eds.), *Studies in dyadic communication*. New York: Pergamon Press, 1972.

Siegman, A. W., & Crown, C. L. Interpersonal attraction and the temporal patterning of speech in the initial interview: A replication and clarification. Symposium paper presented at the International Conference on Social Psychology and Language, Bristol, England, July, 1979.

Siegman, A. W., & Reynolds, M. Gender differences in pausing behavior: Stable markers or situation specific? Symposium paper presented at the annual American Psychological Association meetings, New York, September, 1979.

Zajonc, R. B. Feeling and thinking: Preferences need no inferences. *American Psychologist*, 1980, *35*, 151–175.

Part IV

A sporting goods store, a college classroom, a private hospital room, and an experimental apartment closed off from the world are the contexts of the studies reported in this section. The analyses of interaction are based on macro units of speech and motion. Except for the cycles of conversation determined from continuous sound recordings made over weeks by Donald P. Hayes and Loren Cobb, the patterns of orientation, posture, and action of these studies are perceptible to the unaided eye and ear. They are each about "sharing" behaviors: assuming vis-a-vis orientations (Jones and von Raffler-Engel), mirroring positions (LaFrance), matching various details of speech and motion (Daubenmire and Searles), and sharing conversation periods (Hayes and Cobb). And in different ways they elucidate how mutuality and rapport are reflected and perhaps developed through motion and speech rhythms. Methodologically, they represent advances in the synthesis of ethological observation and quantitative analyses.

In his discussion of the conference presentations, Adam Kendon provides a conceptual framework for the role of orientation and positions in framing and creating the conditions for face-to-face interactions. The concluding remarks by Conrad M. Arensberg bring us back to a discussion of the pervasive significance of interaction rhythms and the need to more vigorously research large groups.

Chapter 13

POSTURE MIRRORING AND RAPPORT

Marianne LaFrance

A decade and a half ago, Albert Scheflen (1964) articulated the compelling notion that people in a group often mirror one another's posture and that such mirroring reflects a common viewpoint. Despite the intuitive appeal of such a notion, there remains little empirical support for Scheflen's conjecture and almost no theoretical elaboration of it.

The present chapter is aimed at remedying this neglect. To that end, the first section reviews the literature on the topic, scant though it is, that suggests that posture mirroring and movement synchrony are regular features of face-to-face interaction and that they are associated with interpersonal involvement. The second section describes two of our studies which examined the relation between posture mirroring and rapport in natural settings. And finally, I will explore some implications of posture sharing for understanding face-to-face interaction.

Let me begin by presenting, quite informally, what I think are some processes underlying the existence of ''interaction rhythms'' to which posture mirroring may contribute and of which it may be reflective. When two or more people come together in an interaction, they need to establish a coordinated system of engagement. When an interaction is appropriately coordinated, the participants might describe the encounter as one in which they appear to be "on the same wavelength" or "in tune with" one another. However, when coordination has not been achieved, these same participants might describe themselves as "not having gotten it together" or as "out of step" with each other.

These expressions suggest some important aspects of interpersonal accommodation. First, a significant feature is the sharing of a common orientation toward the encounter—a common definition of the situation. A second aspect is the need for temporal coordination. Temporal coordination is reflected, for example, in the predictable sequencing of actions such as the "one turn at a time" nature of most conversational exchanges. Temporal coordination is also manifest in the actual co-occurrence of certain actions, such as the handshake. This chapter focuses on this latter form of temporal coordination and puts forth the thesis that a shared stance by people toward each other and/or toward the world may be reflected in simultaneous nonverbal activity. Conversely, the absence of simultaneous action when expected may not only signal discord but may actually instigate it. Note for example, the discomfort when two people are nonverbally negotiating whether they should stand or sit in order to talk. One party starts to sit and finds the other still standing. The standing member notes the discrepancy and begins to sit— just as the other rises. From a distance the two can look like mechanically faulty jack-in-the-boxes. Or let me give you a personal example of temporal miscoordination. Picture if you will the sight of two people jogging together—one who is barely 5 feet in height and the other who is well over 6 feet. Although there is a decided push (sometimes quite literally) to run in unison, the difference in stride makes it very difficult. Each feels that the other has no sense of "rhythm"; and both are exhausted far beyond what the physical activity should induce.

The preceding examples begin to indicate what goes into the coordinated regulation of joint activity. The critical feature is a sharing of functions in time. The regulation of face-to-face interaction depends upon many things including shared rules, shared acts, and shared time. My hypothesis is that posture mirroring may not only be reflective of this sharing but may actually be instrumental to achieving it. And by posture mirroring I mean the degree to which two or more people adopt mirror-imaged postures vis-a-vis each other in a face-to-face interaction. This definition does not necessarily imply that people enter into the same posture at the same time, only that they come to share the same body position during the same period of time. This distinction between synchrous-movement-change points as Condon's work suggests (Condon & Ogston, 1967) and the simultaneous display of particular postural or movement classes as our work illustrates (LaFrance, 1979) is an important one and one which is addressed more fully later in the chapter.

INTERACTIONAL SYNCHRONY

As indicated earlier, Scheflen (1964) suggested that people in a group often mirror one another's posture. In a large gathering, as many as half a dozen people may sit or stand with limbs arranged in an identical or mirror-imaged way. Further, Scheflen postulated that where different postures have been adopted in a gathering, those who share posture usually turn out to share a viewpoint as well.

But this idea has a longer history. As early as 1895, Baldwin was suggesting that motor imitation is an avenue to knowledge of the other. A short time later, McDougall (1908), in one of the first published texts in social psychology, reported his curiosity about the manifest tendency of spectators to assume the postural strains of dancers or athletes they were watching. Blanton and Blanton in 1927 found that postural tensions in the mother tend to be assumed by an infant in arms so that a mother's fear becomes the child's fear. And George Herbert Mead (1934) clearly saw the deeper implications of motor imitation. He regarded it as helping to explain how the individual comes to take the role of another person. We do more than imitate. We perceive what the other is doing, but we note also our own response to it. What occurs is an interweaving process, what Mead called a "conversation of gestures" directed toward mutual understanding.

Although Fromm-Reichman wrote in 1950 that she imitated the postures of clients in order to facilitate her own intuitive inferences of their unverbalized attitudes, the topic of motor mimicry disappeared from the psychological research literature until the middle 1960s when William Condon began his painstaking studies of relation between speech and body movement both within and between speakers. Condon's first discovery was the phenomenon of "self-synchrony" or "the organization of change of a speaker's body motion synchronously with the articulated segmental organization of his speech" (Condon & Ogston, 1967, p. 225).

> ... as a person talks, "blending phone into syllable into word," his body moves in a series of configurations of change which are precisely correlated with the serial transformation of phone into syllable into word of speech. (p. 399)

In other words, the body parts change direction of movement together. This does not mean that all parts of the body are orienting in the same way. The head can be moving down, while the left arm is moving up toward the chin, while the eyes are closing, etc. When the body movement analysis was then superimposed upon the linguistic coding for a given speaker, Condon found that the points of *change* of a speaker's body motion occur synchronously with the articlated changes in the speech. The body "dances in time" with speech.

Further there was the striking finding that speaker and listener body motion change points were synchronized during interaction. Condon and Ogston (1967) reported that while a speaker is speaking and moving, the listener is moving as well. Although sitting relatively motionless and not making any specific gesticulations, he may still be moving hands or head, shifting his gaze or blinking. When these listener movements were compared to the linguistic description of the speaker, it was found that the boundaries of movement waves of the listener coincided with the boundaries of the speech and movement waves of the speaker. The listener may be moving in quite a different fashion from the speaker, but the simultaneity of movement and speech change points is maintained.

At microlevels, Condon's work suggests that communication is facilitated by the continual, shared, kinesic rhythmicity of cointeractants. Following Condon's lead, but moving to a more macrolevel of observation, Kendon (1970) observed body movement of participants in a group discussion. In his examination of listener behavior between those directly addressed by a speaker and those who, although members of the same encounter, are listening to an interchange in which they are not directly involved, Kendon found that the movements of the listener directly spoken to and the movements of the speaker mirror each other at least at the very beginning of the exchange in the speaker-listener roles. Further, Kendon noted that for any given individual, presence or involvement in a gathering may perhaps be judged by the degree to which posture shifts and other movements are coincident with those of others who are also present.

My own work on the speaker-listener turn-taking mechanism of black male speakers also found the presence of movement mirroring just prior to the actual verbal exchange. More specifically, the listener was found to begin a gestural and/or a postural movement at the beginning of the speaker's final utterance which mirrored the movement of the speaker (LaFrance, 1974). The finding that termination signaling is specifically characterized by movement matching is compatible with Kendon's speculation. It appears that movement mirroring may function as an effective and jointly created signal of collaboration. It is interesting that for both these investigations the movement mirroring was particularly visible at exchange points in the conversation. This is not surprising when one considers that it is precisely at these points that coordination is particularly critical. Nevertheless it is not known whether the mirroring is a signal indicating that the coordination has been achieved or whether it is a means whereby coordination is brought about.

The single experimental study of movement imitation was conducted by Dabbs in 1969. Dabbs had one subject mimic another's gestures to investigate the effect of movement similarity. Although mimicry did not directly affect liking for the other, mimicked subjects viewed themselves as more similar to the actor. In addition, Dabbs showed that perceived similarity interacted with intentional imitation, producing liking when the two factors combined. He concluded that:

> When two people are trying to communicate, similarities between them may improve communication . . . this similarity can provide a background or rapport without necessarily being noticed. (p. 338)

Said another way, it is possible that body movement similarity is an early interactional indicator of willingness to communicate. The literature in social psychology has been abundant in the documentation of the importance of similarity to interpersonal attraction (Byrne, 1971). Although similarity has usually been defined as comparability in attitudes, Dabb's (1969) study does imply that movement similarity may tap into the same interpersonal dimension.

Lastly, Charney (1966) focused on the more stationary postural domain in order to test Scheflen's notions regarding posture mirroring. Specifically, Charney analyzed the postures displayed by participants in a dyadic psychotherapy session. He found a significant association between the degree of mirroring in upper-body postures by the client and therapist and positive interpersonal-oriented speech content. In line with Scheflen's suggestion, Charney concluded that postural mirroring was a "naturally occurring interactive unit indicative of a state of therapeutic rapport or relatedness" (1966, p. 314).

While all the aforementioned studies intimate some relation between shared postures or actions and interpersonal involvement, they are more suggestive than definitive due to some methodological shortcomings. In the first place, the analyses have heretofore been more discovery—than verification-oriented. Consequently, the insights need to be taken as worthy and plausible hypotheses rather than as established facts. The issue here has to do with systematically mapping the occurrence *and* nonoccurrence of these phenomena in order to rule out observer and sampling errors. Secondly, the data base while usually intensive is typically not extensive due to small samples. Consequently the generality of the findings is limited. McDowall's (1978) recent nonreplication of Condon's findings has substantiated some of these reservations. In summary, the literature hints at the existence of an important set of phenomena which awaits empirical confirmation.

SYSTEMATIC INVESTIGATION OF POSTURE SHARING

Our research program began by examining the relation between posture mirroring and rapport in natural settings. The first aim was to apply systematic observational methods to the study of posture mirroring. The second concern was to conduct the initial investigations in natural settings so as to glean some information regarding the "ecological validity" of such posture sharing before conducting experimental studies in more controlled settings. The reasoning was that if mirroring of positions did not appear with at least some moderate level of occurrence and in some systematic relation to an important interactional variable in the natural world, then experimental investigations of the phenomenon in laboratory settings would be at best premature and at worst, empty empirical exercises. Another reason for initial observations being carried out in the field was to generate hypotheses not only concerning the relation between overall rates of posture mirroring and interpersonal involvement, but hypotheses having also to do with the conditions under which mirroring occurs.

POSTURE SHARING AND GROUP RAPPORT

The first study sought to explore posture sharing in a social unit larger than the dyadic unit typically used by researchers of nonverbal communication (LaFrance & Broadbent, 1976). More specifically, the question was whether the relation between posture sharing and rapport would be found in a group situation in which involvement may be a critical feature.

Trained coders made *in vivo* observations of posture sharing in a sample of college classrooms. At regular intervals, coders noted which one of a number of possible configurations the instructor had adopted for one body area, such as the left arm. These categories constituted a finite number of discrete and readily distinguishable examples such as left arm bent at elbow across front of body. As such, the observations required little or no interpretation on the part of the observers and no need for inferences to be drawn concerning the intentions or purposes of the participants.

The next step required coders immediately to scan the room and to count the number of students who were simultaneously displaying the same configuration for that particular body part either in congruent or mirroring fashion. The differences between these two is that in the former case, in a face-to-face situation, if the instructor had his left arm bent at the elbow with the left hand behind his neck, the student's left arm would also be so engaged to be coded as congruent. In the case of mirroring, the student's right arm would be so positioned.

In order to obtain a record of the display of posture sharing over the total duration of the encounter, a time-sampling procedure was used. More specifically, during an hour class period, observations began in the fifth minute and were then made every fifth minute until the end of the hour. Time sampling was also employed in order to take the decision of when to code out of the coders' hands. In order to obtain a representative reading of posture sharing for each class, coders observed the same classes on three separate occasions, spread over a week.

At the end of each class period, coders distributed to the

class a 10-item, self-report bipolar scale which asked for students' rating of the class. Of these items, three were selected to measure rapport with the rest constituting filler items. The three scales were: involved-disinterested, apart-together, high rapport-low rapport. Data analysis on 12 seminar-sized classrooms revealed a significant positive correlation ($r = .46$, $p < .01$) between posture mirroring and a combined rating of the three scales. Classes characterized by the students as being in the upper range of the rapport scale were also the ones that displayed higher amounts of posture mirroring. Surprisingly, the correlation between the congruent posture index and rapport was nonsignificant ($r = .09$, n.s.), suggesting important differences in the two forms of posture sharing. Although Scheflen (1964) distinguished between the two types of posture sharing, he nevertheless implied their essential comparability in indicating interpersonal relatedness. It is possible that mirroring is more salient in face-to-face situations, such as these classroom contexts, rather than in parallel seating arrangements, accounting for the found difference in this study. But it is also possible that mirroring is the more significant form of posture sharing in all types of multiperson arrangements. Research is needed to explore these possibilities.

CROSS-LAGGED ANALYSIS OF THE RELATION BETWEEN POSTURE MIRRORING AND RAPPORT

The study just described substantially documented the positive relation between posture mirroring and self–reports of involvement in a group context. The correlational nature of the data, however, did not allow statements to be made about the causality involved. Does posture mirroring affect rapport or is the reverse relation true? Consequently, a second study was undertaken to replicate the previous work in a design that maintained the naturalistic emphasis while allowing the direction of causality to be teased out (LaFrance, 1979).

As mentioned previously in the discussion of movement

mirroring during conversational turn-taking, the causal direction of this posture-sharing rapport relation has been an unexplored issue. Is position mirroring a cue to the presence of interpersonal involvement or is it an interactional device whose purpose it is to establish communality? This is not to argue that the relation must be linear and unidirectional. In fact it is likely that over time the relation is characterized by bidirectionality. Rather the issue is whether mirroring is *only* expressive of an underlying social psychological disposition or whether it contributes to the establishing of that disposition.

To examine this question, the second study used a longitudinal design employing the cross-lag panel technique (Kenny, 1973, 1975). The logic of the cross-lagged analysis is that if two variables, posture mirroring (PM) and rapport (R), are measured at two separate points in time, one can look at the difference between the two cross-lagged correlations ($PM_{time\ one}$, $R_{time\ two}$) and ($R_{time\ one}$, $PM_{time\ two}$) in order to assess the probable direction of causality. In other words if the correlation PM_1R_2 is greater than the correlation R_1PM_2, and if other assumptions are met, then one can interpret it to mean that PM has causal priority over R rather than the reverse.

More concretely, the cross-lag analysis permits one to assess which one of four factors is involved in bringing about a significant correlation between posture mirroring and rapport. The first two are straightforward: First, posture mirroring, by creating interpersonal coordination, could facilitate the subsequent establishing of rapport. Second, rapport once created could become manifest through the display of posture mirroring. Third, both posture mirroring and rapport could be simultaneously caused by an unknown third variable; and finally, both variables could be affecting each other in a positive feedback loop, such that no unitary causal direction can be ascertained.

Videotapes were made on a total of 95 students in 14 college classrooms twice during a six-week summer session, once during the initial week of classes and once again during the final week of classes. Classes were selected to have a maximum of 25 students in order that all or nearly all the participants would be able to be coded. Permission to videotape was obtained from professors and students prior to the first taping. The tapes were made in regular classrooms with the seating arrangements taken as found. The result was that about half the classes were in row seating and half in circular arrangements. The video camera was placed in a stationary overhead corner position and was focused such that both instructor and students were in view at the same time. Rapport was measured as the sum of the following six bipolar scales: in step-out of step, involved-disinterested, high rapport-low rapport, incompatible-compatible, together-apart, congruent-incongruent.

The tapes were coded by two research assistants. As in the previous investigation, a time-sampling method was used to transcribe the tapes. Coders separately transcribed the torso, left arm, and right arm positions for each person at a time at 10 intervals equally spaced across an hour of class time. The second step in the coding procedure then involved placing each student's posture profile alongside his/her respective instructor's posture profile. At each of the 10 observation points, for each of three body positions, a judgment was made whether mirroring was present. In other words, the coding involved making discrete decisions; mirroring was either present or absent at each time point. Scores for each student were the sum of these judgments ranging from a minimum of 0 to a maximum of 30. Interrater reliabilities on the transcriptions and posture-sharing judgments were .92 and .96, respectively. The classroom was used as the unit of analysis. Consequently, individual scores on mirroring and rapport were combined and averaged to obtain measures for each class. These group scores were then subjected to the correlational analyses.

As in the prior investigation, analysis showed that posture mirroring and rapport were significantly correlated with each other at both time points ($r = .63, p < .01, r = .44, p < .09$). In addition, analysis of the cross-lagged differential lent cautious support to the interpretation of the causal priority of posture mirroring over rapport. The correlation PM_1R_2 was .77, whereas the other cross-lagged correlation PM_2R_1 was .58. The difference was marginally significant ($p < .15$, two tailed).

The results of this latter study are important for a number of reasons. First, they confirm that posture mirroring is a systematic and meaningful interpersonal phenomenon. This form of posture sharing occurs naturally, is associated with self-reports of involvement, and may be instrumental to bringing such involvement about. Second, the study demonstrates that posture mirroring is susceptible to objective measurement and can be shown to have high interobserver reliability. Third, these results raise the question of how much postural mirroring actually occurs in interaction. In our classroom situations, the results show that posture mirroring actually occurs frequently enough to be picked up by time-sampling methods but not so extensively so as to make multiple observations redundant. In any case, posture mirroring is not constant nor ubiquitous. The question can now shift from whether posture mirroring occurs to where and under what circumstances does it occur. And lastly, the possibility that posture mirroring is temporally prior to the experience of rapport raises a number of important questions. How does this posture sharing come about? What is its role in regulating interpersonal encounters?

IMPLICATIONS OF POSTURE SHARING FOR FACE-TO-FACE INTERACTION

The studies, taken together, lend themselves also to a number of general observations. First, the salient factor in rapport does not seem to be which particular postures are adopted, but whether two people adopt mirroring postures vis-a-vis each other at the same time. Consequently, two dyads could engage in very different postural forms yet report comparable levels of involvement.

This makes eminently good sense. It has been noted in the research on the psychology of perception that not only is similarity a crucial feature in the detection of what objects seem to go together, but that it outweighs other potential perception cues such as proximity in this determination (Wertheimer, 1958). That two or more people find themselves, albeit probably unconsciously and usually nondeliberately, sharing the same stance, is clearly a more direct route to feeling on track than having to be in a particular postural configuration. Nevertheless, the limits to this hypothesis will need to be tested.

The term synchrony has been used to describe co-occurrence of movement change points (as in the work of Condon) a well as the co-occurrence of body positions (as in our work on posture sharing. There is need to keep the two types of nonverbal co-occurrence distinct. The first says nothing about the content of the movement whereas the latter implies nothing about exactly coordinating onsets or endings of the postures assumed. It falls to further work to explore these and other kinds and levels of nonverbal synchorony. It may be that each serves a unique interpersonal or communicational function. On the other hand, different forms of nonverbal synchrony may be mutually reinforcing or redundant. At this juncture more is likely to be gained by assuming variability and checking for overlap rather then presuming identical meaning.

In the preface to his book, *Relations in Public*, Goffman (1971) argued that "interaction practices have been used to illuminate other things but themselves are treated as though they did not need to be defined or were not worth defining" (p.i). Similarily, Altman (1976) called for the expansion of the definition of social psychology to include not only the study of social behavior but the study of *social units* as well. This proposal is an oft heard, though generally unheeded one; namely, that social interaction cannot be understood by exclusive reliance on the behavior of individuals. It is reductionism to believe that knowledge of an individual is sufficient to explain a phenomenon that occurs in a relation of individuals. The significance of posture sharing and other similar indices of interactional coordination derives from their attention to the dyad or group as the starting point. The literature in nonverbal communication is replete with studies of individual expressive behavior and relatively little attention to what Goffman has called the "with." Posture mirroring may be uniquely helpful in understanding the ongoing formation, change and dissolution of these social units.

Posture mirroring appears to be a reliable and valid indicator of interpersonal solidarity. Time sampling has been our method of choice to date. But continuous time measurements will be necessary as well in order to accurately portray the frequency and duration of posture sharing in groups of various types. Then when we know something about its frequency we can get on with identifying the factors which affect its display as well as the influence of posture mirroring on other aspects of interpersonal engagement. For example, mirroring may enable cointeractants to monitor (albeit probably nonconsciously) the other's level of engagement or relatedness. From an outsider's perspective, an observer might similarly be able to gauge the level of cohesion between and among members of an encounter by noting the amount of mirroring displayed. Secondly, interactional coordination may be more notably present when communication assumes particular importance or when collaboration is necessary to achieve some undertaking. We are currently investigating the impact of intergroup cooperation and competition on the display of posture mirroring. Finally, there may be individual differences in the degree to which people are geared to involvement with others, and thus in their tendency to adopt mirrored positions.

My basic concern has been to understand interaction on its own terms. My sense is that posture sharing may be a route to this understanding. This is not to suggest that this posture sharing preempts other forms of synchrony or other channels of communication but that it may be uniquely reflective of *relationship* dynamics and even instrumental to their creation.

DISCUSSION

Paul Byers: You wrestle with the relationship between sharing postures and rapport. I wonder if you would say that posture sharing *is* rapport. If you have two people sharing all sorts of postures and rhythms in bed, you don't say sex involves intimacy, you say it is intimacy. I'm suggesting that rather than trying to establish a relationship between a behavior and an abstraction, why not recognize that the abstraction is there to label the behavior.

Marianne
LaFrance: Good point, except a couple of important caveats need to be made. First, you equated rapport and intimacy, and I do not see these two as equivalent. In fact, the ratings suggest that they are not related in any perfect sense. There is a distinction between being *involved* in an encounter and *liking* the person with whom you're involved. Scheflen made the same observation a number of years ago when he suggested that two old friends could be having a vicious argument but still adopt identical postures as if indicating that the relationship was still viable though the content of the interaction at the time was anything but positive. Secondly, given the positive but far from perfect correlations between this type of nonverbal behavior and self-reports of subjective experience, to say they are equivalent is to do injustice to the complexity of both rapport and synchrony. I think synchrony may

be related to other kinds of interpersonal dimensions in addition to rapport.

Madeleine Mathiot: Behavior in interaction is very complex, and the question has been asked how many different systems or subsystems should be postulated. I would like to suggest that synchrony between different behavioral flows may indicate that they belong to the same system. If you think especially of the work by Kendon on the maneuverings of the participants when they come into spatial orientational systems, I think that it is very obvious the maneuverings are in synchrony, and this is an indication that you have an isolatable system. I think that this could also be utilized to show that some aspects of the speech flow and body motion flow pertain to a single system, which has been also suggested by many researchers.

Marianne LaFrance: I think much research is needed to see whether all forms of synchrony come from the same system. I feel uncomfortable beginning with the assumption that they are identical. After looking at different movement levels with different measures over different periods of time and in different contexts, it would be lovely to find that they all derive from the same system, but I would not start out assuming that they do.

Participant: In psychodrama when you work especially with schizophrenics who have difficulties with expressing themselves, you can assume the exact posture and get hunches or access to what they are thinking.

Marianne LaFrance: Yes, I think that's what Frieda Fromm-Reichman reported.

Participant: Could you clarify what measures of rapport were used?

Marianne
LaFrance: Let me mention a few of the items we used to measure it. There were synonyms for rapport such as in-step/out-of-step, involved/disinterested, compatible/incompatible, and the like. We did correlate these ratings with positivity ratings such as good/bad, liking/not liking. We found them to be positively correlated but that the rapport items were more highly correlated with ratings assessing an activity dimension, that is, the "energy" dimension rather than pure liking or pure intimacy.

Participant: Do you know what kind of equipment McDowall used in his attempt to replicate Condon?

Marianne
LaFrance: Well, I think that Adam Kendon is going to talk about this later. He reports that he had a standard projector of the type that Bill Condon used to do his analyses.

Adam Kendon: No. The equipment that McDowall used was modified to be a flicker-free projector similar to the Athena, and, thus, it does not do what I would call movement phrase boundary analysis or . . . what happens in movement phrases but looks at them frame by frame. So this technique is in fact a different one.

Participant: That's the point. It is not a replication at all. (And so cannot be used as valid evidence against Condon's observations. — Editor)

Marianne
LaFrance: The real issue with this is neither to throw away the interactional synchrony research as a lot of people would like to do or to throw McDowall away. It behooves us to become much more sophisticated about documenting its occurrence and replicating it.

Participant: Did you say something about an "0" correlation for congruence but a positive correlation for mirroring?

Marianne
LaFrance: The correlation for postural congruency with rapport was low and nonsignificant. My sense is that mirroring is a much more direct sense of knowing that we're together, whereas postural congruence does not directly match the other.

Participant: Are there cases when the rate of postural shifts of the faculty member is so fast the students can't catch up or so infrequent that they can't be shared, and, if so, does that have any effect on the analysis of rapport?

Marianne
LaFrance: Good question. We're doing some analyses on that right now. There are a lot of things that I thought would make a difference that turned out not to make a difference. Certain instructors were incredibly still, others did a fair amount of moving around. That did not seem to affect the nature of the relation between posture and rapport. The other thing is an implication about the instructor's behavior. Posture sharing is, by definition, something that only two people or more can do. We keep slipping into thinking of who is sharing whose posture as though one person does it. I've been phrasing it as students adopting the instructor's posture. It also may be the reciprocal process of the instructor knowing where most of the students are and doing what they're doing.

REFERENCES

Altman, I. Environmental psychology and social psychology. *Personality and Social Psychology Bulletin*, 1976, 2, 96–113.

Baldwin, J. M. *Mental development in the child and in the race*. New York: Macmillan, 1895.

Blanton, S., & Blanton, M. *Child guidance*. New York: Century, 1927.

Byrne, D. *The attraction paradigm*. New York: Academic Press, 1971.

Charney, E. J. Psychosomatic manifestations of rapport in psychotherapy. *Psychosomatic Medicine*, 1966, *28*, 305–315.

Condon, W. S., & Ogston, W. D. A segmentation of behavior. *Journal of Psychiatric Research*, 1967, *5*, 221–235.

Dabbs, J. M., Jr. Similarity of gestures and interpersonal influence. *Proceedings of the 77th Annual Convention of the American Psychological Association*, 1969, *4*, 337–338.

Fromm-Reichman, F. *Psychoanalysis and psychotherapy*. Chicago: University of Chicago Press, 1950.

Goffman, E. *Relations in public*. New York: Basic Books, 1971.

Kendon, A. Movement coordination in social interaction: Some examples described. *Acta Psychologica*, 1970, *32*, 101–125.

Kenny, D. A. Cross-lagged and synchronous common factors in panel data. In A. S. Goldberger & D. D. Duncan (Eds.), *Structural equation models in the social sciences*. New York: Seminar Press, 1973.

Kenny, D. A. Cross-lagged panel correlation: A test for spuriousness. *Psychological Bulletin*, 1975, *82*, 887–903.

LaFrance, M. Nonverbal cues to conversational turn taking between Black speakers. *Personality and Social Psychology Bulletin*, 1974, *1*, 240–243.

LaFrance, M. Nonverbal synchrony and rapport: Analysis by the cross-lag panel technique. *Social Psychology Quarterly*, 1979, *42*, 66–70.

LaFrance, M., & Broadbent, M. Group rapport: Posture sharing as a nonverbal indicator. *Group and Organizational Studies*, 1976, *1*, 328–333.

McDougall, W. *Introduction to social psychology*. London: Methuen, 1908.

McDowall, J. J. Interactional synchrony: A reappraisal. *Journal of Personality and Social Psychology*, 1978, *36*, 963–975.

Mead, G. H. *Mind, self, and society* (posthumous C. M. Morris, Ed.) Chicago: University of Chicago Press, 1934.

Scheflen, A. E. The significance of posture in communication systems. *Psychiatry*, 1964, *27*, 316–331.

Wertheimer, M. Principles of perceptual organizations. In D. C. Beardslee & M. Wertheimer (Eds.), *Readings in perception*. New York: Van Nostrand, 1958.

Chapter 14

A DYADIC MODEL FOR THE STUDY OF CONVERGENCE IN NURSE-PATIENT INTERACTIONS

M. Jean Daubenmire
and Sharon Searles

While there is general recognition of the importance of communication in nursing, there is still much miscommunication or lack of communucation in the everyday world of the hospital. Communicative interaction is a basic practice phenomena in planning and implementing patient care and yet little research has been conducted on communication as a process in health care settings.

We have been involved for the past seven years in the study of nurse-patient communication. Our clinical expertise and the need for well-documented research on effective nursing practice to improve teaching of nurses led us to examine in depth what actually occurs in nurse-patient encounters. The purpose of our study was to develop a methodology for examining the complexity of the interaction processes that occur among nurses and patients in a hospital setting.

Funded for five years by grants from U.S.P.H.S., the Division of Nursing, we developed extensive recording methods using remote controlled audio-video equipment set up in a private hospital room and a postoperative recovery room. Because of the multiple variables ocurring at any one point in time, computer programs were developed and used for pattern analysis and statistical assessment. The research team varied from four to nine persons over the years and primarily included nurse researchers, one person with dance background, a computer programmer, a video technician, and consultants in computer systems and mathematics.

In the study of the interaction process, the focus is shifted from the behavior of an individual to the occurring behavior patterns and processes occurring between persons. In traditional interaction research there has been little or no language for adequately doing this and few strategies for empirically studying these processes. In the initial phase of the project, research methodologies of Ray L. Birdwhistell, Edward T. Hall, and Paul Ekman were explored. Also, several of us traveled to consult and sometimes train with specialists such as Irmgard Bartenieff, Martha Davis, and Warren Lamb. It became clear that we had to evolve our own methodology as each of the experts' input was valuable, but not precisely suited to our area of research.

Ultimately, we collected our data in 21 column recordings of the observable aspects of speech and motion of two or more participants. Entries were made on a second-to-second basis. Time was electronically superimposed on the video recordings in day, hour, minute, and second. Since multiple variables occurred in any one second, there was a great deal of data. Faced with the second stage of analyzing and synthesizing so many bits of information, it became essential to use and/or develop computer programs for pattern analysis. We have made decisions as to what dimensions of the encounter appear most salient for our concerns. In our case, the modes of rapport, contact, and interactions which might bring relief and comfort to the patient—and those, of course, potentially engendering the opposite states of discomfort, antipathy, and alienation—are of prime concern.

We will report only a part of our research dealing with two concepts we found useful and empirically testable—convergence and synchrony. We will particularly focus on what we have termed "convergence."

Both convergence and synchrony are processes which occur between two or more persons as they respond to each other in an interpersonal context. Both appear to be significant interactional phenomena. Convergence is defined as a process of increasing similarity in behavior, literally duplicating the actions and speech patterns of each other in various degrees and ways. Early research related to convergence concentrated on speech, demonstrating that the process of interaction can result in interactions progressing toward more similar patterns of verbal communication (Strupp, 1960; Pepinski, 1964; Lennard and Bernstein, 1969). An outcome of our research is to offer further methods for the study of both verbal and nonverbal convergence using a dyadic model.

There is a growing body of research that indicates interaction usually occurs with some level of synchrony (e. g. Condon, 1967). While there is general agreement that synchrony is a significant interactional phenomena, there is general disagreement on how to define synchrony and, further, how to measure this phenomena in "grosser" observations lasting 1 second or more. Condon's observations of synchrony are based on fractions of a second segments of behavior.

METHODOLOGICAL FRAMEWORK

We have called the methodology we have developed and are presently using "synchronology." Synchronology is the study of presenting behaviors between two or more persons as they occur, change, and develop over time. The framework provides for in-context description and analysis of complex verbal and nonverbal behavior patterns.

Synchronology is composed of five interrelated yet discrete components.

(1) Time Process Model of Human Interaction. A conceptual model to delineate functional units for examining interaction patterns.

(2)   Synchronics. An extensive notation system to systematically describe both verbal and nonverbal behavior. The notation system provides for description of both quantitative and qualitative dimensions of behavior. The quantitative aspect refers to the occurrence or frequency of behavior and the qualitative aspect refers to how a behavior occurs.

(3)   Structure of Events. A structural framework for context delineation, selection of discrete data subsets for analysis, and interpretation of behavior patterns in context.

(4)   Interpretive Concepts. The concepts of convergence and synchrony are being used to provide a conceptual basis for selection and interpretation of interaction patterns.

(5)   Grounded Theory Approach to Data Analysis. A cyclical framework to data analysis which provides mechanisms for large numbers of variables, data-based hypotheses generation, and refinement of the conceptual framework.

Time-series data of patient-health care personnel interactions were collected from admission to discharge via a remote control, audio-video recording system. A total of 1,902 taped interactions were collected varying in length from 10 seconds to over 1 hour. Selected data samples were extracted from videotape, coded, and computerized in both mnemonic word form and numeric files. This interactional data was instrumental in the methodological development and was a key in forcing us to define and describe what was present in the data rather than use methods which were not descriptive of the process.

A more complete description of the framework has been included in a previous article (Daubenmire, et al., 1978). Only the time process model is included in this paper as a basis for presenting the convergence methodology.

Time-Process Model of Human Interaction

As illustrated in Fig. 14-1, the *time-process model of human interaction*, communicative interaction is conceptualized as a dynamic, ongoing behavior process which can be studied by

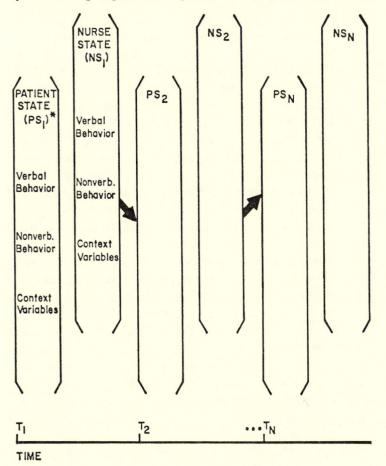

* ( ) = Vector state—includes values of presenting behaviors at given points in time.

Figure 14–1: **Time Process Model of Human Interaction**

identifying the observed effects of presenting behaviors on the participants. States of nurse and patient are described as vectors which include values of essential presenting behaviors at given points in time; for example, patient state 1 (PS$_1$) and nurse state 1 (NS$_1$) at a time 1 (T$_1$). Presenting behaviors are those observable verbal and nonverbal behaviors by which persons communicate with each other. Within any interaction then, the presenting verbal and nonverbal behavior of an individual (PS$_1$) constitutes a message, or transmits information which is received by the second individual. As the second individual responds to the information there will be a change in his observable behavior (NS$_1$). This behavior then transmits a message to the first individual who responds with a change in his behavior (PS$_2$). Feedback, considered a means for altering or clarifyng a message, is conceptualized as occurring in the arrows which go forward in time. Clarification or alteration of a previous message is a new message because there is a different state of both patient and nurse. Therefore, *each message is a new message, each state a new state in time* and the process can be observed as such. While the model indicates nurse state and patient state, it is useful for study of any two or more interacting systems. The unidirectionality of the model also provides for complex data collection and analysis related to the changing presenting behaviors of the participants over time as they respond to each other.

It is important to clarify that this model is not an action-reaction or cause-effect model. In fact, we would not oversimplify the observations by assuming that patient state 1 "causes" nurse state 1 which then "causes" patient state 2, etc. Instead, the model provides a pragmatic method for successive recording of nurse and patient behaviors as they occur over time in an interaction situation.

Based on the time-process model of human interaction, we have conceptualized three levels of behavioral units for observation and pattern analysis:

(1)   Individual. A state of nurse *or* patient at any point in

time; for example, patient state at time 1 (PS$_1$ at T$_1$) on the model.

(2) Interactional. A nurse state *and* patient state at any given point in time; for example, PS$_1$ and NS$_1$ at T$_1$ on the model.

(3) Dyadic. A state in which the nurse and patient are transformed into a new state. The dyad describes a different state which is more than the sum of individual behaviors. The patient in a given state (PS$_1$) and the nurse in a given state (NS$_1$) influence and respond to each other in a variety of ways. These two states, PS$_1$ and NS$_1$, are transformed into a new state referred to as the state of the dyad (DS$_1$); for example, DS$_1$ at T$_1$ on the model.

Patterns are defined as recurring sequences of the above behavioral units.

It is our contention that the dyadic level of analysis has the most potential for gaining insight into the communication process we are most concerned with. The conceptualization of the dyadic level provides for a different level of analysis. Dyadic behavior is more than the sum of individual behavior. Dyadic behavior is described as a unit rather than as behavior of individuals responding to each other. It is important to note that in most reported studies the dyad refers to two interacting persons. In this study, the dyadic state is described as one unit; the nurse and patient are one system.

There is however, a growing awareness by some authors of the importance of what we refer to as dyadic state. Byers, while not naming the phenomenon, describes it as "when two people get to the same state through communication (talking, dancing, singing, massage, etc.), certain physiological processes become synchronized and the two interactants function, in part, as a single organism" (Byers, 1977, p. 138).

Condon, in describing interactional synchrony of speakers and listeners, indicates that even following silence "at the precise

1/48 second the speaker resumes talking, the listener begins his or her series of synchronized movements'' (Condon, 1975, p. 43). This seems to imply much more than an action response pattern, but rather becoming a part of one system. In the study of mother-infant interactions, several researchers refer to the strength of the dyad. ''In other words, the strength of the dyadic interaction dominates the meaning of each member's behavior'' (Brazelton, Koslowski, and Main, 1974, p. 55).

The activity-inactivity model was based on modification of ideas from Chapple's (1970a) extensive research measuring rhythmic patterns of activity-inactivity in speech frequency and duration. The investigators believed a dyadic activity-inactivity model could provide a basis for further study of phenomenon like convergence and synchrony. While both concepts have been studied in the verbal mode, nonverbal variables such as eye contact, limb movement, body movement, gestures, and touch have received little attention.

The initial coding process included detailed coding of verbal behaviors and quantitative and qualitative measures of nonverbal behaviors on a second-by-second time frame. For example, any limb-movement notation included a description of the part of the anatomy used, the duration of the movement, the directional pathway, and the amount of energy used in relation to force, space, and timing. This was true for all nonverbal behaviors. Many types of analysis were used and will be reported in future papers.

For this study of convergence, the data were compacted via computer and the dyad was examined for patterns of activity or inactivity. Measures of convergence were based on similarity/ dissimilarity of nurse-patient behaviors within an encounter. Convergence is defined as a process of increasing behavior similarity; divergence indicates decreasing similarity of behavior and stationarity denotes a process of little or no variance in behavior. The technique can be used for any number of verbal and nonverbal variables, both in the initiation and duration mode.

This technique was developed to provide a measure of

convergence that applies uniformly to interactions of varying length. It uses a dyadic model for comparison of nurse-patient behavior based on activity/inactivity duration. Four possible states are coded for each of the variables, body movement, limb movement, and eye contact. The four states include:

(1) mutual activity — nurse active, patient active
(2) nurse active, patient inactive
(3) nurse inactive, patient active
(4) mutual inactivity — nurse inactive, patient inactive

States 1 and 4 describe periods when the nurse and patient are involved in similar activity. States 2 and 3 describe periods when the nurse and patient activity are not similar.

Using this model, convergence is defined by the following steps: (1) each interaction is divided into segments of 1 minute each plus a final segment of less than or equal to 1 minute; (2) in each segment there are 60 observations of each variable relative to activity/inactivity duration; (3) states 1 and 4 are combined into a similarity state (S) and the frequency of occurrence of S in each time segment is divided by 60 to obtain a measure P (S) of the time fraction that nurse and patient are involved in similar activity; and (4) the similarity measures from each time segment are then compared to determine rate of change of similarity from one time segment to the following time segment. The rate of change provides an index of trends toward increasing or decreasing similarity across time segments.

The computations are dramatized by: $M(S) = [P(S) - .5] \times 2$ then $-1 \ M(S) \ 1$, $M(S) = -1$ when $P(S) = 0$, $M(S) = 1$ when $P(S) = 1$, and $M(S) = 0$ when $P(S) = .5$. In this manner, a similarity/dissimilarity measure is constructed with the property of being -1 for totally dissimilar activity and $+1$ for completely similar activity. To derive a convergence measure C from $M(S)$, one denotes by $M_i(S)$ the similarity measure in the ith segment and define C_i by: $C_i = M_{i+1} (S)] / 2$, $i = 1, 2, \ldots$ The component $M_{i+1}(S) - M_i(S)$ gives the rate of change of similarity, and dividing this by 2 puts C_i in the range of -1 to $+1$. C_i $= -1$ designates a change from completely similar activity to completely dissimilar activity (divergence), $C_i = +1$ designates a change from completely dissimilar activity to completely similar activity (convergence) and $C_i = 0$ denotes no change in activity (stationarity). Thus, a positive rate of change means that the measures of similarity are becoming closer and the process is converging. Negative rate of change indicates measures of similarity are becoming increasingly different and the process is diverging. Zero rate of change implies stationarity.

Figure 14-2, a graphic display of the S_1 and C values, demonstrates a visual representation of similarity (S) and convergence (C) over time. The solid line connecting S values provides an index of increasing and decreasing similarity in behavior from minute to minute. The C value, which is graphed between two S values, provides an index of the extent to which two S values are *becoming* similar. Any interpretation of convergence, therefore, requires attention to both S and C scales. For example, from minute 1 to minute 2 nurse-patient behavior similarity increases to a $+0.27$ C value, that is, some convergence has occurred. From minute 2 to minute 3 there is a slight decrease in similarity; however, the behaviors remain relatively similar. The C value -0.05 indicates the process is primarily stationary because it is closest to 0, i. e. 0 equals stationarity. From minute 15 to minute 23, nurse-patient body movement is completely similar; behavior has converged. The C values 0.00 again indicate a stationary process. During this time, the S values are no longer increasing in similarity because convergence has occurred and the process is stationary. A stationary process could also occur if behavior remained dissimilar over a period of time. Both S and C scales then are necessary for interpretation of convergence. The decrease in behavior similarity from minute 4 to minute 5 leads to a $-.55$ C value, and example of divergence. Results of convergence analysis for one encounter are presented in Figs. 14-2, 3, and 4 to exemplify how this analysis is applicable for study of nurse-patient interactions.

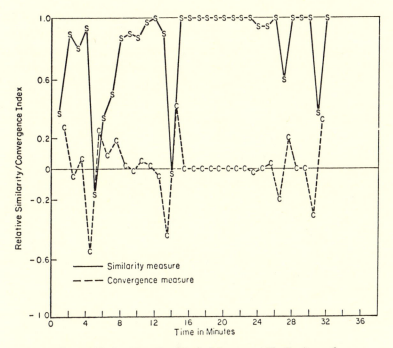

Figure 14–2:   Graph of Body Movement Similarity and Convergence for a 32-Minute Encounter Between Mr. B and RN3

Before describing this encounter, it is important to explain that the patients in our study were ill and had been hospitalized in order to have some type of surgery. The project was done at The Ohio State University Medical Center, a teaching hospital supportive of this long-term project. Patients are frequently from out of town, have suffered serious illness, and have come to Ohio State because of the expertise available for treatment.

We believe that nurse-patient relationships developed under stress have the potential for being intensified in time in either a positive or negative way. Relationships are developed very quickly in the hospital which might take days or weeks to develop under other circumstances. Of course, each patient and staff member fully consented and was informed about the project and the cameras. Patients and staff seemed to adjust to the

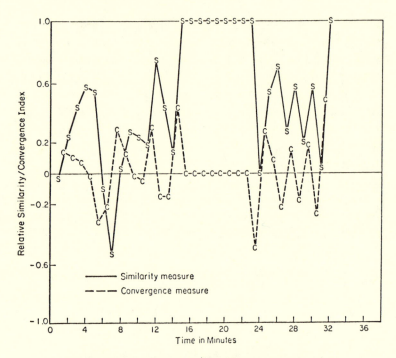

**Figure 14–3:   Graph of Limb Movement Similarity
and Convergence for a 32-Minute Encounter
Between Mr. B and RN3**

presence of the cameras readily. All persons were given the option of asking to have the cameras turned off. Only one orderly made this request throughout the rather lengthy time of data collection.

For some critically ill patients such as Mr. B, whom we will discuss, the project was in a small way a means of feeling useful and giving some value to his suffering. He cheerfully stated, "I'd like to help improve patient care." He understood that he had cancer and on several occasions discussed dying as well as ways to make living more comfortable. Of course, such situations as these are the critical challenge in nursing, the most demanding and important, and hence the most urgent to study and understand.

We will focus on a 32-minute encounter between the

patient, Mr. B, and RN3 which occurred nine days ofter the patient had undergone surgery for removal of recurrent abdominal wall carcinoma. Mr. B has experienced numerous surgical interventions for tumor removal, a colostomy, and a nephrostomy. He was addicted to morphine secondary to severe abdominal pain. During this encounter, he continued to complain of surgical pain and abdominal distention, which necessitated increased dosages of morphine. Mr. B received fluids and vitamins intravenously. He remained sitting in bed throughout the encounter. The nurse, RN3, had visited Mr. B 10 previous times. During those visits, Mr. B expressed some concern over the increased dosages of morphine required for postoperative pain.

During the encounter illustrated in Figs. 14-2, 3, and 4, one

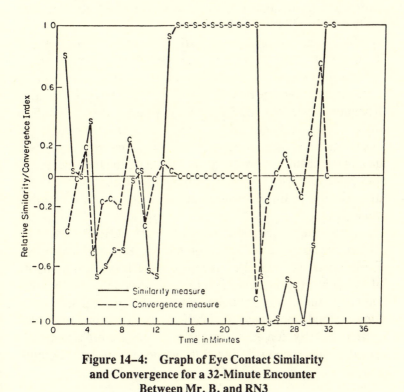

Figure 14–4: Graph of Eye Contact Similarity and Convergence for a 32-Minute Encounter Between Mr. B. and RN3

can see that the pattern of nurse-patient body movement is more similar and the process remain more stationary throughout the encounter in comparison to limb movement and eye contact. For the first 7 minutes RN3 is standing in the patient's exploratory space, a distance of 7 to 12 feet from the patient. Verbal exchange includes evidence of entry and approach behaviors and a discussion on mouth care to relieve some of Mr. B's discomfort. During minute 7, Mr. B mentions he slept well and was able to go six to eight hours without much pain. At this point, RN3 moves into the patient's interpersonal space, a distance of 4 to 7 feet from the bed and sits down facing the patient. She also verbally recognizes Mr. B's comment and Mr. B discloses his concern about taking morphine, ''Cause I think if there's any way in the world to get off the stuff you have to start stretching it out you know, move it out farther and farther and farther and eventually try to get off it.'' Patterns for eye contact, limb and body movement show an increase in similarity from minute 7 to 10. The discussion of pain medication also continues until minute 10 when Mr. B attempts to change the subject and RN3 directs him back to the discussion by a question about how he plans to ''stretch out'' the time between medications. At this point, another RN enters the room and Mr. B again changes the subject. The most dramatic changes during minute 10 occur in the patterns for eye contact and limb movement. One initial interpretation might be that the change in similarity in eye contact and limb movement was related to Mr. B's verbally expressed discomfort with the discussion of pain medication and/or the presence of another person.

The second RN leaves during minute 12. RN3 once more returns the conversation to the topic of Mr. B's pain medication. From minute 12 to 13, there is a measurable increase in similarity of eye contact, or increased mutual gazing. By minute 15, the S value $+1$ indicates continued mutual eye contact. Patterns for limb and body movement also show a shift to $+1$ similarity. This total similarity for all three variables lasts until minute 23. Verbal conversation during this period of interface includes further discussion of Mr. B's fears concerning morphine, his chemotherapy as it is related to nausea and the need for continued relief of pain. The nurse verbally clarifies, reflects, and assists the patient to interpret his thoughts and feelings. During minute 23, the nurse moves toward Mr. B and touches his arm. The conversation centers around how Mr. B will specifically talk with his physician about nausea from chemotherapy and his concerns about spacing dosages of morphine. Mr. B begins to manipulate his nasogastric tube, break eye contact, and move around in bed. From minute 26 to 29, Mr. B begins to express his feelings about how difficult it has been for him to live during the past several years. "... my life the way it is right now, I just live from day to day; I don't try to make plans for tomorrow ... other than going to bed and hoping I wake up the next morning." Nurse responds, "You and I can do something about the quality of your life or what you do with your life. You have that choice in determining what it is that you will do with your day . . . . You've got some control over that." During this conversation, Mr. B continues to look away from the nurse. The break in eye contact, increased limb and body movements, and verbal content suggest Mr. B was very uncomfortable with talking about these problems. This shift in similarity during minute 23 is somewhat similar to the shift observed in minute 10 (see Figs. 14-3 and 14-4). In both patterns, there appears to be a period of self-disclosure which lasts for several minutes, the patient apparently becomes uncomfortable with the conversation, and similarity of eye contact and movement decreases. This suggests that during periods of self-disclosure there is a tendency to converge until the disclosure becomes too stressful for one or both persons. Analysis of this data set also suggests limb movement and eye contact are more likely to show fluctuations in convergence patterns than total body movement.

One further example is included in another encounter between Mr. B and another nurse, RN2. Only the graph of eye contact (Fig. 14-5) is included because of space. This preoperative interaction pattern is somewhat similar to the example given above. Although the variable relationships are different, there is a trend toward increasing similarity until minute 19. Verbal conversation centers around Mr. B's preoperative concerns and his life style resulting from recurrent carcinoma. A radical decrease in similarity occurs during minute 19, particularly for eye contact as the patient mentions suicide. This example appears to support the suggestion that convergence tends to increase during self-disclosing conversation until a certain point when more disclosure becomes too stressful and leads to divergence. It is important to note that this is dyadic analysis and both nurse and patient behaviors indicate discomfort at the point of divergence.

These examples have been included only for demonstrating specific points relating to the methodology. There was no intent to criticize the relationships. Mr. B later remarked that these two

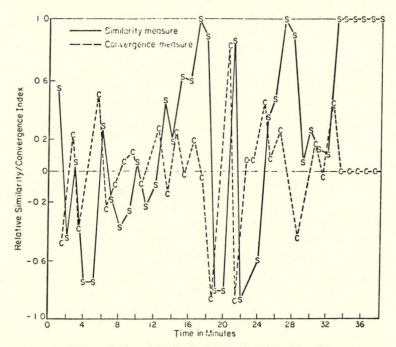

Figure 14–5:   Graph of Eye Contact Similarity and Convergence for a 38-Minute Encounter Between Mr. B and RN2

nurses had been most helpful to him throughout the hospitalization. Obviouly, he trusted them to be able to discuss dying and suicide with them. About a week later, the patient was able to return home to continue treatment on an outpatient basis.

Seventeen nurse-patient encounters were analyzed for patterns of convergence. The patterns identified for most data sets were essentially different; however, some commonalities began to emerge. Limb movement and eye contact showed more variability in patterns of similarity than did body movement for encounters longer than 15 minutes. Both variables appeared more indicative of or related to changes in conversation and context. For short interactions, lasting 6 minutes or less, specific patterns of similarity were not clearly delineated because the technique of obtaining one similarity and convergence measure each minute did not yield enough values for accurate pattern description. Perhaps similarity and convergence measures computed every 15 seconds would be more appropriate for short interactions.

Firm conclusions cannot be drawn at this time; however, certain patterns and variable relationships suggest potential for further investigation. The phenomena of self-disclosure in verbal content should be studied to determine: (1) extent to which convergence is associated with disclosure, and (2) how nonverbal convergence facilitates disclosure.

One should investigate whether specific patterns of convergence are common to broad patient populations or whether patterns are more individualized to specific nurse-patient dyads. For example, some nurses might attain higher measurements of convergence than others. A comparative study of one nurse interacting with numerous patients or the same patient interacting with numerous personnel would be appropriate for additional pattern identification.

Research which defines convergence in context of a total relationship is also needed. Both examples presented above represent nurse-patient dyads which had established a relationship over several encounters. Perhaps a tendency for behavior similarity occurs over several encounters as the relationship develops, and thus pattern identification should be made wth reference to context phases rather then specific encounters. Pepinski and Kurst (1964), for example, suggest convergence in values and attitudes develops over time throughout a therapeutic client-therapist relationship. Within this framework, one could also examine patterns of convergence as they relate to outcome.

Potential also exists for incorporating other nonverbal behaviors in convergence analysis. Areas of space, spatial relationships, touch, and specific activities might significantly correlate with type and extent of convergence. For example, convergence may occur most frequently in the interpersonal space.

An important methodological consideration is that while the nurse-patient communicative interaction process is considered to be extremely complex, interaction patterns can be statistically differentiated using a dyadic model which is not complex.

Synchrony

In this study we defined synchrony in terms of the intensity, frequency, rate, or duration of one person's patterns rhythmically matching the patterns of another person. Several methodological issues related to the development of the concept of synchrony were addressed in a previous article (Daubenmire, et al., 1978, p. 308). These included factors such as variable dependency, context dependency, and time process, or the time frame required for observation and measurement of synchrony.

Although synchrony appears to be a significant interactional phenomenon, it may well be an outcome rather than a process. The investigators are presently examining synchrony as an outcome of convergence. For example, patterns of convergence, divergence, and stationarity, specific C/D/S units over time in an encounter appear useful in identifying the rhythmic quality of similar nurse-patient activity.

In summary, the time process model provides a means of

examining the flow of behavior between two persons in an encounter. The dyadic level of analysis takes into account the continuous change and transformation occurring and yet may provide further insight into the basic unity and dynamic characteristics of the interaction process. While other authors press for an interactionalist approach to the study of communication, it is the investigator's belief that further research of the dyadic phenomenon is essential to understanding convergence and synchrony in the communication which occurs in interpersonal relationships. As greater understanding of this total process is gained, the outcomes will be invaluable to fields such as nursing.

REFERENCES

Brazelton, T. B., Koslowski, B., & Main, M. The origins of reciprocity: the early mother-infant interaction. In M. Lewis and L. A. Rosenblum (Eds.), *The effect of the infant on its caregiver*. New York: John Wiley and Sons, Inc., 1974.

Byers, P. A personal view of nonverbal communication. *Theory into practice: Journal of the School of Education*, 1977, *16* p. 138.

Chapple, E. D. *Culture and biological man*. New York: Holt, Rinehart and Winston, Inc., 1970a.

Chapple, E. D. Experimental production of transients in human interaction. *Nature*, 1970b *28*, pp. 360–633.

Condon, W. S. & Ogston, W. D. A segmentation of behaviors. *Journal of Psychiatric Research*, 1967, *5* pp. 22–235.

Condon, W. S. Multiple response to sound dysfunctional children. *Journal of Autism and Childhood Schizophrenia*, 1975, *5* p. 43.

Daubenmire, M. J. Nurse-patient-physician communicative interaction process. In H. Werley (Ed.), *Health research: A systems approach*. New York: Springer Publishing Company, 1976.

Daubenmire, M. J., Searles, S., & Ashton, C. A. A methodologic framework to study nurse-patient communication. *Nursing Research*, 1978, *25* pp. 303–310.

Lennard, H. L. & Bernstein, A. *Patterns in human interaction*. San Francisco: Jossey-Bass, Inc., 1969.

Pepinski, H. B. & Kurst, T. D. Convergence: a phenomena in counseling and psychotherapy. *American Psychologist*, 1964, *19* pp. 333–388.

Strupp, H. *Psychotherapeutics in action*. New York: Grune and Stratton, 1960.

ACKNOWLEDGMENT

While all team members have contributed to this research project, the convergence methodology was developed by the authors with Carol Ashton, Dr. James Gemma, and Dr. David Penniman. Their excellent contributions are acknowledged. This research project was funded by a Public Health Service Grant No. NU-00401-05, Division of Nursing.

Chapter 15

CYCLES OF SPONTANEOUS CONVERSATION UNDER LONG-TERM ISOLATION

Donald P. Hayes and Loren Cobb

INTRODUCTION

Social interaction, and particularly conversational behavior, is an activity that would seem, at least on the surface, to be independent of the physiological processes by which life is maintained in the body. Certainly it would be absurd to make the reductionist argument that the decision to engage in or terminate social interaction is solely caused by a change in a physiological state or system. Nevertheless, the claim can be made that the tendency to engage in conversation is detectably modulated by a cyclic physiological process that goes through an entire cycle in roughly 90 to 100 minutes. We make this claim, and cite evidence from a unique series of long-term isolation studies of couples in a natural but controlled environment.

From the perspective of biochronometry, all the processes of life are modulated by a loosely coupled network of physiological oscillators whose cycle times range from roughly 4 weeks (the menstrual cycle) down to 1/10th of a second (the alpha rhythms), and beyond. The strongest of these oscillators have cycle times of approximately 24 to 25 hours, and are therefore called "circadian." Oscillators with longer cycle times are called "infradian," while oscillators with shorter cycle times are called "ultradian." The popular literature on biorhythms notwithstanding, these ocillators are not as stable and regular as clockwork: quite the contrary. All known physiological oscillators can be perturbed and entrained by exogenous stimuli, and all exhibit some degree of autonomous irregularity. This is particularly so in the analysis of 90 to 100-minute sleep cycles. Kleitman (1967) proposed that cyclic changes in EEG and rapid eye movement during sleep were nighttime manifestations of a hypothesized physiological basic rest/activity cycle (BRAC). Since then, there have been a number of studies on daytime cycles of this length, including studies of "oral" behavior (in the psychoanalytic sense) by Friedman and Fisher (1967) and Ostwalt, et al. (1970); on day-dreaming by Othmer, et al. (1969) and Kripke and Sonnenschein (1978); and on human performance by Klein and Armitage (1979). At issue is whether these processes with similar cycle lengths are coupled to each other in-phase, suggesting a single master oscillator, or whether these processes are oscillating independently of one another. Such research is typically carried out in an environment where all exogenous sources of entrainment or perturbation have been controlled or eliminated. Since the purpose of such research is to determine if the cycle is endogeneous to the organism or is induced by some exogenous cyclic process, subjects under these controlled conditions are said to be "free-running." Under free-running conditions, any oscillatory trend in the observed data can reasonably be ascribed to an endogenous (hence physiological) process.

Do the daytime ultradian biorhythms affect social interaction? In order to answer this question, first posed by Chapple (1939, 1940, 1970), it was necessary to define the concept of a free-running *social* environment. Merely isolating a natural unit, such as a married couple, behind one-way glass in a typical laboratory proved to be irreparably inadequate. In a series of studies beginning in 1970, we found that a high level of reactivity to continuous monitoring by observers produced too many artifacts to yield valid conclusions. Subtle forms of subrosa interaction between subjects and observers developed (e. g., comments addressed to observers, cookies left out for observers). Furthermore, observer reliability was unacceptable, in part because of the dullness of the task. Finally, the sense of violating the couples' privacy, though agreed to by them, led to a decision to design a fully automatic telemetry and recording system to replace the human observers. Thus our operational definition of a "free-running social environment" calls for the isolation of couples in as naturalistic an apartment as we could devise. They were cut off from all social contacts, were isolated from all time cues, were free to schedule all their own activities, and where there were no observers behind one-way glass, without even the presence of the investigators in the instrument room adjacent to the apartment, except for delivery of mail and groceries and occasional checks on the equipment. Under these living conditions, the spontaneous interaction would be independent of the world outside and presumably approximates their own free-running behavior pattern.

SPECTRUM OF CONVERSATIONAL ACTIVITY

The spectrum of oscillatory phenomena in conversational activity covers a very broad range of frequencies. In this context the term "*frequency*" does not have its usual statistical meaning: it refers instead to the number of cycles per second, etc. The reciprocal of a frequency, a "*period*," refers to the time taken to complete a full cycle. Periods, therefore, are expressed in terms of days per cycle, or seconds per cycle, etc. A period consists of two phases: a silent phase and a speech phase. Individuals may vary in the relative duration and amplitude of these phases and in the ease with which these can be changed in adapting to others.

The hypothesized physiological rhythm which modulates conversational activity has a period of about 90 to 100 minutes per cycle, and thus a frequency of about 16 cycles per circadian day (a free-running circadian day is apparently the lunar day, approximately 24.8 hours, thus the circadian rhythm has a period of about 1,500 minutes per cycle). However, oscillatory phenomena in conversational activity have been noted at a number of different frequencies. One major group exists by virtue of the give-and-take nature of dialogue, and has been studied by many social scientists (Chapple, 1939, 1940, 1970; Chapple & Lindemann, 1941; Jaffe & Feldstein, 1970; Kimberley, 1970; Cobb, 1973; Warner, 1978, 1979). These rhythms of dialogue have periods ranging from roughly 30 to 360 seconds per cycle. Lastly, phonemic-like rhythms have been described (Byers, 1972), which have frequencies on the order of 10 cycles per second. Thus the conversational spectrum spans the range of frequencies between 1 and 100,000 cycles per day, as depicted in Fig. 15-1. These frequencies may be organized as a hierarchy in which short cycles operate within longer cycles within still longer cycles.

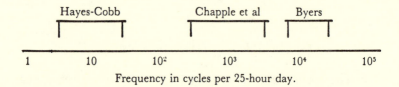

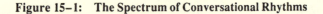

Frequency in cycles per 25-hour day.

Figure 15–1:   The Spectrum of Conversational Rhythms

PRIOR RESEARCH

The hypothesized 90 to 100-minute oscillation between the silence and conversational phases was first noted in our pilot studies whose primary purpose was to test the newly developed telemetry equipment and social environment. In this study two female friends were isolated in the laboratory for three nights and two days. Fig. 15-2 shows their levels of conversational activity over the first 12 hours of each day. The two days have been aligned so that the two time series appear to start at the same time, but the actual clock time is also indicated for each day. The second day began 90 minutes later than the first day because of the free-running environment in the laboratory. Visible within these two time series is an irregular but persistent cyclic tendency in the ebb and flow of their conversational activity. The period of this particular rhythm is closer to 120 minutes than it is to 90 to 100 minutes, but it is within the range of generally accepted values for ultradian biorhythms.

Later in a series of studies, Hayes & Cobb (1979) provided the first evidence for such 90 to 100-minute interactional rhythms in conversation. Over a period of several months, eight volunteer couples were isolated in a specially designed apartment for durations of from 2 to 12 days, under identical conditions. A period of roughly 92 minutes per cycle was found in the time series of 42 days of confinement. The oscillatory patterns were *not* found in every day of every couple, and in two couples confined for short durations, it was missing altogether. Three explanations for those days where couples were arrhythmic seem likely:

(1) It may be perfectly normal for some people to have no cyclic pattern to their interactions.
(2) The individuals concerned may not have been confined long enough to have adapted to the free-running regimen of the study.
(3) Transient, perturbing events occurred which temporarily upset an otherwise periodic pattern of conversation.

All three of these explanations are possible, and could have been the case either separately or in combination. In part, as a result of this state of affairs, the decision was made to conduct a much longer confinement than any that had yet been attempted thus far in order to eliminate the second possibility and establish evidence for the third.

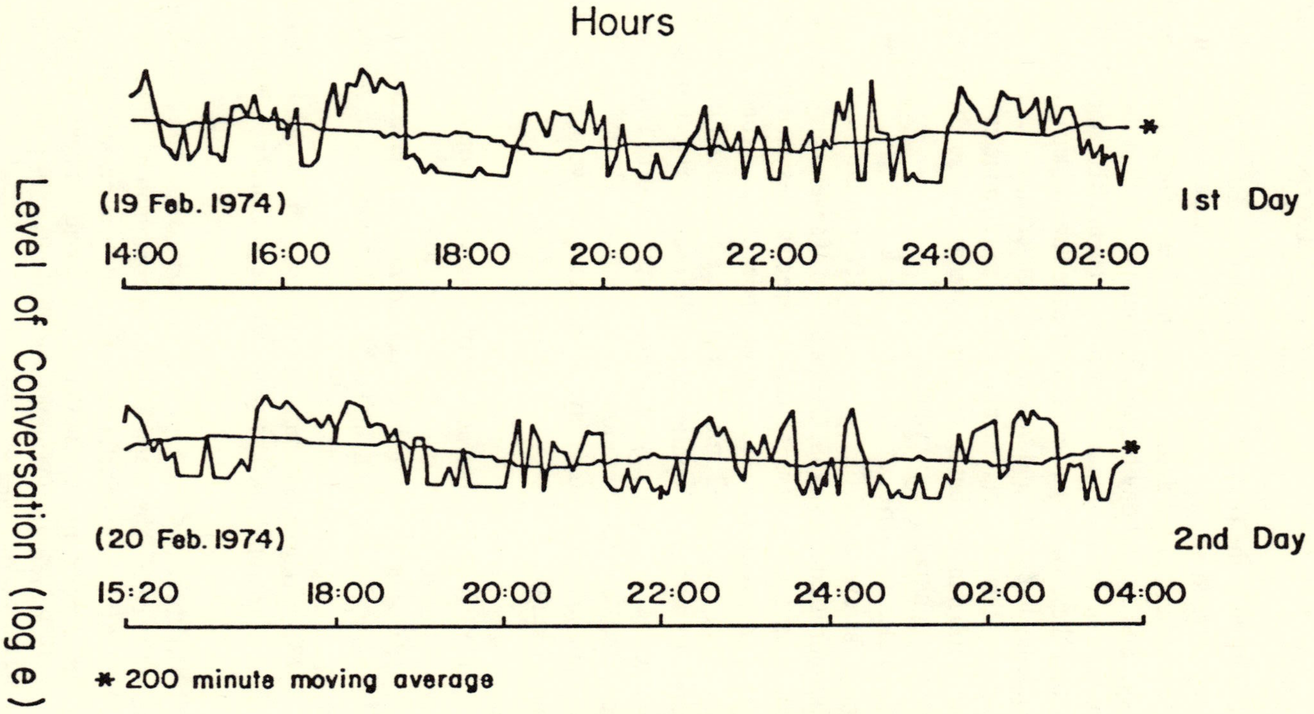

Figure 15-2: Conversation Activity Time Series for Two Days

Hours

(19 Feb. 1974)

14:00 16:00 18:00 20:00 22:00 24:00 02:00 1st Day

(20 Feb. 1974)

15:20 18:00 20:00 22:00 24:00 02:00 04:00 2nd Day

* 200 minute moving average

Level of Conversation (log e)

LIVING ARRANGEMENTS

A man and a woman of 25 years of age, who were living together, were recruited from a state unemployment office. They, like all previous couples, were isolated around the clock in the large, specially designed three-room laboratory apartment. As in the earlier studies, we excluded all clocks and other time cues, separating the couple from external contact with others, except by notes to the investigators. Aside from some simple rules governing the use of their microphones and equipment, they controlled all aspects of their life, including temperature, lights, eating, bed and arising times. Not all perturbing events or agents were eliminated, of course, because each could perturb the other and their physical condition could upset their behavior and temperament.

The apartment's construction provided complete privacy and a high level of sound control. They previously had selected their own food before the study began and prepared it in their kitchenette. To make the apartment home-like they brought their own large record collection, library, wall decorations, plants, sewing machine, musical instrument, macrame—whatever they needed to feel at home in this apartment. Additional fresh milk, produce, and miscellaneous articles were delivered on written request. An exercise bicycle was available, but infrequently used. Most subjects exercised regularly but according to a schedule of their own design. Neither was on drugs at the time of the study, except for those used for fertility control.

Each person was paid $100/week plus a food allowance. Both were given an extensive screening interview and medical examination before and after the experiment. Fully informed as to the purposes of the study, they signed formal agreements outlining their own and the investigators' rights and responsibilities, with special attention given to the issues of privacy in the primary data.

In recording speech and silences, two microphones were used for each person: a bone oscillator pressed to the throat by a neck band and a boom-mounted dynamic microphone attached to a golf hat. The throat unit oscillates only when there are vibrations in the larynx, and is not activated by airborne sounds. Unless sound is detected synchronously by both units, the person on whom these units are attached is declared ''silent.'' This system ensures that loud background noise, such as phonograph music, cooking sounds, or another's voice, is not falsely detected as the person's speech. Signals from all four microphones were transmitted by miniature telemetry units so that the subjects could move about freely. Instruments in an adjacent room preprocessed these signals and sent them to an on-line microcomputer for further compression and recording. A decision on each person's speech or silence was made 10 times per second. After each minute, the 600 decisions per person were aggregated into a single value and recorded on tape along with identifying timing information.

The essential feature of this environment and recording system is that there are no human observers behind one-way glass monitoring the couple's every word and action. The fact that couples can be assured of their privacy increases the naturalness of their behavior and communications, thereby increasing the validity of recordings designed to identify the hypothesized free-running conversational cycles.

THIRTY-DAY STUDY

It was not difficult to find a couple willing to spend 30 days in our laboratory apartment. Indeed, at the conclusion of the confinement this couple stated what others before them have said—that they could and would be willing to stay on another month if desired. Confinement like this was not a difficult thing to do once one gets over the first few days when the experience of being cut off from the outside is still novel. A period of adaptation is essential and probably limits the value of our earlier short-term confinements.

Throughout the 30 days, this couple lived "days" averaging 25-hours, 4-minutes long, but with a large daily variation (SD = 73 minutes). This coincides with previous reports of circadian day lengths under free-running conditions (Ashoff, 1965). Their sleep phase was estimated (from apparatus which detected movement and sound in the bedroom) to average 7 hours, 52 minutes (SD = 60 minutes), while their waking phase averaged 17 hours, 12 minutes (SD = 77 minutes). The couples in our earlier studies had similar day, sleep, and wake lengths, and similar levels of variability.

ANALYSIS OF THE THIRTY-DAY CONFINEMENT

For the purpose of spectral analysis of the 30 days of data, the time series were initially aggregated so that a 6-minute interval is the smallest time unit of observation. At this level of aggregation, there are 250 observations per 25-hour circadian day and 15 observations per hypothetical conversation cycle. An unbroken series of 26 days of error-free observations was available for the female subject, while the male series was interrupted by occasional equipment failure. Fortunately the two time series at this level of aggregation are nearly perfectly correlated, so the female's time series was used for statistical analysis.

The statistical technique appropriate for this and similar studies of periodic patterns of behavior is known as spectral analysis. Although rarely used in sociology, its use is growing (e. g. Warner, 1979; Hibbs, 1975). The primary purpose of spectral analysis is to break down the total power (variance) in a time series into a sum of independent periodic components, each component being a sine wave with a particular frequency. The "power spectrum" of a time series shows the power attributed to each periodic component in a fashion analogous to the way in which the analysis of variance attributes a portion of the total variance of a variable to each of several independent effects. An excellent introductory text on spectral analysis has been written by Bloomfield (1976), and Hibbs (1975) has written an article especially for sociologists.

The analysis proceeded as follows: each 25-hour circadian day was transformed with the Fast Fourier Transform (FFT) algorithm found in Bloomfield (1976). The 26 complex transformed daily series were then averaged, a procedure that is justified by the linearity of the FFT. The power spectrum of the average FFT was computed and smoothed with a 3-point smoothing formula (.25, .50, .25). The resulting power spectrum for the first two weeks of the study is depicted on a *logarithmic* scale in Fig. 15-3.

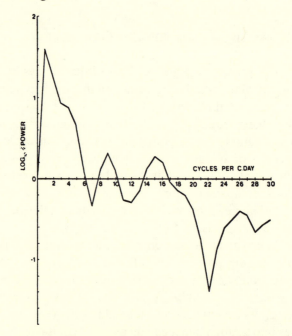

Figure 15–3:   Power Spectrum for the Couple's First
12 Days of Confinement (Power is expressed as
percent of total variance on a logarithmic scale.)

The conversational activity power spectrum is dominated by the very strong 25-hour circadian biorhythm (as should be expected—few people talk in their sleep on a regular basis).

There are some other very low frequency (2–5 cycles per day) components, reflecting the unequal lengths of sleeping and waking episodes and the irregularity of the circadian rhythm itself. The low-frequency band from 5 to 25 hours (representing 1–5 cycles per day comprises some 85 percent of the total power (variance) in the conversational activity time series. This low frequency range is of nominal interest in this research. Our focus is on the power spread across the band between 12 and 250 minutes per cycle. This is the area where we expect interactional rhythms modulated by physiological cycles to be found. Fully 14 percent of the remaining power in this couple's conversational behavior is concentrated in the spectral peak centered at 16 cycles per circadian day alone (94 minutes). The signal at this peak is approximately four times as strong as the power at adjacent higher or lower frequencies. This peak, though much smaller than the circadian peak, clearly indicates the presence of an ultradian rhythm with the hypothesized period: in this case, 94 minutes per cycle. Prewhitening the time series (a procedure which compensates for possible nonstationarity in the series) had virtually no effect at all on the shape of the power spectrum. The 94 minute period in the first 12 days of this long confinement coincides closely with the 92-minute period found earlier in eight couples isolated for 3 to 12 days. A second spectral peak exceeding background levels at 166 minutes per cycle (9 cycles per day) was somewhat shorter than a similar 183-minute period found in the earlier studies, but it is difficult to find a satisfactory biological, psychological, or sociological explanation for this feature. Detailed examinations of the still-frame pictures taken every 40 seconds eliminated the hypothesis that this 166 to 183-minute cycle is related to eating.

In evaluating these results, it should be noted that spectral analysis shows only the linear components in time series while biological oscillators are notoriously nonlinear. A strong, well-established cycle of 94 minutes may be perturbed by some event, resetting the oscillation in such a way as to put the earlier cycles out of phase with those that follow. The linear spectral solution will underrepresent the regularity of the rhythm in such a series. In short, it is fair to say that these results, if anything, underrepresent the strength of the periodic character of spontaneous episodes of conversation in these couples.

EFFECT OF PERTURBATIONS

An unplanned set of natural events during this 30-day study may cast some light on the three interpretations of arrythmia in conversational behavior alluded to earlier. After 12 days of the clear pattern described above, the woman of the pair sent a note to the investigators reporting that she was experiencing a yeast infection. This was making her increasingly uncomfortable, both day and night. It was subsequently controlled by medication from her doctor, but the symptoms did not go away for several days. At almost the same time, the apartment house in which they normally lived was unexpectedly sold by their landlord, and we had to inform the couple (by note) that the new owner insisted that the couple remove their belongings or he would throw them out. We were able to arrange new housing for them, and had their belongings moved to it.

These unplanned events were upsetting to the couple and had a powerful perturbing effect upon their behavior. Their sleep phase was greatly shortened, the standard deviation of their day lengths tripled, and the roughly 94-minute per cycle ultradian rhythm disappeared entirely (see Fig. 15-4), though the 166-minute rhythm remained unaffected. Several days elapsed before the effects of these perturbing events began to disappear. In the final week of the study, the couple had almost recovered the type of pattern seen during their first two weeks, as shown in Fig. 15-5. Noteworthy is a subtle shift in the points in the spectrum having maximal power. The couple's former conversational periodicities of 166 and 94 minutes shifted to somewhat shorter periods, as though both oscillators had speeded up slightly.

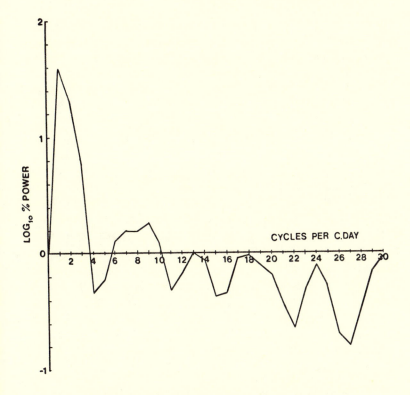

**Figure 15–4: Power Spectrum for the Couple's
Third Week (During this week perturbations
described in the text occurred.)**

CONCLUSIONS

This study, taken together with our previous research, indicates that there is a rhythmic character to the daily pattern of conversational behavior in couples isolated under free-running conditions. The rhythm is irregular, but seems to have periods of 90 to 100 minutes and 166 to 183 minutes. Since the former is the period of the nighttime REM sleep biorhythm, and since this periodicity has also been found in important physiological vari-

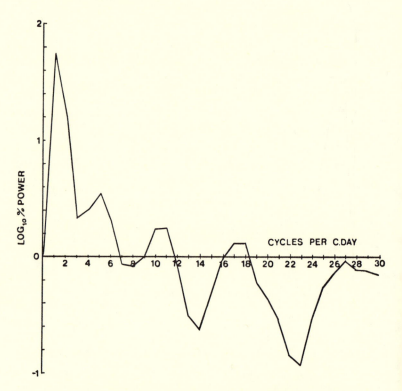

Figure 15–5:   **Power Spectrum for the Final Week (During
this week the couple were recovering from the perturbations.)**

ables (e. g. heart rate) during waking hours, it may be reasonable to conclude that the cause of the 90 to 100 minute cyclic modulation of conversational activity is the common underlying physiological process. Our daily behavior is thus superimposed upon and responds to waves of physiological change. Where manifestations of this biorhythm in conversational activity are absent in our data, it now appears plausible to suppose it had been perturbed (suppressed) by transient events. The side effects of such a suppression, if any, are unknown. Whether all such cases can be explained in the same way is also unknown. Like biorhythms, the 30-day study reported here establishes that the interactional rhythm does tend to reassert itself after the perturbations have ceased, although it will probably not be "in phase" (on the same schedule) with its prior appearance.

How important are these results for theories of social interaction? This is very difficult to answer without equivocation. Under the controlled conditions of our research, interactional rhythms have been repeatedly demonstrated, but the evidence is often of a statistical nature only, due to the irregularity of the manifestations of the underlying physiological processes. Indeed, in some couples there is no evidence for any periodic pattern in their conversational activity. On the other hand, in others it is plainly apparent in the raw data. Under the uncontrolled conditions of everyday life it is reasonable to suppose that manifestations of the latent rhythm are all but undetectable (which is why they must be studied under free-running conditions). However, close friends and married couples interact with a degree of intensity that suggests that these physiological processes become important as a factor in determining compatibility, as was first suggested by Chapple (1970). It is also possible that the temporal requirements of one's job may interfere with these processes, with unknown consequences for job performance.

These empirical findings linking sociology and biochronometry have four theoretical implications for our conception of the nature of human social behavior:

(1)   Social interaction, and in particular conversational activity, does not occur solely as a function of the conscious decisions of the participants. The alternations between activity and inactivity are not entirely unpredictable—on the contrary, it is an oscillation which has a rhythmic character.

(2)   The unique free-running social environment in which these couples lived excluded all known *exogenous* influences which might have induced these rhythmic patterns, leaving as the most plausible explanation of their presence, *endogenous* physiological processes.

(3)   The endogenous oscillator must somehow adapt to a

person's normal social environment in which interactions are constrained by daily schedules of work and play. Synchrony between a person and his/her environment is possible if the adaptations are minor. At other times, they are out of synchrony, thus perturbing the underlying endogenous rhythms much as extensive east-west flight induce transient disturbances in our circadian cycles of physiology and performance. We do not know what the consequences of these disturbances are for social interaction though Chapple (1970) has proposed several which have interpersonal consequences.

(4) If the rhythmic pattern of social interaction is based on underlying physiological processes, then it is very likely that human social behavior is "phase dependent." In other words, our response depends upon the phase of the cycle at which the potentially perturbing event occurs. This last implication (which is not demonstrated in our research to date) is based upon considerable research on phase dependencies in human physiological, pharmacological, and medical research showing how strikingly the effects of the same dosage of drugs, or a common surgical procedure, depends upon the phase in the cycle at which these "treatments" were administered.

The mechanisms or processes by which two individuals living together adjust their own rhythms so that they can be in reasonable synchrony with each other needs further elucidation. Unsystematic analyses of our couples' experiences and behavior lead us to suspect that some people are much more able to adapt than others. It may well be that research into this adaptability variable will be essential in trying to link physiology and human social interaction.

DISCUSSION

Participant: Would you comment more on how much com-
                munication you have with your subjects   ɔe-
                cially during that perturbation period. Were
                they really upset about their apartment? How
                much conversation did you have with them?

Donald Hayes: It is very important to clarify that we never
                talked with them. We do pass messages. Com-
                munication is all done by written letters. They
                were very upset about the apartment disturb-
                ance.

Participant: Could you discuss in more detail how you
                view conversation and interaction, your inter-
                pretations of this research.

Donald Hayes: Our expectation is that each individual will
                have phases which are the active phases in
                which direct conversation will take place and,
                for most people, a much longer quiet phase. If
                Chapple is right, the presumption is that ul-
                timately we somehow find persons with whom
                we can be congenial in our own on-and-off
                phases. To put it another way, if there are no
                periodic processes, then presumably a behav-
                ior would at any point be equally responsive to
                a stimulus from the outside. But, if the behav-
                ior is rhythmic, it has a phase response curve.
                In that case, the responsiveness of the organism
                depends upon which phase it is in. So the pre-
                sumption is that, if you're at one phase, you
                may be perfectly comfortable about convers-
                ing, but a little later it might be harder to get

you to interact. It's as if you have a "slow-as-molasses" respondent for a portion of the period, but a very quick and easily reacting person at the other part. That's a speculation. We certainly know that's true in many physiological studies. We're not sure it's true in human interaction.

Loren Cobb: I'd like to comment on the question of synchrony that has been brought up several times here, and I think these records shed a little more light on it. For example, in our data at the level of aggregation, at say five minutes, there can be a high degree of synchrony in the sense that they're either both talking or they're both not talking. But at a much lower level, such as Jaffe and Feldstein's classic work on rhythms of dialogue and, of course, Eliot Chapple's work in the 30s, units of time are measured in seconds, and a person is talking while the other is silent. If they are both talking simultaneously, that's actually an interruption. So it all has to do with the level of aggregations. A high level of conversational activity in our larger units could be considered as one kind of synchrony.

Participant: I wonder whether you contemplate looking at aspects of their moods or whatever you want to call that.

Donald Hayes: Not in the immediate future. We'd love to do what Kripke does, and I think in some short experiments we can do that sort of thing, but it would involve stopping their interactions in the course of the free-running behavior. I think we'd rather not do that. Kripke deliberately perturbs them by introducing a task such as answering those kinds of questions. Are you suggesting some ways we might do it from voice automatically?

Participant: It occurred to me you might run some kind of correlate with intensity.

Donald Hayes: We do record speech on audio tape for subsequent analysis if we ever wanted to do that.

Participant: Have you considered doing an effort-shape analysis of the movement?

Donald Hayes: We don't have continuous film footage. We only have the still frames. If we had video, we could do something like that, but can you imagine what 30 days of videotape would cost?

Participant: You expected to find these particular cycles?

Loren Cobb: We started out with the hypothesis inspired by previous physiological research which suggested that there might be a 100-minute rhythm in things like this. (Donald Hayes: That's the Kleitman hypothesis.) But we've looked at the whole spectrum from 1 cycle per day up to about 30 or 40 cycles per day, and we were willing to go with anything that appeared.

Donald Hayes: To supplement that, it's suggested that the periodicities that we're finding, somewhere around 180 minutes and 90 minutes, with a hint, especially in the last week, of another periodicity on the order of about 45 minutes, are also fractions of the circadian day. We wonder if, in fact, the circadian day isn't the ultimate driver of each of these periodicities, one at 180 minutes, one at 90, one at 45, one at 22, 11, and so on. The one at 11 minutes has already been reported by Kimberly (1970). A periodicity at about six minutes or a little less than six minutes and one at three minutes have also been noted by Kimberly (1970). Rebecca

Warner (1979) had similar results. It looks as if these are all multiples of each other with the largest oscillator being the circadian day, and it is conceivable that only one master oscillator is driving the whole system. We intend to test that hypothesis.

Participant: Have you analyzed any nonverbal behavior?

Donald Hayes: The only analysis we've done from the photographs thus far has been to test whether Kleitman's notion that there's a basic rest-activity cycle on the order of 90 to 100 minutes would be reflected in the physical movements. There is reason to suppose that that would work out because there's an article by Hobson, et al. in *Science* (29 September, 1978) in which people have been reporting physical movements associated with sleep stages. We have analyzed two weeks of this 30-day experiment to see if the couples have a tendency to move about, changing their site or major gross body movements on the order of 90 to 100 minutes, and the answer is no, for reasons that I don't understand.

Participant: Do you think there are differences in this rhythm culturally?

Donald Hayes: Well, if Kleitman's hypothesis is correct, then the answer would be no, but we're not assured that that is the case.

REFERENCES

Ashoff, J. Circadian rhythms in man. *Science*, 1965, *148*, 1427–1432.

Bloomfield, P. *Fourier analysis of time series: An introduction.* New York: John Wiley & Sons, 1976.

Byers, P. *From biological rhythm to cultural pattern.* Doctoral Dissertation, Columbia University, 1972.

Chapple, E. D. Quantitative analysis of the interaction of individuals. *Proceedings of the National Academy of Sciences—U.S.*, 1939, *25*, 58–67.

Chapple, E. D. Personality differences as described in invariant properties of individuals in interaction. *Proceedings of the National Academy of Sciences—U.S.*, 1940, *26*, 10–16.

Chapple, E. D. *Culture and biological man*. New York: Holt, Rinehart and Winston, 1970.

Chapple, E. D. & Lindemann, E. Clinical implications of measurements of interaction rates in psychiatric patients. *Applied Anthropology*, 1941, *1*, 1–10.

Cobb, L. *Time-series analysis of the periodicities of casual conversations*. Doctoral Dissertation, Cornell University, 1973.

Friedman, S. & Fisher, C. On the presence of a rhythmic, diurnal oral instinctual drive cycle in man. *Journal of American Psychoanalytic Association*, 1967, *15*, 317–343.

Hayes, D. & Cobb, L. Ultradian biorhythms in social interaction. In A. Siegman & S. Feldstein (Eds.), *On time and speech*. Hillsdale, New Jersey: Lawrence Erlbaum Associates, Inc., 1979.

Hibbs, D. A. Problems of statistical estimation and causal inference in time-series regression models. In H. L. Castner (Ed.), *Sociological Methodology*. San Francisco: Jossey-Bass, 1975, Chapter 10.

Hobson, J. A, Spagna, T. & Malenka, R. Ethology of sleep studies with time-lapse photography: postural immobility and sleep-cycle phase in humans. *Science*, 1978, *201*, 1251–1253.

Jaffe, J. & Feldstein, S. *Rhythms of dialogue*. New York: Academic Press, 1970.

Kimberly, R. P. Rhythmic patterns of human interaction. *Nature*, 1970, *228*, 88–90.

Klein, R. & Armitage, R. Rhythms in human performance: 1½ hour oscillations in cognitive style. *Science*, 1979, *204*, 1326–1328.

Kleitman, N. *Sleep and wakefulness*. Chicago: University of Chicago Press, 1967.

Kripke, D. F. & Sonnenshein, D. The biological rhythm in waking behavior. In K. S. Pope & J. L. Singer (Eds.), *The stream of consciousness*. New York: Plenum Publishing Corp., 1978.

Ostwald, I., Merrington, J. & Lewis, H. Cyclic 'on demand' oral intake by adults. *Nature*, 1970, *225*, 956–960.

Othmer, E., Hayden, M. & Segalbaum, R. Encephalic cycles during sleep and wakefulness in humans: a 24 hour pattern. *Science*, 1969, *164*, 447–449.

Warner, R. *Temporal Patterns in dialogue*. Doctoral Dissertation, Harvard University, 1978.

Warner, R. *Synchronized vocal activity rhythm in conversation*. Unpublished manuscript, 1979.

Chapter 16

TRANSACTIONS AT A STORE COUNTER

Judson P. Jones
and Walburga von Raffler-Engel

SCOPE OF RESEARCH

The study of nonverbal interaction is still in its beginning stage, and we feel that in order to lay the foundations for a general framework in this field, research should meet four basic conditions: (1) it should be done within a culture with which the researchers are thoroughly familiar to limit misinterpretation of the data; (2) it should be naturalistic to avoid laboratory and experimenter bias; (3) it should lend itself to generalization; and (4) it should be easily replicable.

To satisfy the above conditions, we selected the sales transaction in a sporting goods store selling items appealing to both men and women from a broad range of social classes and ethnic groups. As store customers are accustomed to the sight of video cameras for theft detection, we felt that in this situation the presence of a camera for research purposes was as unobtrusive as possible. In a retail store the presence of an additional person does not create an intrusion as customers hardly notice the number of employees present in the store at any particular time.

Focus of Research

The focus of our research is the patterning of postural change during a speech event. It is based on the idea first proposed by Scheflen (1964, p. 320) that postural shifts function as markers of discourse segments. The most stringent documentation of this hypothesis is offered by Erickson (1975), and we ourselves had previously explored this idea and found it fully confirmed (von Raffler-Engel, 1975).

The sales transaction in a retail store involves certain well-defined procedures which are not necessarily separate nor occur in a fixed sequence:

(1) The customer must make a decision on what, if anything, he wants to buy; sometimes a sales person aids the customer in that decision.

(2) A store employee must be made aware of that decision, and, if the salesperson acts also as cashier, the customer and the employee usually move together toward the cash register.

(3) The employee must inform the customer of the total amount of the purchase either spontaneously or in reply to the customer's request.

(4) The customer must indicate, explicitly or implicitly, in what mode he or she wishes to pay, by cash, credit card, or any other of the modes of payment acceptable to that particular store.

(5) The employee must take the payment and finalize the transaction by providing the customer with official acknowledgment that the transaction has been accepted.

(6) The customer must accept the merchandise either by taking it with him or her by indicating some mode of delivery.

The present study does not encompass all of the above components. Complete coverage would have necessitated several recording cameras. This was not financially feasible, and, mor\ importantly, such a setup would have violated the naturalness condition. With only one camera in use it was not possible to cover the customer's decision-making process while he walked around the various merchandise exhibits. The recording range of the camera was restricted to the area immediately surrounding the sales counter and the cash register. This allowed us to cover the end of the movement towards the cash register and to cover payment as well as leave taking in their entirety.

EXPERIMENTAL METHODOLOGY

Videotaping was done on a Saturday in October in a Nashville, Tennessee sporting goods store. The store specialized in bicycles, backpacking gear, and whitewater boating equipment.

The camera was placed 4.0 m from the interactants so that they were viewed from the side as they faced each other. The light in the store was sufficient for recording; therefore, no artificial lights were used. The field of view of the camera covered the sales counter, the cash register, and the store entrance.

The experimenter-observer sat at the far end of the L-shaped sales counter, 3.0 m from the interactants, operating the videotape equipment. He was a 20-year-old white male, dressed in blue jeans and an orange T-shirt. His attire was similar to that of the store employees. The videotape equipment was set up so that it could be activated and deactivated by a discreet flip of a small switch. Since the observer spoke to no one during recording, persons in the store did not know when the videotape machine was on or off.

Five employees were working that day, all white males between the ages of 20 and 32. The employees in this store serve a dual function of salesman and cashier. We recorded 1 to 4 interactions for each employee. After having been granted permission to perform the experiment by the store owner, the experimenter informed the store employees three days prior to the experiment that he was to record the behavior of the customers. Only after the recording sessions were completed did he debrief the employees about the true nature of the experiment.

About 70 people entered the store during the 5½-hour recording session (11:00 A.M.–4:30 P.M.). To keep the naturalness condition, we avoided signed consent forms and demographic data forms. After consultation with a lawyer, the legality of the experiment was assured by posting a sign on the front door which read:

> This store is participating in a study of marketing behavior. You will be videotaped while you are in the store. If you do not wish to be videotaped, please inform the cashier.

Only one person entering the store objected to being videotaped, and that interaction was not recorded.

The recording device was activated when the employee and the customer were approaching the sales counter and deactivated when one or both interactants left the counter. In instances in which one subject left the counter and subsequently returned to it, the recorder was left running or reactivated whenever the movement had not been immediately detected.

A total of 15 interactions were recorded on a total of 1,250 feet of videoband. These represent all actual sales transactions disregarding transactions involving exchange of previously bought merchandise, persons simply cashing a check without intent of purchase, and customers whose perusal of the merchandise did not end in purchase. Among the 15 customers were seven white males, four white females, two black males, and one chicano male. Various social classes were represented, with the majority being middle class.

Timing was done with a stopwatch and statistical computations done on a computer. The postures of the interactants were observed at 2.0-second intervals, yielding a total of 332 observations for all 15 interactions.

DATA ANALYSIS

The audio part of the data collected on the videotape was transcribed. Subsequently, the 15 interactions between employee and customer leading to the buying of merchandise were analyzed according to Hymes' (1974, pp. 52–53) speech event model. The speech event was divided into three speech acts. As our main concern was the payment transaction, the speech act preceding that transaction was termed "speech preparatory" (SP), the paying transactions "speech central" (SC), and the speech act following payment "speech final" (SF).

In order to allow for reaction time, SC was said to begin upon utterance by the employee of the last syllable of the total price. Thus, if the amount was $15.64 the syllable "four" marks the beginning of SC. Everything preceding this syllable was considered SP. SC terminates when the employee gives an indication that the transaction has been completed. In the case of a cash purchase, handing of return change to the customer indicated the end of speech central. (No instance of exact amount payment was observed.) In the case of a credit card payment, the end of SC was marked by the handing of the receipt slip. The exact point for recognition of the marker for the end of SC by either the handing of return change or a credit card receipt was considered when the arm or arms of the employee had reached their fullest range of foreward extension. In the case of purchase by check, the marker was the audible bang made by the cashier in stamping the check with a rubber stamp. Everything following SC was considered SF. The end of SF was easily identified by the end of the last utterance proffered by either of the interactants.

A typical interaction went as follows (see Fig. 16-1):

Emp: "Okay, so (3 second pause) $16.96 with tax." (19 second pause)
Emp: "$17.20. Thanks a lot. Do you want a bag for these?"
Cust: "No, that's all right."
Emp: "Okay, thanks a lot."
Cust: "Yeah, thank you."

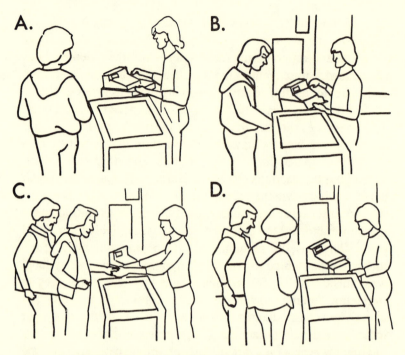

Figure 16–1: Orientations during a Sales Transaction. A) A moment during the speech preparatory phase (SP) .8 sec. before the beginning of speech central (SC). Both distances are 3 (arm's length), and will remain so. The customer has his shoulders rotated 90° away from the employee (orientation 2). The employee is facing the customer (orientation 2). The employee is facing the customer (orientation 0). B) The beginning of speech central (SC). The customer has turned to face the employee, assuming orientation 0. C) The end of speech central (SC), employee returning change to the customer. D) Drawing made 1.0 seconds after the end of SC, during speech final (SF). The customer has turned away from the employee, signaling the end of the transaction.

The leave-taking formula was invariably pronounced by the employee on a falling intonation contour. Paralinguistically it was strongly distinguished from any other utterance. At the end of the leave-taking formula the employee had a marked postural turn away from the customer.

The notational system used to describe the posture is based on a slight modification of Hall's (1963) sociofugal-sociopetal (orientation) and kinesthetic (distance) scales. In the present study, the subject's postures are determined relative to a fixed object, the sales counter. The distance from the center of the sales counter was recorded on a scale of 3 to 5, and the rotation of the subject's shoulders was recorded on a scale of 0 to 7.

RESULTS

The four drawings of Fig. 16-1 illustrate the application of these codes and demonstrate the postural course of a typical interaction. Figure 16-1a is a drawing made from the videotape .8 seconds before the beginning of speech central in this particular interaction. The cashier is uttering the first syllable of the price, which is $16.96. He has just finished making a shift in orientation from the cash register to facing the customer. The customer, however, has his shoulders facing 90°away from the employee. They are both within arm's reach of each other and will remain so throughout the course of the transaction.

Figure 16-1b is a drawing made at the beginning of SC, upon the utterance of the second "six" of the price, .8 seconds after time A. The customer has made a marked change in orientation to face the employee. The interactants maintain this relative posturing throughout the 18−seconds SC.

Figure 16-1c and d are drawings made at the end of SC and 1.0 second after SC, respectively. In this 1−second interval the customer again alters his orientation so that he is facing about 45° away from the employee, presumably a postural signal of the end of the formal interaction.

Results indicate that customers maintained orientation 0 (facing the cashier) throughout the duration of SC. Only two exceptions to this general rule were observed; both during a third-party intervention into the interaction. Since orientation was observed 189 times during SC, and many observations included third parties, these two instances are not considered significant, but as exceptions to the rule. Customers normally maintained a distance of 3 (arms length) away from the employee, with only 6 exceptions in the 189 observations.

Employees maintained orientaton O (facing the customer) 45.5 percent of the time during SC and orientation 1 (facing the cash register) 50.3 percent of the time. They assumed other orientations only 4.2 percent of the time. The distance maintained was 3 (arm's length), with only 6 exceptions to this in the 189 observations. We should also note that interactions in which the cashiers were apparently familiar with the customers did not differ noticeably from interactions with unfamiliar customers in terms of these postural shift patterns (although there was more conversation during them).

Our findings support the hypothesis that postural change occurs at the moment of transition between the three parts of the sales transaction, from SP to SC and from SC to SF. They also suggest that the postural behavior within each of these three parts differs from that of the others.

During SC the employees assumed two postural orientations: facing the cash register or facing the customer. The customer in this study assumed only one postural behavior: facing the employee in a vis-à-vis. These postures are reliably maintained during the entire SC, with only a few deviations. During SP and SF, the same postural behaviors are common, but a greater variety of distances and orientations are observed, and postural changes occur more frequently.

As our criterion for classification of the three speech acts is based on verbal language and on nonverbal factors other than distance and orientation, we feel confident that we have observed the postural behavior of this interacton without danger of circularity.

CONCLUSION

Our research provides further documentation of Scheflen's (1964) finding that postural change accompanies a change in topic and is support for Kendon's (1977) finding that a change in spatial arrangement between interactants takes place when the participants change from one kind of interaction to another. The present study further demonstrates that a category-specific body orientation system obtains for the participants in a sales transaction and, most importantly, that this orientation is context-free of sex, age, and social class. It remains stable under changes in the environment, such as crowding of the setting or changes in the activity of others nearby, which have been suggested by Kendon as potentially altering the transactional arrangement (1977, p. 191). It also occurs independently of the presence or absence of third parties. We suggest replication of our study in other parts of the United States and in other countries to determine if the transactional orientation we have observed is culture-specific and to further examine other properties of behavior within this setting.

REFERENCES

Erickson, F. One function of proxemic shifts in face-to-face interaction. In A. Kendon, R. Harris, & M. R. Key (Eds.), *Organization of behavior in face-to-face interaction*. The Hague: Mouton, 1975, 175–187.

Hall, E. T. A system for the notation of proxemic behavior. *American Anthropologist*. 1963, *65*, 1003–1026.

Hymes, D. *Foundations in sociolinguistics, an ethnographic approach*. Philadelphia: University of Pennsylvania, 1974.

Kendon, A. Spatial organization in social encounters: the F-F system. In *Studies in the behavior of social interaction*. Bloomington, Indiana: Research Center for Language and Semiotic Studies, and Lisse, The Netherlands: Peter de Ridder Press (Indiana University Studies in Semiotics, Vol. 6) 1977.

Scheflen, A. E. The significance of posture in communication systems. *Psychiatry*, 1964, *28*, 126–136.

von Raffler-Engel, W. Kinesics and topic. *The language sciences*, 1975, October, p. 39.

Chapter 17

COORDINATION OF ACTION AND FRAMING IN FACE-TO-FACE INTERACTION[1]

Adam Kendon

The idea of 'rhythm' in interaction has, with one or two exceptions, been addressed quite indirectly in these chapters. Each paper has pursued quite different questions, each one assessing a different aspect of behavior and each one approaching the phenomenon of 'interaction' from a different perspective. Hayes and Cobb measured fluctuations in the amount of talk that occur between the same two people, living together but isolated from others over a long period of time. Siegman examines measures of verbal output and verbal fluency in interviews. Marianne LaFrance examines postural relations in college seminars. Judson Jones and Walburga von Raffler–Engel look at sales transactions in sporting goods stores. Condon examines the minute structure of movement in conversation. Lomax, finally, contrasts rhythmic patterns in human movement and speech from widely separated cultures throughout the world.

All of these studies, with the exception of certain aspects of

[1] This chapter is based on a formal discussion of some of the papers. (Ed.)

Lomax's, have been concerned with occasions when two or a few individuals come to sustain together a common focus of attention and, in doing so, they come to jointly engage their behaviors in a system of behavioral relationships which govern them jointly. That is, the participants in the occasions studied, whatever their separate individual motives or intentions may be, insofar as they are participants in interactional events, must be regarded as entering a particular complex of behavioral relationships. We may observe how, on such occasions, people orient their attention to one another and to a topic of joint concern in a particular way. The spate of actions between them becomes, for them, bounded from the rest of the world around them. So, for half an hour or so, Siegman's interviewer and interviewee engage together in the joint enterprise of an interview. Judson Jones' customers and service personnel align their actions and attentions in a particular way to bring off a sales transaction. Students and instructor in Marianne LaFrance's seminars jointly sustain a presence and a pattern of relationship of attention and action around the task of the seminar.

It seems to me that an issue of central concern to students of interaction is the question of how it is that people succeed in bringing their lines of action into the more or less coherent, patterned relationships that characterize an encounter. Human beings have so many different options in how they may deploy their attention, they have so many different ways of attending to and dealing with each other's behavior, that unless they are able to adjust their attention each to the other so that the actions and utterances of one have the same relevance for both, a coherent social encounter would not be possible. Goffman (1961, 1963, 1974) has said that people engaged in what he has called "focused interaction" together may be said to put a "frame" around the events that occur between them. It seems to me that to understand how such "framing" is achieved is, for students of interaction, a really crucial question.

One place to begin our inquiries into this is to observe that occasions of interaction are always distinguished by particular spatial and orientational arrangements. How people place themselves in relation to one another makes a difference in how they make themselves available to one another and how they may affect each other's behavior. Two people facing one another at close range will be able to observe each other's actions and to hear each other's sounds in a way that is quite different from a situation in which they are facing away from each other or in which they are far apart. Spatial and orientational placement, thus, can be crucial for creating the conditions suitable for particular kinds of interactional relations.

It appears that, when people enter into a *focused* encounter, they come to participate in a system of spatial—orientational relations in which the participants face their bodies in relation to one another in such a way that the space to which they have immediate access overlaps. An area of shared "transactional space" is thus created and its creation and sustainment constitute one kind of behavioral process by which a shared attentional frame can be established and maintained. Studies of such spatial-orientational arrangements, which Scheflen and I have termed "facing formations" or "F-formations" (Scheflen and Ashcraft, 1976; Kendon, 1977) suggests that they are often sustained through a dynamic process of mutual spatial-orientational adjustment. F-formations show a considerable variety of spatial pattern or arrangement. What pattern or arrangement is adopted appears to be related to the kind of interaction occurring within them. Within the course of an encounter, furthermore, the specific arrangement adopted may undergo relatively abrupt change. These changes in arrangement appear to occur in association with other changes in the systems of relationship obtaining between the participants. For example, in examining greeting encounters one finds that the "close salutation" is always enacted in a spatial-orientational relationship that is distinct from the one that is adopted for whatever focused interaction that follows it (Kendon & Ferber, 1973). If one looks at standing conversational groups one can see how they rearrange themselves in relation to shifts in topic (Kendon, 1977).

Judson Jones' and von Raffler-Engel's study is a further and rather nicely documented demonstration of this phenomenon.

There are several features of their study which I like and will comment on. Most notable was their decision to begin a systematic observation of naturally occurring interactional events with a structural analysis. Their measurements of aspects of behavior were taken in scrupulous regard for the natural structure of the event. They further had the sense to examine an event of great simplicity. It is my belief that it will be from looking at events of just this sort of routine and simple nature that we shall best be able to see, in a clear way, how the different aspects of behavior contribute to the structure of an interactional event.

What Jones and von Raffler-Engel show is that for each phase of the sales transaction, a different spatial-orientational relationship between the participants is sustained and that changes from one phase to the next are associated with changes in this arrangement. I should be very interested to have details of the relationship between the initiation of spatial-orientational change here, and the progress within the utterance and actonic exchange systems that are also proceeding in these encounters. For example, does the postural change that leads into the speech final phase of the encounter begin prior to the speech final talk or after it? My own expectation is that the spatial-orientational arrangement change would come in advance of the beginning of the next phase of the event, as defined by the utterances of actions being exchanged. This is because I think it likely that the spatial orientational position a person moves into provides the frame for the line of specific activity that he or she will follow—and that *general* frames or brackets tend to be established first, before frame-relevant actions are begun. More microscopic kinds of analysis requiring continuous assessment of utterance occurrence and spatial-orientational structure are required here. But it seems to me that now that Judson Jones and von Raffler-Engel have established the general phenomenon of contrastive spatial-orientational relations framing successive phases of a transaction, they could now proceed to a more refined analysis that might throw light upon the part that spatial-orientational arrangement plays in the process of frame establishment.

The transactions Jones and von Raffler-Engel have been

concerned with are, as I have already said, quite simple. The information that is exchanged is small in amount and not complex. The period of time for which the two participants must sustain a joint perspective on the same set of events is brief and the amount of ''frame maintenance'' work that is required for such transactions to be successful is relatively small. Other kinds of interactions can be much more demanding, however. Siegman's interviews or Marianne LaFrance's seminars are much more complex. It is in the context of settings of this sort that Scheflen originally made his observations on the possible importance of posture in interaction (Scheflen, 1964)—posture here can be thought of as how people arrange their bodies within the context of a particular location and orientation. Postural arrangements can be regarded as further refinements within a spatial-orientational arrangement, and they may function in reference to sub-frames within the more general frame the spatial-orientational arrangement serves to define.

Marianne LaFrance's work is of relevance here. She is concerned with the relationship between postural arrangements between participants in an encounter and reportable ''rapport.'' LaFrance's observations were all made within one phase of a particular kind of social occasion—the seminar—and the spatial-orientational arrangement remained constant, at least so it would appear. What could and did vary, however, was how the participants arranged their bodies. Thus within the general frame of the ''business phase'' of a seminar we can expect further refinements, further precision in the attunement of the common attentional frame.

''Rapport'' is, I think, a rather elusive concept. However if, when people are *en rapport* they share, to a high degree, a common perspective on current events between them, LaFrance's general observation that the more postural similarities there are between instructors and students the more the students report there is good ''rapport'' is certainly what one would expect if one supposes that bodily arrangements in interaction are employed to an important extent in the process of joint frame establishment and maintenance.

There are two specific points from LaFrance's findings that I would like to emphasize. First, that her observations provide some indication that the establishment of postural sharing *precedes* the development of a reportable perception of rapport is just what I would expect. As I said, in commenting on Jones and von Raffler-Engel's paper, I would expect change in spatial-orientational arrangement to precede the onset of the next phase, as indicated by speech or action exchanges. So here, it is my expectation that postural sharing will serve to create the conditions for the emergence of a higher degree of coordination in respect to those aspects of interaction that deal with the sharing of information and interpretation.

Secondly, her finding that *postural mirroring* has the highest correlation with her measures of rapport is of considerable interest. As I shall suggest in a moment, the maintenance of joint perspective depends ultimately, I believe, not on the assumption of similar *static* postures and orientation. It depends upon the participants coming to allow the tempos of their actions to be governed by the same rhythmical pattern. Thus, what is important here is not so much that you have the same posture as I do — though this is certainly important — but also that you and I seem to be jointly coordinated in action. Mirrored postures, I suspect, provide a much more powerful visible indication of a functional relation between oneself and the other than other kinds of postural similarity — for example, postural parallelism.

Marianne LaFrance's observations, then, support the notion that the pattern of bodily arrangement that participants in encounters enter into has a part to play in the process by which participants become attuned to one another, sharing a common interpretative frame to each other's actions.

There is one further observation that seems to be in LaFrance's data which I would like to comment on. In the study in which she measured both posture sharing and rapport at five-week intervals, it appears that whereas posture mirroring and rapport were quite reliably correlated in the data from the first week, this correlation in the fifth week was much less reliable. This may reflect the tendency for postural relationships to become *less* important as frame attunement devices with the development of familiarity with a situation. When a situation is young, or when people are less acquainted, external devices such as set routines and explicit rules will be relied upon to sustain procedures in a situation. I also suspect that spatial-orientational and postural discipline will be much more closely observed. With the development of familiarity with the procedures of a situation or of familiarity with people, the information that participants need from one another does not have to be as complete. In fact, a commonality of view, a jointness of perspective can, in such circumstances, be taken for granted and it does not have to be expressed in observable behavioral relations.

If this consideration has any weight at all here, it suggests that in attempting to further investigate the role of postural relations in the establishment and maintenance of definitional frames, we must be sensitive to the possibility that what aspects of behavior in each other that participants rely upon for frame establishment and maintenance may alter with degree of familiarity or with degree of acquaintanceship. This means that we shall have to take into consideration the history of the group we are concerned with.

Although neither of these studies address the issue of rhythmicity in interaction directly, they do both support the idea that a coordination of spatial and orientational arrangement is important in the establishment of the commonality of perspective I have referred to, the "joint frame" that interactants must establish. William Condon's work does deal with rhythmicity more directly. His remarkable demonstrations of fine-grained synchrony between speakers and listeners in interaction are well-known. Although there are a number of difficult methodological issues that surround his work, I think that anyone who made even some degree of the same effort that Condon makes to closely examine how the actions of one person in interaction are temporally related to those of another will be struck by the high degree of coordination, it not perfect synchrony, in Condon's sense, that can very often be observed.

The phenomenon of synchrony has, in my view, been

clearly demonstrated. Whether it is a continuous and inevitable feature of conversational interaction as Condon appears to believe, or whether it tends to occur at some points in the interaction process and tends not to occur at other points, remains unresolved. Condon would appear to hold the view that synchrony, in his sense, will arise whenever anyone is in receipt of auditory input. He sees synchrony as a manifestation of a "primary response phase," a consequence of the spreading to the motor muscular system of the activity in the auditory system as it processes input. The two individuals in interaction, thus, are synchronized because each is "driven" by the rhythmic structure of the other's vocal outputs. For Condon, thus, the presence of synchrony is symptomatic of nervous system functioning. He has not explored the possible role of temporal coordination of action between interactants in the process of interaction itself.

Condon's synchrony is rarely perceptible to the ordinary participant, and people are generally very surprised at his demonstrations. It seems likely that we do not perceive Condon's synchrony as a rule because, in our perception of each other's action, we process stimulus input in terms of high-level action units, to which component movements are subordinated. Accordingly, we perceive action in units at a much higher level of organization than that with which Condon is dealing. When we do become aware of the coordination of action between ourselves and our co-interactants it seems that this can have quite powerful consequences for our feeling for and apprehension of the other. As Alan Lomax pointed out in his paper, the highly organized and sustained shared rhythmicity of action in song and dance is not something that we observe in ordinary everyday interaction. He suggested, indeed, that such "overrhythmicity" may be distracting and get in the way of any information exchange functions of the interaction.

Nevertheless, high-level synchronization of action in interaction does occur and it may play an important role in the process of frame alignment that I have here been discussing. I refer here to the choreographic-like maneuverings one can observe in people as they come to form an F-formation or as they manage a transformation in the spatial arrangement of an F-formation; to the highly formalized rhythmical coordinations that can be observed in greeting salutations; and to the sustained "dialogues" of gesture and vocalization that have been described for interactions between mothers and their infants (e. g., Brazelton, Kaslowski, & Main, 1974). Such a high-level coordination of action, sometimes fleeting, sometimes cyclic, occasionally sustained, is a form of synchrony, but it seems likely that it comes about through processes somewhat different from the "primary phase response" processes suggested by Condon. Stern, in his description of mother-infant dialogues, suggests that this kind of coordination comes about as a consequence of each participant's capacity to comprehend the rhythmical structure of each other's flow of action and to modify the rhythmic organization of their own flow of action in terms of this. He suggests that the processes involved in apprehending the rhythmic structure of a piece of music and then organizing one's own flow of movement to fit are the same processes as those involved in synchronizing one's actions with those of another. This means that people have a capacity to anticipate the temporal trajectories of each other's current actions and to adjust their own actions accordingly. This suggests that synchronization of action comes about as a consequence of active cognitive processes and not as an inevitable consequence of the processing of stimulus input, as Condon would appear to suggest. It should be noted, by the way, that such processes of active coordination of action with another to produce a synchronization does not exclude the possibility of a "primary response phase" synchroncity as well.

An important issue to explore is that of the possible role of synchronization in interaction. In my own work on this phenomenon I have observed it in adult conversations and interactions such as salutation exchanges in greeting and in the coordination of spatial maneuverings in the transitional phases of interactional events. It becomes especially conspicuous in phases of interaction where the interactive relationship between the participants is changing. For example, if one examines instances where two participating members of a multiperson conversational group establish an utterance exchange axis together, in many cases one may observe how the bodily orientation of each to the other is accomplished prior to any exchange of talk and it is done synchronously, suggesting that the two interactants, in advance of any explicit exchange of utterance or gesture, had come to share each other's tempo of action. The bringing of orientational and other movements into synchrony at these points may be of importance in establishing the jointness of orientation necessary for each other's acts to become the shared focus of attention. Presumably, by coming to share each other's tempo, each perceives that the other's tempo, behavioral pace is linked to his own, and it is by this that the jointness of attention is conveyed (Kendon, 1970, 1973).

Such synchronies may be observed, too, when people greet. It is notable that close salutations are usually simultaneously performed. In this way the two participants become rhythmically linked to one another. Such initial rhythmical coordination, provided for here by a formalized behavior pattern, establishes each as one who is guiding his behavior by that of the other. They are jointly attentive, therefore. Likewise, in the incorporation of a new participant into an already continuing conversational group, or F—formation, the newcomer approaches and stops just a little distance away. He does not resume his approach until a current member orients to him and begins to move his body. This provides a movement with which the newcomer may join and so become linked, rhythmically, to the system by which the spatial-orientational system of the F-formation is maintained (Kendon, 1977).

Such synchronization of action at transitions to new interactional frames can readily be found. However, they do not *always* occur. A problem for future work is to establish the conditions under which they do occur and to work out the consequences of their occurrence.

Keeping pace, moving in the same tempo as another, then,

may be a way of keeping "frame" with him. It may well be that people in interaction fluctuate in the degree to which they are closely coordinated in action and that such fluctuations have consequences for the degree to which they are able to apprehend each other's attentional perspective on the situation and on what each is doing.

I will now turn briefly, and finally, to a few comments on the paper by Siegman. Siegman's careful experimental studies produce very interesting findings and I was especialy interested in the early studies that he reports, those concerned with the effect of ambiguous questions and of various types of questions on the verbal output of interviewees. I have always been interested in Eliot Chapple's approach to the analysis of interaction by chronography (Chapple, 1940) and at one time I did some research that employed that approach (Kendon, 1963). Chapple's work has shown what a close interdependency there is between the rhythmic structure of the temporal patterning of one person's speech and that of another. Siegman now shows that we have also got to take into account features of the *content* of what is being said as well, to have a full understanding of how one person's verbal output is dependent upon the other's. Chapple, incidentally, was well aware of this, and he devised very careful rules for the construction of utterances by interviewers in his Standard Interview procedure (Chapple, 1953, 1959) to ensure that they would be equivalent in terms of content for all interviewees. Siegman, however, has provided us with interesting experimental explorations of this. Siegman's more recent findings that he reported today, those concerned with the effect of "warm" and "reserved" interviewers are also of interest, but I must confess I find them very tantalizing. They are tantalizing because Siegman has told us so little about how the *interviewers* in his study actually behaved. Measures of the *interviewees'* vocal activity only are presented, not that of the interviewers. Yet, as Siegman himself acknowledges, there is a considerable body of material to suggest that how one person patterns his speech in an encounter is very closely coordinated with how the other does so. In view of the fact that the "warm" and "reserved" interviewers were the same people, it would be most interesting to know to what extent the temporal organization of their utterances altered from one manner to another. For example, how much difference was there in the lengths of the interviewer's questions in the two conditions? Siegman says that in the neutral condition the "interviewer displayed interest in the interviewee's responses, but refrained from any social reinforcers." What is it to "display interest"? In the warm and friendly condition, on the other hand, the interviewer "smiled and nodded on an intermittent but non-contigent basis." I confess myself mystified by this description. In view of the fact that conversationalists tend to modulate their performance in respect to that of their partners in a highly sensitive fashion, often adjusting it moment by moment, I feel that before we can truly understand the findings Siegman reports, we need to know in much more detail about just how the *interviewer's* performance is related to that of the interviewee.

As for Siegman's finding that there was no clear effect on amount of speech by interviewee, according to whether the interviewer was "warm" or "reserved" which, he says, contradicts clinical experience, I feel that, before we challenge the clinicians further on this we ought to gather real examples of clinical interviewers who are regarded as "warm" and examples of those who are "reserved." I would like to know if the two kinds of interviewers *adapt* the temporal patterning of their speech units to the temporal patterning of the speech units of their clients *differently*. It may well be, for instance, that part of being "warm" or "friendly" involves being more flexible in utterance patterning, being able to adjust one's own style of speaking to the style of one's client in such a way as to maximize his output. "Reserved" interviewers, on the other hand, are more inflexible, less able to adapt. In other words I want to know more, in terms of the detailed way in which the interviewer's behavior interrelates with that of the interviewee in real clinical settings, before applying Siegman's findings generally.

REFERENCES

Brazelton, T. B., Koslowski, B. & Main, M. The origins of reciprocity: the early mother-infant interaction. In M. Lewis & L. A. Rosenblum (Eds.), *The effect of the infant on its caregiver*. New York: John Wiley and Sons, Inc., 1974.

Chapple, E. D. Measuring human relations. *Genetic Psychology Monographs*, 1940, *22*, 3–147.

Chapple, E. D. The standard interview as used in interaction chronograph investigations. *Human Organizations*, 1953, *12*, 23–32.

Chapple, E. D. *Training manual for interviewers and observers*. Noroton, Connecticut: The E. D. Chapple Co., Inc., 1959.

Goffman, E. *Encounters*. Indianapolis: Bobbs-Merrill, 1961.

Goffman, E. *Behavior in public places*. New York: The Free Press of Glencoe, 1963.

Goffman, E. *Frame analysis*. New York: Harper, 1974.

Kendon, A. *Temporal aspects of the social performance in two-person encounters*. Doctoral dissertation, Oxford University 1963.

Kendon, A. Movement coordination in social interaction: some examples described. *Acta Psychologica*, 1970, *32*, 100–125.

Kendon, A. The role of visible behavior in the organization of social interaction. In M. Von Cranach and I. Vine (Eds.), *Movement and social communication in man and chimpanzee*. London and New York: Academic Press, 1973.

Kendon, A. Spatial organization in social encounters: the F-formation system. In A. Kendon (Ed.), *Studies in the behavior of social interaction*. Indiana University and Lisse: Peter DeRidder Press, 1977.

Kendon, A. & Ferber, A. A description of some human greetings. In R. P. Michael and J. H. Crook (Eds.), *Comparative ecology and behaviour of primates*. London and New York: Academic Press, 1973.

Scheflen, A. E. The significance of posture in communication systems. *Psychiatry*, 1964, *27*, 316–331.

Scheflen, A. E. & Ashcraft, N. *Human territories: How we behave in space-time*. Englewood Cliffs, New Jersey: Prentice-Hall, 1976.

Chapter 18

CONCLUDING REMARKS

Conrad M. Arensberg

The papers of this conference deal with kinesics and human rhythms and with the ethology of human beings. In such a focus, we of the human sciences move away from the too−simple current models of human culture and communication as primarily verbal. Moving away from models of communication primarily as language took shape in the thirties, particularly in the work of Eliot Chapple and others (Collins and Collins, 1973) who have provided the background for the studies to be reported here. Chapple and I, in long discussions and in diverse research experience, became convinced that the major, strong stimulations in human interaction, the impetuses that lead to change states in human action and affect, come from interpersonal contact and conduct. We were convinced that the patterns of such interpersonal interaction and communication were as much biological and physiological as they were linguistic or semantic. As we found then and you will find again from the papers of this conference, these interaction patterns have a richness and an intricacy at many levels of observation. They show diverse and

365

unexpected rhythms and periodicities, and they are regularized in individual and social behavior in rigorous and productive ways. When these ways are followed out, they yield as much about the culture as the anthropologist, sociologist, and social psychologist are concerned to explain through assessment of language.

The papers of this conference with the exception of those by Chapple, Lomax, and LaFrance are about the observationally simplest of human events: interaction between pairs of persons. Dyads are the first relationships to yield interpersonal behavior patterns and have been the easiest to submit to close–up observation.

We must start where we can and where the best research rigor and control can be achieved, but there are everywhere, of course, other events to be seen and to be explored; events acted out by many more persons then pairs. Triadic and more populous events have their regularities and yield their structures, too, though following them is a much more difficult observational task. Patterns can be detected of simultaneous and ordered, rhythmic response among large sets or groups of people, what I would call "set events" (Chapple and Arensberg, 1940; Arensberg, 1972). These also have their physiological bases and yield predictable social organization and culture. As you will see, the dramas of collective behavior and of expressive artistic performance and participation also owe much of their form and their force to stimulation and rhythm far beyond the verbal, the oratorical, and the language of "meaning." The present conference, of course, cannot cover the whole range of interaction rhythms. It deals with the larger patterns only implicitly.

Many of the papers cite novel and original discoveries. But many of them, too, are highly specific illustrations of more general points to be found in the decades of interaction research summarized by Eliot Chapple. For example, Chapple has discussed the phenomenon of the intermeshing of rhythms at various levels of behavior between interacting persons and the achievement of a synchrony of their rhythms as a necessity of successful, adaptive communication. I believe that considering this synchrony as a matter of individual, personal adjustment is too narrow a view. It certainly is personal adjustment for each of the participants, taken one by one. But, as the evidence shows time and time again, when the reciprocal adjustments take place, it is something else: It is the emergence of a synergetic product of interpersonal communication, a cooperative behavior or activity which was not there before. We are still relying too much on models of adaptation, stimulus−response and personal adjustment of persons (or animals for that matter) considered alone, one by one. Therein lies solipsism. We must attend to the system that interaction makes between and among persons, synergizing them into a common resultant, a systems−product of their rhythmic intermeshing of behaviors.

This point is crystal clear in the film and interaction analysis of mother and baby presented by Beatrice Beebe. In finding their rhythmic meshing, mother and baby both found a reward and a pleasure in mutual adjustment. They entered upon a reciprocity that could and did continue. There was a result that was not there before and would not have arisen if the reciprocity of alternative stimulations—baby of mother and mother of baby—had not found the rhythm that worked.. The healthy, learning baby and the happier, teaching mother—a new two−way interaction frequency—was a cooperative, systems product.

We have moved a long way from the solipsistic mechanism of Harlow and his wire−and−cloth monkey mother and her baby. Growth and health are not a trade−off of the baby's search for warmth and softness, but a reciprocity of response to each other's rhythms, which, if not learned in infancy, cannot be easily achieved with other partners later in life.

So it is too with larger−scale communication patterns and their synchronies. When many people mesh in successful social interaction and regularize their behaviors and rhythms in the institutionalized conduct of human culture and organization, this is not only a successful arousal of motivation and morale or an individual adjustment of a pleasurable or tolerable kind. Out of the pleasure comes a new result: productivity, creativity. We share a social science with economists, engineers, administrators, other people who must work in the world and get a result out of the cooperation and coordination of persons. That too comes from the intermeshings and synchronies about which we are conferencing. The study of rhythms in human behavior could lead to a better and healthier understanding and management of ourselves, and, since these rhythms are physiological and biological as well as social and cultural, they somehow mesh with the rest of the biological and ecological realm. There has been a tendency in much of modern science to treat biology as the physiology of single organisms, the same kind of solipsism I have warned against here in interaction research. We must move on to the rhythms and the synchronies not only of man and animals among each species but also between and across the species in the web of life.

REFERENCES

Arensberg, C. M. Cantometrics in retrospect. In *Folk Song, style and culture*, by Alan Lomax, Washington, D. C., American Association for the Advancement of Science, 1968.

Arensberg, C. M. Culture as behavior: structure and emergence. *Annual Review of Anthropology*, 1972, *1*.

Chapple, E. D. & Arensberg, C. M. Measuring human relations. *Genetic Psychology Monographs*, 1940.

Collins, O. & Collins, J. M. *Interaction and social structure*. The Hague: Mouton Corp., 1973.

Kimball, S. T. & Arensberg, C. M. *Culture and community*. New York: Harcourt, Brace and World, 1965.

INDEX